From Communicative Action to the Face of the Other

Levinas and Habermas on Language, Obligation, and Community

Steven Hendley

LEXINGTON BOOKS
Lanham • Boulder • New York • Oxford

LEXINGTON BOOKS

Published in the United States of America
by Lexington Books
4720 Boston Way, Lanham, Maryland 20706

12 Hid's Copse Road
Cumnor Hill, Oxford OX2 9JJ, England

British Library Cataloguing in Publication Information Available

Library of Congress Cataloging-in-Publication Data

Hendley, Steven, 1956–
    From communicative action to the face of the other : Levinas and Habermas
  on language, obligation, and community / Steven Hendley.
        p. cm.
    Includes bibliographical references and index.
    1. Habermas, Jürgen. 2. Levinas, Emmanuel. I. Title
    ISBN 0-7391-0140-4 (cloth : alk. paper)
    ISBN 0-7391-0141-2 (pbk. : alk. paper)

B3258.H324 H46 2000
170'.92'2—dc21   00-028576

Printed in the United States of America

⊖™ The paper used in this publication meets the minimum requirements of American
National Standard for Information Sciences—Permanence of Paper for Printed Library
Materials, ANSI/NISO Z39.48–1992.

for my daughters,
Johanna and Sarah

Contents

Preface

Of all those who have influenced the contemporary revival of moral theory in continental philosophy, Jürgen Habermas and Emmanuel Levinas are surely the most important. Finding resonances in quite different and often opposing schools of thought, Habermas's discourse ethics has brought a new level of energy and sophistication to cognitive, Kantian approaches to ethics, while Levinas's meditations on the moral significance of the other have informed, though not uncritically, a wide range of postmodernist attempts to get beyond that Kantian legacy.[1] But though they are both inescapably important for an array of debates in contemporary moral theory, they are rarely assessed in relation to each other.[2] There are, no doubt, many reasons for this. The differences in their philosophical styles, for example, are like night and day, with Habermas practicing a rigorously argumentative and technical mode of critical theory while Levinas engages in his own often poetic and always dense version of phenomenological analysis.[3] Their basic agendas are different as well, with Habermas's discourse ethics framed in terms of a general concern with democratic political theory while Levinas's work is largely indifferent, if not hostile, to political concerns.

Such differences as these make a critical study of Habermas and Levinas an unlikely endeavor inasmuch as one is initially hard-pressed to find points of convergence or some sort of common ground between them that could make such a critical study productive. I propose to undertake such a study in this work out of the conviction that this first impression is mistaken, that beneath the surface there is a remarkable degree of convergence in their work that is usually overlooked as scholarship on the two go their own ways. Both Habermas and Levinas understand the most basic sense of moral obligation we have to the other, the adoption of a moral point of view onto life itself, as grounded in our capacity for language. There is a moral dimension to language, to communicative action, for both thinkers, which opens us up to a moral point of view onto life and makes it unavoidably binding on us. But the conceptions of language with which they work, or, more precisely, the conceptions of the significance of the moral dimension of language that both recognize, are profoundly different, posing important questions as to how we are to understand what it means to take a moral point of view onto life, what is implied in adopting such a point of view. Whereas Habermas understands the moral point of view in terms of the procedural imperatives at work in communicative action that oblige us to an attitude of impartiality, Levinas understands it as grounded in a relationship to the other person that is constitutive of speech, a sense of the "height" of the "face of the other" that emerges for us in taking the other as interlocutor. Habermas, in other words, recognizes a moral dimension to language understood purely in terms of a rule-governed social practice whereas Levinas operates with a more expansive conception of language as a substantive relationship, a morally laden mode of "proximity" to the other person. It is this difference in their conceptions of language and its relation to their understanding of our sense of moral obligation that interests me in this work.

What, if anything, does Levinas's reference to the face of the other add to Habermas's understanding of language as a rule-governed social practice? Is Levinas attentive to a dimension of our moral experience that escapes Habermas, or is his account of the other merely a superfluous gesture, a quasi-poetic amplification of insights already elaborated in a more precise way in Habermas's account of communicative action? It is through attention to these sorts of questions that we can best get at, by my reckoning, what really divides Habermas and Levinas. Once we get beyond the more obvious differences of their philosophical styles and projects, it is this issue of how to pitch our analysis of the moral significance of language that offers the most productive possibilities of a dialogue between the two. And, as we shall see, though both have much to teach each other, I believe the most basic lesson we stand to learn from such a dialogue is the need for a Levinasian correction to or qualification of Habermas's otherwise well-founded theory of communicative action. As I argue, Levinas's references to the face of the other contain important insights into the moral point of view that Habermas overlooks. It is as if, focused on an analysis of the procedural imperatives we take for granted in speaking with another person, Habermas forgets the visage of the other person, the interlocutor, whom we address in speech.

In reflecting on the importance of Levinas's account of the face of the other for our understanding of language and the moral point of view, I draw extensively on Charles Taylor's observations concerning the shortcomings of a procedural understanding of ethics. Conceiving the moral point of view in exclusively procedural terms, centered in Habermas's case in the adoption of an impartial point of view that takes into account the objections of all concerned in the justification of our normative commitments, misses what Taylor calls the point of those procedures, the substantive good that is at stake in adopting such impartial procedures. We lack an answer to the question of why we should be moral in that sense, why it is important to adopt a moral point of view onto life, if we fail to recognize the substantive good those procedures serve. Reading Levinas in the context of these concerns, I argue that his articulation of what he calls the "always positive value" of the face of the other may be understood as an attempt to retrieve our sense of the good that is at stake in our moral sensibilities. In losing sight of the face of the other in his procedural analysis of language, Habermas loses sight of the point of the moral point of view, why it is important to be moral.

Of course, Habermas has his reasons for adopting what he chracterizes as a postmetaphysical perspective in moral and political philosophy that eschews what he believes would only be hopelessly controversial commitments to substantive conceptions of the good. In a pluralistic age in which we have to deal with diverse cultural and ethical points of view, the best we can achieve in the way of a moral consensus that would be equally acceptable to all may be a consensus on fair procedures, a consensus on the right rather than the good. And so, to reproach Habermas for the way his work eclipses what Levinas calls the face of the other is to critically challenge this postmetaphysical dimension of Habermas's work, to suggest that for all the otherwise justifiable reasons we may have for wanting to eschew controversial substantive normative commitments, they are not finally compelling. In this way, this work is something of a sustained reflection on the gains and loses of the postmetaphysical perspective that Habermas brings to moral and political philosophy and, in the end, an argument for abandoning that perspective in order to do justice to the insights that inform Levinas's account of the face of the other.

I begin, in chapter 1, by making a case for the convergence of Levinas's and Habermas's accounts of language. In particular, I argue that the theory of meaning that Habermas assumes in his account of communicative action provides us with a way of bringing to fruition what remain, at best, pregnant but largely undeveloped insights into language in the work of Levinas. For all their differences, we will see that Habermas and Levinas work from a shared understanding of the power of language to establish a morally significant connection between us that is unavoidable for anyone competent with language. It is only when it comes to their understanding of that connection that they part company. The next four chapters assess this parting of the ways through an examination of what I argue are four shortcomings in Habermas's discourse ethics that can be corrected by attending to Levinas's account of the face of the other. As such, these chapters form the heart of the book, exploring the two philosophers' divergent conceptions of the moral point of view as well as making a case for the validity of Levinas's insights as an important correction of some of the insufficiencies of Habermas's postmetaphysical emphasis on procedures. Chapters 2 and 3 focus on problems arising with Habermas's moral theory, beginning, in chapter 2, with an examination of his response to questions raised by Carol Gilligan's account of care in our moral experience. Chapter 3 deals with Taylor's critical assessment of Habermas's proceduralism and his argument for a substantive conception of the good that would give us a sense of what is at stake in adopting a moral point of view onto life. Chapters 4 and 5 turn to issues more germane to political theory, with chapter 4 dealing with Habermas's attempt to construct a balanced account of our rights to private and public autonomy in a liberal constitutional democracy and chapter 5 concerned with his conception of constitutional patriotism as the glue that knits a liberal political community together in support of a liberal-democratic conception of justice.

In these four chapters, I try to show how Habermas's procedural understanding of ethics and democratic politics generate an array of problems that can be resolved by expanding his account of communicative action to encompass Levinas's account of the face of the other. By conceiving language, as Habermas stresses, as a rule-governed social practice oriented, as Levinas stresses, to the face of the other with whom we speak, we are able to overcome the procedural myopia of Habermas's theory of communicative action without abandoning its most important insights. For though it does entail that we can no longer take the postmetaphysical distance that Habermas does from substantive goods, it does not require abandoning the moral universalism or the idea of the priority of the right to the good that Habermas seeks to underwrite with his postmetaphysical stance. To the contrary, the heart of Habermas's deontological concerns with moral and political theory are preserved with Levinas's account of the face of the other. The key is in seeing how Levinas's account can supplement rather than contradict Habermas's theory of communicative action, how it goes beyond it in constructive ways that a more adequate discourse ethics can and should appreciate.

In arguing for the relevance of Levinas's work for discourse ethics, it is also important, however, to address an array of troubling questions that have been raised concerning the epistemic viability and coherence of his account of the face of the other. I conclude by turning my attention to these questions in chapter 6, arguing for the epistemic integrity of Levinas's account as an important contribution to moral and political theory, in general, and Habermas's discourse ethics, in particular. It is this concern with the value of Levinas's work as a contribution to discourse ethics that remains my focus throughout. As critical as I am of the procedural limitations of Habermas's work, my interest with Levinas is framed entirely in terms of what I believe is his relevance for discourse ethics as what is, arguably, the most developed and sophisticated moral and political theory available today. There are many aspects of Levinas's work to which I do not attend, therefore, based in what I believe is their lack of direct relevance to the concerns with moral and political theory that drive discourse ethics. Such a selective appropriation of Levinas's work should not, however, be construed as dismissive of the importance of those dimensions of his work. To the contrary, Levinas's work with such issues as temporality and mortality, to mention just two topics that remain wholly neglected here, are rich in phenomenological insights into the nature of human subjectivity that deserve their own independent study. But their relevance to my concerns with discourse ethics is negligible.

My aim in this work is, therefore, modest. I do not intend to undertake a wholesale comparison of Habermas's and Levinas's work, but only to selectively appropriate some of what I believe are Levinas's most crucial insights concerning what he refers to as the face of the other in the context of concerns with moral and political theory that remain centered in Habermas's discourse ethics. I trust I do not do Levinas a disservice with such an endeavor. But my aim is not one of faithfully presenting and transcribing the totality of his far-reaching concerns but only of attempting to take what I believe is most instructive from his work for contemporary moral and political theory, especially as it has been developed in the work of Habermas. We have much to learn from Levinas. This work forms an attempt to isolate just one particularly valuable lesson concerning the importance of the face of the other for our reflections on the constitution of a moral point of view onto life and our concerns with a liberal-democratic conception of justice, to help us retrieve a sense of what Taylor refers to as the substantive point of the moral point of view and the ideal of justice we derive from it that is too easily lost in our postmetaphysical preoccupation with moral and political procedures.

I want to express my appreciation to Birmingham-Southern College for the January sabbatical I was given to work on the manuscript; to *Philosophy Today* for permission to draw on my essay, "From Communicative Action to the Face of the Other: Habermas and Levinas on the Foundations of Moral Theory" (*Philosophy Today* 40, no. 4 [winter 1996]: 504-530); to my colleagues at Birmingham-Southern, Judy Cox (German) and, especially, Renée Norell (French), for their help with questions regarding translation; to Kenneth Baynes for his insightful commentary on a paper that was an earlier version of part of chapter 5; to William Rehg and Vic Pederson, whose comments on a paper that was an earlier version of chapter 4 aided me greatly in my development of that earlier paper into its present form; and, finally, special thanks to Jim Marsh and Todd May, whose correspondence and conversation proved essential in helping me to clarify some of the key ideas and arguments that form the basis of this essay.

Notes

1. For example, there is the work of such Habermasians as Seyla Benhabib, *Situating the Self: Gender, Community and Postmodernism in Contemporary Ethics* (New York: Routledge, 1992), and James Marsh, *Critique, Action and Liberation* (Albany: State University of New York Press, 1995). On the postmodernist scene, Levinas has been crucial for the work of Jean-François Lyotard, *Just Gaming*, trans. Wlad Godzich (Minneapolis: University of Minnesota Press, 1998), and *The Differend*, trans. Georges Van Den Abbeele (Minneapolis: University of Minnesota Press, 1988), and, in conjunction with Jacques Derrida, the work of John Caputo, *Against Ethics* (Indianapolis: Indiana University Press, 1993).

2. The few exceptions that I know are George Trey, "Communicative Ethics in the Face of Alterity: Habermas, Levinas and the Problem of Post-Conventional Universalism," *Praxis International* 11 (January 1992): 412-427; Arne Johan Vetlesen, "Worlds Apart? Habermas and Levinas," *Philosophy and Social Criticism* 23, no. 1 (1997): 1-20; and Max Pensky, "The Limits of Solidarity: Discourse Ethics, Levinas, and the Moral Point of View" (paper presented at the annual meeting of the Society for Phenomenology and Existential Philosophy, October 1994, and forthcoming in *Philosophy Today)*. I am indebted to Professor Pensky for a longer version of the paper he read at the meeting.

3. Levinas's style of writing can provoke quite strong reactions in those who are unfamiliar with it. See, for example, Roger Gottlieb, "Levinas, Feminism, Holocaust, Ecocide," in *Artifacts, Representations and Social Practice*, ed. Carol Gould and Robert Cohen (Dordrecht: Kluwer Academic Publishers, 1994), 365, where he writes, "my intellectual background often makes reading his work a sort of extended theoretical hallucination." This is a rather widespread response, I believe, to which I am not unsympathetic.

Chapter 1

Conversational Deference and Communicative Action

For all that divides them, the parallels between Emmanuel Levinas's and Jürgen Habermas's conceptions of language are remarkable. Language plays a pivotal role in the constitution of the moral point of view in each of their work. And both make a case for the universal validity of the sense of obligation that informs that point of view primarily in terms of language as a constitutive dimension of what it means to be a human being. Because we are, as Aristotle commented, animals with logos, creatures who articulate our relation to ourselves, the world, and one another in and through language, we share a sense of justice.[1] But unlike Aristotle, who thought this shared sense of justice depended on a shared form of life, a common ethos providing a substantive horizon of interpretation for our experience, both Habermas and Levinas seek in different ways to identify a dimension of language that would be common to every ethos as the root of a universally shared sense of justice.

This parallel in their concerns with language has led both thinkers to what are, at least in part, convergent conceptions of language and its relation to the moral point of view, though this point has tended, and not without reason, to be overlooked. Beyond the virtual incommensurability of their respective philosophical registers and styles, Levinas's work, in particular, has never easily given itself to such a comparison. This is because Levinas makes what is arguably his most original contribution to philosophy with his phenomenological articulation of the significance of our ethical relation to the other, the sense in which it opens up what he evokes as a relation to the "face of the other." It is easy, therefore, to

1

neglect the significance of his attempts to specify the conditions of our ethical relation to the other and, hence, the limits and extent of the validity of his analysis in a particular conception of language.

The account of language to which Levinas appeals, moreover, is largely undeveloped, more a promising insight than a fleshed out theory. It is for this reason that I begin in this chapter with an examination of Levinas's account of the relation between language and our sense of moral obligation and then proceed to Habermas's more developed theory of language in order to work out some of the unfinished horizons of Levinas's account. The parallel or convergence between their two conceptions of language and its relation to the moral point of view may best be seen in the way many of Habermas's ideas enable us to constructively develop what is left only suggested in Levinas's work, the way Habermas can be productively brought to the aid of Levinas's project without doing violence to it. Though Levinas's and Habermas's accounts of language and obligation may in no way be identified with one another—a point I examine in the next chapter—I hope to show here how Levinas's reflections on language anticipate themes that are only fully developed in Habermas's theory of language as communicative action. In this way, I aim to establish the presence of a shared terrain between their otherwise disparate philosophies that will enable us to better understand what is at stake in the differences they bring to the question of the nature and grounds of moral obligation.

1.1 Conversation and Obligation

Levinas begins his reflections on the moral relevance of language in *Totality and Infinity* with a particular use of language as conversation. "The very fact of being in a conversation (*discours*)," he writes, "consists in recognizing in the Other a *right* over (one's) egoism, and hence in justifying oneself."[2] This point is of tremendous importance in understanding Levinas's work. The "face of the other" that he evokes as the ground of our sense of moral obligation is always essentially the face of my interlocutor, the one who addresses me in speech.

> The word that bears on the Other as a theme seems to contain the Other. But already it is said to the Other who, as interlocutor, has quit the theme that encompassed him, and upsurges inevitably behind the said. . . . In discourse (*le discours*) the divergence that inevitably opens between the Other as my theme and the Other as my interlocutor, emancipated from the theme that seemed a moment to hold him, forthwith contests the meaning I ascribe to my interlocutor.[3]

Though I may attempt to present the other as an object I comprehend in my word about the other, to present the other in terms of something true that can be *said* about the other, a conversational relation to the other always establishes a divergence between the other as the theme of my speech and as my interlocutor, the one to whom I present this theme. As my interlocutor, the other always has the right to contest what is said of her/him and, indeed, to contest whatever is said.

This is a part of what it means to be in a conversation. It is to be in a relationship with the other in which s/he, as Levinas puts it, "is called upon to speak" and in so doing "'come(s) to the assistance' of his word."[4] Herein lies what Levinas refers to as the essentially "magisterial" character of speech, the way in which my interlocutor presents her/himself *as* interlocutor, as irreducible to anything said insofar as s/he always maintains the right to say more, to comment on what is said.[5] To this extent, my interlocutor is my master, my teacher, the one to whom I am obliged to be attentive.[6] Not that being in a conversation implies being gullible, naively accepting whatever my interlocutor says without question, as a pliant student might write down whatever the teacher says simply because the teacher says it. But it does imply responding to my interlocutor *in terms of* what s/he has said no matter what is said. Should my interlocutor say something so off the wall or embarrassing that I simply ignore it, changing the subject as if s/he had not said anything at all, then, arguably, I have simply quit the conversation, or, at least, *that* conversation, precisely by changing the subject, which is to say, by initiating a new conversation. To remain in a conversation with the other is to accept, then, an obligation to respond to the other in terms of what s/he says to you.

Hence, Levinas's reference to the conversational duty to justify oneself.[7] To converse with another person is to find oneself called into question,[8] called precisely to question what one would say in the light of what the other has said, to say only that which takes into account what the other has said and, in this way, genuinely respond to the other. Though I might not be inclined to concern myself with what my interlocutor has said, I find that inclination called into question, called to justify itself in the light of the commitments I have undertaken by virtue of entering into a conversation with the other. And so I might try to move the conversation to my own interests, but only insofar as I can justifiably do so, which means in a way that is responsive to the other, which finds a way of connecting my concerns with what the other has said so that I pay the other the consideration I owe her/him as my interlocutor.

For Levinas, it is the emergence of this critical relation to myself in and through a conversational relation to the other that constitutes the birth of reason, not so much as a way of acquiring knowledge, a way to make present the truth of the objective world around us, but as an elementary "critique of spontaneity," the recognition of a duty to speak only in terms of what I can justify in the light of what the other has said regardless of what I might otherwise be spontaneously inclined to do. For even when I try to argumentatively show how what the other has said is without merit, I have, at least, taken the trouble to consider what has been said by the other, to weigh its potential merits, if only to propose that it lacks any. Even this dismissive kind of consideration of the other is qualitatively different from an unqualified dismissal that simply ignores the other. Reason, even when it is dismissive, is never completely dismissive, but presupposes the kind of consideration of the other and obligation to respond to the other characteristic of a conversational relationship.

A conversational obligation to respond to the other is, of course, hardly equivalent to an obligation to, say, care for the suffering of the other, "to take the bread out of one's own mouth," as Levinas says, "to nourish the hunger of another with one's own fasting."[9] But Levinas's point is, I believe, just that this distinctively moral sense of obligation is inconceivable outside of an essentially conversational relation with another person. When I see another human being who is suffering and find myself called to assist, even when it is not convenient, even when it entails some, however minor, degree of sacrifice on my part, I am effectively in a conversational attitude. I grasp the other as someone who could speak to me or does speak to me in the transparent presence of her/his suffering, asking me, in effect, how I can justifiably turn aside in indifference to that suffering. I can, of course, turn aside and in that way relate to the suffering of the other as if it were merely an interesting theme, a curious object, to take up and then put aside. But this is an option inconsistent with the kind of consideration of the other demanded in a conversational relationship. Indeed, lacking a genuinely compelling justification for why I should not or cannot come to the other's aid, failing to try to alleviate the suffering of the other will always be nonresponsive, a matter of breaking off the conversational relationship that opens up between us when I grasp the suffering of the other as making a claim on me, as demanding a kind of consideration that no object or theme can conceivably demand of me, but only another who speaks to me. It is only as my interlocutor, if not in fact then at least in principle, that the other shows me her/his face as one to whom I am obliged to give a kind of consideration that, in some contexts, can only be characterized as moral.

1.2 "Meaning Is the Face of the Other"

Locating our ethical proximity to the face of the other in a conversational relationship to the other is helpful in specifying how a particular use of language may implicate me in a form of obligation to the other. But Levinas wants to claim more. It is not just *a* use of language but language itself that implicates me in an ethical relation with the other. "Meaning (*Le sens*)," he writes, "is the face of the Other, and all recourse to words takes place already within the primordial face to face of language."[10] There is, however, quite a gap between the first point regarding a conversational use of language and this second, more ambitious point regarding "all recourse to words." Not every recourse to words is conversational. Sometimes, as with reading a book, there need be no one around with whom to converse. And sometimes, even when I could be conversing with someone, I am doing something else with words, such as insulting someone or giving an order. Jacques Derrida, in particular, has amplified the first point with his reflections on the noncommunicative dimensions of language, and Speech Act theory has emphasized the second point with its insight into language as a kind of performance that may take many forms.[11] But the general point is surely evident without having to appeal to any particular *theory* of language. Linking our ethical proximity to the other to conversation is not yet to link it to language generally, to "all recourse to words."

And yet, it is possible that we have overlooked the implicitly conversational character of some of these nonconversational uses of language. This seems to be the idea Adriaan Peperzak pursues in an attempt to defend Levinas's position regarding language and the other with respect to the activity of reading. Though cognizant of the independence of the text from its author, the way "the author leaves it to the reader, who may do with it whatever he wants," Peperzak emphasizes the way a text must be *presented* in order to be meaningful. "Left to itself, a text does not mean anything. *Someone* is needed—a loud or silent reader, a commentator or believer—in order to be presented with a meaningful paper." And this presentation of the text by the reader, Peperzak argues, "not only reminds me of its known or unknown author, but represents and revives the author's position as someone who calls to me." This is the key for Peperzak in linking the act of reading to the ethical proximity to the other opened up in conversation. Even though the author who wrote the text may be absent and so unable to "come to the assistance of his word" as my interlocutor can, in reading the text I am presenting it *as* the address of the author to me, soliciting my response to the address just as my interlocutor would. Reading is, as it were, a virtual conversation with the author, a response to her/his summons to consider what has been written not in any way it might please me but in the way the author wrote it. Alluding to the gathering at which he presented his paper, Peperzak concludes, "Our discussing 'Levinas's presupposes and implies our addressing his writings to one another and when we are doing this, the master's voice is echoing in ours."[12]

Peperzak makes a compelling case here. But its compelling character seems to stem largely from the way he presupposes a certain form of reading in his analysis, exemplified by his reference to the scholarly reading and discussion of Levinas's text to which he and his audience are devoted. In a public and scholarly reading of an author's text my reading *is* a response to the author that takes upon itself the obligation to justify itself in the light of what the author has said or what others could say in the place of the author. It is far from clear, however, how this model would apply to less public or scholarly readings. When I read a light novel to pass the time on a long flight, for example, I am not concerned with what the author or anyone else has to say of my reading. The public validity of my reading is irrelevant here, and I would find it annoying if someone, standing in for the author, challenged it, arguing that I had failed to appreciate the novel's true worth. The public validity of my reading, I might honestly respond, was not my foremost concern.

How, then, can Levinas generalize his insights into conversation to language generally? Levinas wants to claim, using the terminology that will come to dominate his discussions of language, that every "said" presupposes a "saying" that is directed toward the other, that everything that can be said only takes form against the background of a saying which is responsive to the appeal of the other in the conversational manner we have been examining.[13] To this end, he devotes much of his critical attention in *Totality and Infinity* to conceptions of language that by his account overlook the way in which language is embedded in this conversational relation with the other. Martin Heidegger's and Maurice Merleau-Ponty's views, in particular, come under fire for the way in which they "remain bound to the process of comprehension," as Levinas puts it, privileging language as a practically grounded disclosure of the world to the neglect of the "ethical event of sociality" that makes that disclosure possible.[14] For the most part, however, these criticisms presuppose the cogency of his own view of language rather than provide evidence for it.[15]

But in the course of these criticisms Levinas expands on his perspective with a reflection on the idea of a *proposition*, which, at the very least, takes us farther along toward the conclusion he wishes to draw. He writes, "the proposition that posits and offers the world does not float in the air, but promises a response to him who receives this proposition, who directs himself toward the Other because in his proposition he receives the possibility of questioning. . . . A proposition is maintained in the outstretched field of questions and answers."[16] Certainly, a proposition always makes what it proposes open to question in a way that it would not be prior to being proposed. To this extent, a proposition always exists in a *possible* field of questions and answers regarding what it proposes. But why is this "possibility of questioning" essential to a proposition?

We see an answer suggested in the lines that follow the passage just cited: "A proposition is a sign which is already interpreted, which provides its own key. The presence of the interpretive key in the sign to be interpreted is precisely the presence of the other in the proposition, the presence of him who can come to the assistance of his discourse, the teaching quality of all speech."[17] Here Levinas seems to be suggesting that our interpretation of the meaning of a proposition is a function of its being placed in "the outstretched field of questions and answers," that a proposition provides the keys to its own interpretation only insofar as it makes an essential reference to the one "who can come to the assistance of his discourse" by answering my questions about it. But how so? Can I not understand a proposition without having its author present, able to respond to my queries? How, if this were necessary, would reading be possible, where the author typically is not there to respond?

Levinas seems to respond to our queries regarding his own proposition when somewhat later in the same section of *Totality and Infinity* he emphasizes a connection between speech, in which one maintains the ability to come to the assistance of one's discourse, and the overcoming of dissimulation or equivocation.

"Speech," he writes, "consists in surmounting, in a total frankn ess ever renewed, the dissimulation inevitable in every apparition. Thereby a sense—an orientation—is given to every phenomenon."[18] This seems to be the key to Levinas's ideas. Every proposition taken on its own apart from a context that would help to fix its meaning is subject to equivocation and manifold interpretation. The meaning of any linguistic sign, as Derrida among others has taught us, is never one, simple, univocal thing but something that is always different as it disseminates from context to context.[19] It is only as we define the relevant contexts for how to take the sense of what is said or read that we may overcome this inevitable dissimulation, establishing a more or less univocal meaning through this process. But if we imagine this process of contextualization as a private act, a matter of the personal assumptions each of us brings to bear on what we hear or read that enables us to make some sense of it, we only complicate the problem of the polysemy of language, as what is said or read can mean different things to its different recipients as they bring different assumptions to bear. Only a public contextualization of language can make inroads on this problem by establishing shared contexts for the interpretation of what is said or written and, consequently, a more or less shared, univocal meaning. But this is impossible apart from the questions and answers we raise to each other concerning what we say or write. It is only through the possibility of questioning you and taking your response concerning what you say into consideration that I can develop with you a shared sense of the context in which to take what you say to me. Only the deference[20] I show to you as my interlocutor, allowing your commentary to set the appropriate context for what you say to me, allows us to construct a shared context in which a more or less univocal meaning for what you say can emerge for both of us.

This, moreover, seems to be a point that is true of even the most solitary uses of language, such as the example of reading a light novel by oneself on an airplane. To be reading a book that is recognizable by other readers of that book *as* the same book, with enough minimally shared meaning to allow those other readers to recognize it as the same book they themselves have read,[21] we must read each sentence with an eye toward the internal context the author has constructed in the other sentences that populate the book, reading it as the author has presented it, in other words. Much as Peperzak showed with respect to more public readings, we read the book in what amounts to a *virtual* field of outstretched questions and answers, questions we raise about the meaning of what we read that we allow to be answered by the other things the author has written in the book. There is, of course, nothing preventing us from opening the book randomly and reading the first sentence we come to apart from its textual context and, in that sense, encountering a proposition that really does "float in the air," as Levinas puts it. But then we would be forced to imagine our own context for it in order to make any kind of determinate sense of it—a process that, as noted above, only complicates the problem of the manifold things the sentence could mean to manifold readers.[22] To be reading what is recognizable by many readers of the book as the same book, to be reading, in other words, in a way that strives to overcome the inevitable dissimulation of language that could, past a certain point, make it difficult to even identify what we read as the same as what someone else has read, we must defer to the author as our virtual interlocutor at least insofar as we allow her/his other sentences in the book to answer our initial questions about the determinate meanings of each particular sentence we read within it.

In his essay, "Meaning and Sense," Levinas gets at what is in part the same point when he writes of a "unique sense" ("sens unique") as the ground of any otherwise culturally constituted meaning.[23] Exploiting the ambiguity in the French phrase "sens unique," which can mean both a unique meaning or direction,[24] Levinas appears to want to claim that the *unique sense* of a publicly shared meaning that would not be abandoned to the otherwise inevitable dissimulation of language is always a conversational achievement, a matter of the *unique orientation* or sense of deference to the other we find in the social practice of conversation. Taken on its own, this is not an insignificant point, as it suggests that every linguistically mediated shared understanding within a community is a product of such a conversational relation with the other, that a community could not share in any univocal way an understanding of what is meant by the words they use without resorting to a conversational use of language (or, at least as we saw with the reading of the novel, a *virtually* conversational use of language). This point, if true, would go a long way to establishing a degree of universality to Levinas's claim regarding our ethical proximity to the other as it would imply that no linguistic community with relatively univocal shared linguistic understandings could be completely alien to a conversational relation to the other. But it does not establish the more demanding point that Levinas sets for himself, that meaning itself is impossible apart from a conversational relation with the other, that "all recourse to words," every "said," is in some way said *to the other*. After all, a proposition that "floats in the air" apart from any shared context may be inherently equivocal. I may be able to project a number of different contexts in which it might mean a number of different things, but it still has meaning in terms of the different contexts in which I can project its use.

Admittedly, it does not seem plausible to imagine someone who *only* had recourse to words in such a way, wholly indifferent to the unique sense they would have for others, content to make whatever sense s/he could of the discourses s/he finds scattered around her/him as so many ambiguous relics, so to speak, of a civilization no longer able to comment on them. This would seem to be more the position of a permanent observer of the practices of some linguistic community than a genuine participant. To the extent that such a permanent observational position is implausible, Levinas has provided some grounds to suggest that no linguistic agent could be completely alien to the sense of the other as my interlocutor as this arises in our conversational practices. But it is not yet clear *why* genuine participation in this sense of being concerned with a shared and unique sense of what we say or write to one another and, consequently, implicated in a conversational relation to the other is a prerequisite of being able to make *some* sense of what we say or write. Indeed, when viewed not as a permanent position but only as an occasional possibility, the perspective of the observer would seem to be inevitable, as we often come across what are, in effect, fragments of language that have been severed from the commentary that would make it possible to establish a unique sense for them. Certainly all written language is like this at some point. Even if we read with a sense of deference to the author's presentation of the text, allowing the author's complete text to serve as commentary for each sentence within it, the text must end somewhere without resolving all our questions as to its meaning. Then, it would seem, we are own our own to make whatever sense we can of it.

If Levinas is to redeem his claim that "meaning is the face of the other" he must show how this position of the pure observer, even as only an occasional perspective, is unsustainable; that my ability to make some sense of language without access to or even without apparent concern for its unique sense still presupposes a conversational perspective toward the other implicating me in a sense of obligation toward the other. In what way is the very possibility of a meaningful proposition, not merely the possibility of a proposition with a unique meaning, a possibility that is only maintained in "the outstretched field of questions and answers"? The insight embodied in Levinas's conception of language, an insight that is never adequately developed or justified by him as far as I can see, is that language only has meaning by virtue of its place or role in a field of questions and answers, its relation to other things that can be said of relevance to it, that can serve as answers to questions we might have concerning it. We have seen how this seems to be true with respect to a shared and unique sense for what we say and write. Unless I am prepared to defer to your commentary as authoritative for setting the context in which I hear what you say to me, the range of possible contexts I could myself project for it will open up a range of multiple potential meanings for what is said. But as each of these potential meanings seems accessible to me without deferring to the other, it is hard to see how Levinas has made his point.

We should, however, examine this ambiguous semantic potential of language more carefully before proceeding. If I do not defer to your commentary to set the context for what you say or write, say, by simply reading a sentence at random in one of your books, then I must project a context in which to understand it. But what could we mean here in speaking of "projecting a context"? If I open a book at random and read, "It's a blue day," I will probably understand the sentence to mean that the day to which the sentence refers provokes sadness in some way. But this is not, of course, the only thing it could mean. It could mean that the day was literally colored blue in that everything as far as the eye could see had, for that bizarre day, been somehow rendered blue. The difference between these interpretations will, of course, depend on the context we project for it. This is, however, only a matter of what *answers* we imagine a person in a position to utter such a statement making to us in response to our *questions* concerning it. We anticipate, as it were, what such a person would say if we responded to the statement with "How so?" asking her/him to elaborate, to comment on it. With the first interpretation, we suppose that the most common answer would refer to the sadness the day somehow provokes in the speaker. With the second, less likely interpretation, we suppose that someone might refer to the color of things in the perceived environment. But in any event, we will only be able to understand the sentence *as* meaningful insofar as it plays a relevant role in a field of questions and answers that remains implicitly or virtually conversational insofar as I defer in each interpretation to the commentary of a possible interlocutor to establish the sentence's meaning.

This may be as much as Levinas could say for his claim that "meaning is the face of the other." But it also may be as much as he needs to say. For it does not make good sense to claim much more than this. To suppose that what is said or written can only mean something insofar as I am in an *actual* conversational relation with the speaker or author, deferring to her/his actual commentary to establish its meaning, is ridiculous. At that rate we would never be able to read anything. But to recognize that meaning is dependent on, at the very least, a virtual conversational relation with an other I imagine as my interlocutor is to recognize that linguistic meaning would be inaccessible for anyone who was not competent with a conversational use of language, who was not familiar with what it means to defer to an interlocutor and so was not capable of reproducing that sense of deference even when there is no interlocutor to whom to actually defer—that the position of the pure observer, even as only an occasional rather than a permanent possibility, is incoherent, and no interpretation of language is possible that would completely abstract from our conversational competencies as genuine participants in a linguistic community. And this implies that we could not find anyone who could speak with us or understand what we say or write as meaningful who would not appreciate the sense of obligation to another person that emerges insofar as s/he is my interlocutor. Though they may be oblivious to it in this and many other cases, refusing in this instance for any number of possible reasons to take me as their interlocutor, they could not be absolutely oblivious, in principle, to such a conversational mode of proximity to the other.

1.3 Communicative Action

At this point, however, all we really have is a rather pregnant insight into language rather than a fully developed theory of language. And this is, as I have mentioned, about all that we can expect from Levinas on this point. But Levinas's insight into the way in which linguistic meaning is only established in an "outstretched field of questions and answers" may be seen as theoretically developed in Habermas's claim that "we understand a speech act when we know what makes it acceptable."[25]

The theory of meaning implied in this claim complements and develops Levinas's insights into language as well as plays a key role in Habermas's own account of the relation between moral obligation and language. Following a path similar to Levinas's, Habermas argues that the grounds of a moral[26] sense of obligation to others emerges in our competence with language, in particular, in the way language implies a capacity for communicative action oriented to mutual understanding and communicative action implies a capacity for argumentative speech or communicative reason in order to achieve understanding. It is in the constraints of the practice of communicative reason that we find an unavoidable commitment to what Habermas dubs "the principle of universalization," which he argues underlies all cognitive or Kantian-inspired approaches to ethics, providing a foundational normative perspective for the justification of any practical norm as morally valid. Before proceeding, then, with an examination of Habermas's theory of meaning and the account of communicative action in which it is embedded, we should briefly consider what Habermas means by the principle of universalization and his argument for its roots in communicative rationality in order to grasp the role his theory of meaning plays in the broader context of his views on language and moral obligation.

As Habermas proposes it, the principle of universalization is just the idea that no norm can be valid unless "*all* affected can accept the consequences and the side effects its *general* observance can be anticipated to have for the satisfaction of *everyone's* interests."[27] It is this principle that essentially constitutes the moral point of view for Habermas, requiring of everyone a willingness to take the concerns of others who might be affected by a norm into account in its justification. It demands a willingness to take the objections of others seriously by only accepting such a norm as valid after it has been shown to be defensible in the light of those objections. A morally justified principle is, in short, one that could be rationally shown as fair to the interests of all concerned. But the principle of universalization is, as he argues, only a particular expression of a more general commitment to communicative rationality. For the endeavor to rationally convince anyone of the validity of a proposition essentially involves a commitment to answer all objections to it. It involves a commitment to consider seriously the questions and concerns of others, taking them into account in the rational formation of one's own position. As applied to the question of moral norms, however, this is just the principle of universalization itself—a commitment to only accept as a valid moral norm, legitimately applicable to all, one that can be defended as such in relation to the concerns of anyone who would be subject to it.[28] Our commitment to a basic sense of fairness with others stems, then, directly from our commitment to being communicatively rational with others.

1.3.1 Habermas's Inferentialist Theory of Meaning

Our commitment to communicative reason stems, in turn, from our capacity for communicative action, for achieving mutual understanding through language, which presupposes a capacity for being communicatively rational. And it is Habermas's theory of meaning, in particular, that is the linchpin in this connection, that enables us to see why communicative action presupposes communicative rationality. The key to his theory of meaning is to be found in the idea that the understanding of a speech act is dependent on a knowledge of what makes it acceptable, that we only understand a speech act when we know the sorts of reasons that could be given for it, what could give someone good reason to believe her/himself entitled to make it. It is in this sense that our capacity for communicatively achieved understanding depends on a capacity for reason, the capacity to propose and assess reasons that could be advanced for the claims we make. And so, when we understand the meaning of the sentence, "It's a blue day," as involving a reference to a sadness the day somehow provokes, what we have done is anticipated the kind of reason someone could appropriately give for believing her/himself entitled to the utterance; in this case *because* of the sadness s/he feels in confronting the day. The sentence, "It's a blue day," can be appropriately understood as following as an inference from the sentence, "I feel sad confronting the day." Or, rather, to understand its meaning in the particular way noted here *is* to understand it as an inference from a sentence such as that. In this way, Habermas's conception of language appears to draw from the same insight as Levinas's, that the meaning of a sentence is always a function of the role it plays or can play in an "outstretched field of questions and answers." Habermas's articulation of this insight serves, however, to specify the distinctively *inferential* role a speech act must play in this field. We only understand a speech act when we can understand it as inferentially related to other speech acts or appropriate circumstances that could serve as reasons for it, that could provide an answer to our questions concerning it in the sense in which we ask for the speaker or author's entitlement to it. To understand the meaning of a speech act is to understand the role(s) it could play in an essentially conversational "practice of giving and asking for reasons."[29]

The basic idea at stake here is, as Habermas explains, an expansion of the insight behind truth-conditional semantics, in particular, the version arrived at by Michael Dummett, who emphasizes as essential to our understanding of the meaning of any sentence a knowledge of the sorts of reasons that could be given for one's entitlement to propose it as true.[30] To know the meaning of a sentence such as "The sky is blue" is simply to know the reasons that could be given as entitling one to assert it as true, in this case, being in a position to reliably report on the obtaining of appropriate perceptual circumstances (a recognizably blue sky) that provide one with a reason to claim it as true. Habermas's major criticism of this idea is just that it is too restrictive to explain our understanding of linguistic meaning generally. Tailored to assertions or statements which can be appropriately evaluated as true or false, what J. L. Austin dubbed "constative" utterances, it is inappropriate for the other sorts of things we can do with language that cannot be so easily characterized as true or false, what Austin dubbed "performative" utterances, such as making a promise or giving a warning.[31]

Taking Austin's developed model of speech acts as always involving a generally constative and performative dimension, a locutionary act "of" saying something with a specific propositional content or meaning and an illocutionary act "in" saying something with a distinctive force, such as stating something to someone or warning someone about something, Habermas argues that we can generalize Dummett's truth-conditional semantics by expanding our recognition of the sorts of validity claims that can be raised in a speech act as we expand our recognition of the different things that can be done with our speech acts. And so, to take an example from Austin, we could be perfectly clear about the conditions of acceptability for the truth of a sentence such as "It is going to charge" and so, in this way, grasp the meaning of the propositional content of that sentence without clarifying at all how the sentence is used, as a statement of fact or as a warning.[32] The illocutionary significance or force of the sentence can only be captured by a knowledge of the conditions that would make it acceptable as a normatively appropriate performance, as valid in this normative rather than cognitive sense. To understand "It is going to charge" as a warning, for example, would be to understand how uttering it *as* a warning would be a justifiable use to make of this sentence given the circumstances—something that cannot be gleaned from the propositional content of the sentence but only from its use in a particular context, say, referring to a large bull coming at us in an open field where the normative appropriateness of drawing attention to this fact in order to avoid it would be all too evident. With this generalization of Dummett's idea, however, linking our understanding of linguistic meaning to conditions of acceptability in this expanded sense, Habermas argues that we can adequately account for both aspects of the meaning of a speech act, the meaning of its propositional content as well as the illocutionary force of what is done with the utterance.[33]

1.3.2 The Case of Simple Imperatives

In this way, Habermas proposes an internal link between meaning and validity, our ability to understand the meaning of a speech act and our capacity to rationally assess it as raising a validity claim that could be redeemed with specific sorts of reasons. As one would expect, however, it is not difficult to find examples of speech acts that seem to defy this model. In particular, there is the troubling case of what Habermas dubs "simple imperatives," commands that are not authorized by a normative context, such as a bank robber's "Hands up!" In this case, we understand the speech act *as* an imperative but without an understanding of any legitimate reasons that could be given to normatively entitle the robber to issue it. It is different, then, from normatively authorized imperatives, such as the "No Smoking" sign on airplanes, which we understand as a command precisely insofar as we understand the airline or its representatives as having legitimate reasons to issue such a command. In this latter case, meaning and validity are still inescapably linked, as understanding the "No Smoking" sign *as* an imperative involves understanding it as raising a validity claim concerning the normative appropriateness of performing such a speech act under those circumstances that could be redeemed with reasons. But with the bank robber's "Hands up!" the connection between meaning and validity appears to be severed, as there is no validity claim to the normative appropriateness of that speech act being raised at all, only a threat that we will regret it if we fail to comply. And yet we are still able to easily understand it as a command.

Habermas's approach to this specific problem has undergone substantial development.[34] His most recent approach, however, centers on a sociological analysis of, as he puts it, the "continuum between de facto power relations that are merely habitual and power relations that have been transformed into normative authority."[35] The normative authority, for example, of the airline to prohibit smoking on its flights is not wholly distinct from its *de facto* power to enforce the prohibition, as its authority essentially involves a power to impose sanctions, to refuse to honor our ticket if we do not comply with regulations. Thus, the naked assertion of power in the bank robber's "Hands up!" backed only by the threat of force as a sanction without any normative authority, can be understood as an extreme in this continuum. Rather than providing normatively valid reasons for the imperative in conjunction with sanctions, simple imperatives offer sanctions as a substitute for reasons.

But, and this is the point of Habermas's analysis, the simple imperative of the bank robber is only intelligible as an imperative because of its place in this continuum with normatively authorized imperatives for which reasons are available. I recognize the bank robber's speech act as a command despite the apparent lack of any reasons that could be given to normatively authorize such a command, to normatively entitle the robber to make such a command, because I recognize it as the same sort of speech act I am familiar with in normatively authorized contexts, such as the airline flight where smoking is prohibited, except that with the bank robber's command the threat of sanctions has been emphasized to such an extent as to make the provision of reasons unnecessary. Simple imperatives are, therefore, "parasitic" on normatively authorized imperatives, a use of language that takes for granted our competence with imperatives for which reasons can be provided.[36]

This analysis is, admittedly, far from conclusive. It does enable us to see, though, how even in this extreme case it is difficult to get too far away from a grasp of the inferential role a speech act could play in an "outstretched field of questions and answers" and still make sense of its meaning. I can only understand the robber's "Hands up!" as a command insofar as I understand how the threat of force can substitute for a reason as to why I ought to accept the robber's entitlement to issue such a command. It is as if we grasp the threat of force as an answer to our question regarding the robber's entitlement to the speech act, but one that explicitly acknowledges that the sorts of reasons that might ordinarily be available to authorize such a command are absent, making a different sort of response necessary, not a reason for accepting the robber's authority to make the command but a powerful motive for obeying it. Habermas's point is just that a motive can be intelligibly substituted for a reason here only because of the way they are already closely connected in our understanding of imperatives for which reasons can be provided. But without the capacity to ask for and comprehend the sorts of reasons that could ordinarily be given for commands it is difficult to see how we could understand it *as* a command.

1.3.3 Understanding a Reason Implies Assessing Its Validity

It is never sufficient, however, to merely understand the *motives* someone might have for a speech act in order to grasp its meaning. In this case, the robber's offer of a motive for accepting her/his speech act *is* sufficient only because we understand how such a motive can intelligibly substitute for a reason that ordinarily could be understood as valid. This is a point Habermas stresses with what remains one of the more controversial aspects of the development of his theory of meaning[37], his claim that understanding the meaning of a speech act involves a critical evaluation of the validity of the reasons that could be offered for it. As he puts it, understanding a reason that could be given for a speech act implies "judging the soundness" of those reasons.[38] What this sort of evaluative stance involves precisely, however, is more difficult to say. Habermas goes out of his way to distinguish the sense in which we need to take a position on the validity of the reasons offered in order to interpret the meaning of a speech act from the sense in which a participant in some practical context of action would take a position on the validity of a claim that has been raised, agreeing or disagreeing with it and consequently incurring "certain obligations with regard to the further course of interaction. The role of interpreter and of actor are not identical. Understanding does not of course mean agreement."[39] Taking an evaluative position as an interpreter does not, therefore, entail coming to a conclusion regarding validity that would entail agreement or disagreement and the consequent assumption of "obligations with regard to the further course of interaction." But it does involve more than simply noting what are advanced as reasons without concerning ourselves with the question of their validity.

Situated between these extremes it seems plausible to suppose that what Habermas is claiming is just that understanding a reason that could be advanced for a speech act *as* a reason must involve the exercise of our evaluative capacities at least insofar as we can recognize what is advanced as a *potentially* valid reason for that speech act, as what would provide good reason for the speech act *were* we to come to agreement on its validity. Understood in this way Habermas's point is very well made. If we were utterly unprepared to evaluate the potential validity of the reasons offered for a speech act it is hard to see how we could even grasp them *as* reasons relevant to the meaning of the speech act. A part of what enables me to understand the legal authority of an airline to regulate issues of health and safety *as* a reason that could be advanced for an imperative prohibiting smoking is my ability to see how it would indeed provide a sound reason for the acceptability of that imperative *if* the authority is valid. But this means that I must be prepared to critically distinguish this sort of appeal that could provide a sound reason from other sorts of appeals that could not. For example, suppose I was confused as to the meaning of the "No Smoking" signs on my flight, wondering whether they might not be statements describing the typical absence of smoking that obtains on flights of this sort rather than commands not to smoke. If I questioned the flight attendant it would be of no help to me if the attendant launched into an otherwise interesting explanation of the aerodynamics of flight as opposed to an explanation about legally mandated health and safety regulations because I cannot understand the explanation of aerodynamics as providing a sound reason to issue a command prohibiting smoking. I must be at least this evaluative in my assessment of reasons that could be provided for the speech act, critically distinguishing the sort of appeals that could from the sort that could not serve as genuinely sound reasons.

Anything more than this, however, seems an implausible demand for a theory of meaning to make. If, to continue playing with this admittedly forced example, I was not sure about the validity of my attendant's explanation about legally mandated health and safety regulations, having doubts as to whether such laws had really been passed or whether the airline was actually authorized to enforce them,[40] this would not prevent me from understanding what was meant by the "No Smoking" sign. I recognize that *were* the explanation to be valid, it would constitute a sound reason for the imperative prohibiting me from smoking. Hence, Habermas's conclusion that understanding the meaning of a speech act involves a capacity for rationality in this specific sense, involving the ability not merely to discern the presence of what others might take as good reasons for a claim in the capacity of an observer, but also the capacity to evaluate the validity of those reasons from the perspective of a participant in an argumentative exchange. Discerning the inferential role of a speech act is simply not possible for a pure observer of the practice of giving and asking for reasons. It is only possible for a participant, someone who actually has this capacity and, if only implicitly, exercises it by taking a position on what could or could not serve as a sound reason for a claim.

1.3.4 "Understanding Is the Inherent Telos of Human Speech"

To establish the necessity of communicative reason for achieving understanding, as Habermas attempts with his inferentialist theory of meaning, is not yet, however, to establish it as a presupposition of our capacity for language generally. As Habermas recognizes, some uses of language do not appear to be oriented to achieving understanding. Insulting someone or making a false promise, for example, are both primarily oriented to achieving strategic effects in the world: making someone feel bad or motivated to do what you desire. And yet Habermas insists that "reaching understanding is the inherent telos of human speech," "an original mode of language use" in relation to which any other uses are "parasitic."[41] As such, he aims to show that every use of language, "all recourse to words," is dependent on the aim of achieving understanding, which involves a capacity for communicative reason and, as a consequence, a commitment to the moral point of view as it is implicit in the universalizing constraints of the practice of rationality.

Habermas's argument to this end relies on Austin's distinction between illocutionary and perlocutionary aims in speech. Drawing a rough[42] line between illocutionary aims, which concern "bringing about the understanding of the meaning and of the force of the locution . . . securing (its) uptake,"[43] and perlocutionary aims, which seek to realize strategic goals that go beyond merely achieving understanding, he argues that perlocutionary objectives with language can only be achieved on the basis of successfully realized illocutionary aims. One cannot have perlocutionary aims that go beyond achieving understanding without also taking for granted illocutionary aims that concern securing the uptake of one's speech. To seek to influence you to give me money on the basis of a false promise to repay you or to make you feel bad about yourself on the basis of an insult does not aim primarily at achieving an understanding of the meaning and force of the promise or insult. But it must take such a successfully secured understanding for granted as the necessary means to achieve such influence as you will not be motivated to give me money or to feel bad about yourself if you fail to understand the promise or insult.[44] As Habermas concludes,

> speech acts can serve this *nonillocutionary aim of influencing hearers* only if they are suited to achieve illocutionary aims. If the hearer failed to understand what the speaker was saying, a strategically acting speaker would not be able to bring the hearer, by means of communicative acts, to behave in the desired way. To this extent, what we initially designated as "the use of language with an orientation to consequences" is not an original use of language but the subsumption of speech acts that serve illocutionary aims under conditions of action oriented to success.[45]

It is not possible, therefore, to use language strategically without first having a competence with its properly communicative use to achieve understanding. The strategic use of language presupposes its communicative use. This is not, moreover, merely a point about how we *learn* language.[46] It is true that no one could learn how to use language strategically without first having learned how to use it communicatively. But Habermas's argument also entails that there can be no *completely* strategic use of language that could be abstracted from its communicative use. It is not as if having learned a communicative use of language we are then prepared to learn a strategic use that would enable us, at least at times, to leave its communicative use behind. It is, rather, that even as we use language strategically we must also use it communicatively, if only as a necessary condition for accomplishing our strategic goals. In insulting you I may be explicitly aiming only at the strategic goal of making you feel bad. But I would not be able to achieve that goal if I were not also, if only implicitly, aiming to secure an understanding with you as to the meaning and force of my words, which I hope, of course, will have the consequence of making you feel bad.

1.4 Between Communicative Action and Conversational Deference

As a properly communicative use of language used to secure understanding is a necessary presupposition of any use of language and a capacity for communicative reason is a necessary presupposition of communicative action, the principle of universalization is, therefore, a normative principle to which all who are capable of speech find themselves unavoidably committed as a function of the constraints of being communicatively rational. In this way, we find a universal sense of justice knit into the very fabric of human speech. But Habermas's account of communicative action may be seen to advance Levinas's aims with language as well, to establish a conversational sense of deference to the other as a condition for the possibility of language itself, of "all recourse to words." To begin, Habermas's inferentialist theory of meaning strengthens and develops Levinas's claim that a conversational relationship to the other as interlocutor is a presupposition of understanding the meaning of any speech act. The sense of rationality to which Habermas traces our hermeneutic competence with language, the capacity to give and ask for reasons we are prepared to evaluate as sound or unsound, must involve the conversational deference described by Levinas. To reason in this sense is, as Levinas argues, to find myself called into question by the other, called to take what the other says into account in what I say. As previously noted, even a dismissive argument aiming to show what the other says is unreasonable is qualitatively different from a truly dismissive attitude that would treat the other as if s/he did not deserve even that consideration. To advance reasons for what I say in the light of the objections of others is to accept that I am not really entitled to what I say until I can say something else capable of convincing the other of my entitlement. Though there is certainly more to a conversational sense of deference as Levinas understands it, our capacity to reason in this sense is an expression of it, a type of conversational practice that would be unintelligible apart from it.

Habermas's argument for the priority of communicative to strategic uses of language also clarifies how every use of language, not merely those in which the achievement of mutual understanding is a foremost concern, takes place, as Levinas would say, in proximity to the other. Inasmuch as a conversational sense of deference to the other is an essential moment in any attempt to use language communicatively, and no use of language is possible without some, if only instrumentally necessary, reference to its communicative use, then "all recourse to words" can be seen to presuppose a sense of obligation to the other, my interlocutor, to whom speech is addressed. This may be, of course, a rather distant presupposition whose appreciation is obliterated by our strategic concerns with language. When I make a false promise to repay you money I am trying to get you to lend me, I certainly do not recognize in any explicit manner an obligation to a form of consideration of you that would be inconsistent with the purely instrumental attitude I adopt in making such a false promise. My strategic attitude toward you as a resource I could exploit to my advantage overwhelms any conversational attitude that may be implicit in my communicative act of trying to make myself understood to you. But should I cease to be able to take that communicative achievement for granted, should I, for example, find that you do not quite understand what I am promising or even, perhaps, that what I am doing is making a promise, I will find myself forced by virtue of my strategic project to attend more to the conversational requirements of that communicative achievement. I will have to solicit the basis for your lack of understanding and attempt to provide you with reasons for what I say that are responsive to your questions and, in that way, may clarify what I mean to say to you. And though this would certainly not, in and of itself, constitute any sort of moral awakening on my part as to the injustice of my false promise, it would—and this is the point of Levinas's analysis—place me in a relationship with you that provides the potential for such a recognition, a conversational relationship to you as my interlocutor.

1.4.1 Reciprocity and Asymmetry in Our Ethical Proximity to the Other

Before proceeding, however, it is important to stress that I have no intention here of suggesting a perfect parallel between Levinas's and Habermas's accounts of language and our sense of moral obligation. Many divergences remain to be examined. And so in what remains of this chapter, I want to address *some* of these divergences beginning, in particular, with two that I believe are not as significant as they might first appear, so as to more precisely delineate the shared conceptual terrain between Levinas and Habermas and to prepare to place into relief the major divergence between them that is the central concern of the next four chapters. To begin, there is at least one implication of my argument that may appear to overtly contradict one of the more definitive aspects of Levinas's account of our ethical relation to the other. In proposing Habermas's inferentialist theory of meaning as a more articulate development of Levinas's insights into language, a moment of reciprocity and critical judgment is introduced into our moral relation with the other. To understand the speech acts of the other I must be able to evaluate their potential validity, asserting myself as an equal in the relationship with my interlocutor to this extent, subject not only to the judgment of the other but subjecting the other to my judgment as well.

This appears to contradict, however, Levinas's emphasis on what he characterizes as the asymmetrical character of my proximity to the other. As I have already noted, Levinas conceives of the other who would be my interlocutor as my master or teacher, the one to whom I am obliged to attend. It is this "orientation" toward the other that Levinas suggests is asymmetrical. "Responsibility, the signification which is non-indifference, goes one way *(est à sens unique)*, from me to the other."[47] I find myself responsible to the other but not, at least at first, the other responsible to me. Though Levinas is not entirely clear as to everything that is implied for him by this thesis, the main point seems to be to emphasize the "gravity"[48] of our responsibility to the other, the unconditional manner in which I am solicited by the other apart from any symmetrical service from the other, any tit for tat arrangement with the other. My responsibility, as Levinas understands it, is not conditional upon a reciprocal agreement with the other that might lead me to voluntarily undertake such a commitment, to be for you *if* you will be for me—hence, his references to responsibility for the other as a form of "persecution" in which I have been singled out as responsible prior to any "commitment" I might voluntarily undertake.[49]

In initiating a conversation with another person, for example, I may have my own reasons for deferring to the other in the way that practice demands. Perhaps I want to gain your confidence so I can rely on your aid in the realization of some project of mine. Perhaps I need information from you that I can attain only through conversation with you. We often have our own reasons for undertaking a conversational relationship with someone with all that entails in the way of a commitment to defer to the point of view of the other. But whatever our reasons, once we embark on that conversational relationship, we find ourselves bound to a sense of deference to the other that is not limited by those reasons, that remains unconditional precisely insofar as it may call into question any of the reasons we might intend as limiting conditions for our commitment to the other. In seeking the information I need from you, I may find that what you say to me calls into question the very aim that drew me into conversation with you. I may find myself called to justify an aim I cannot really justify from your perspective insofar as it was formed from a point of view entirely indifferent to your concerns. But insofar as I continue to converse with you, to relate to you as my interlocutor, I find myself called to reconsider my aims, called to an unconditional mode of deference to you, a form of consideration for you that is not and cannot be limited by the reasons that may have brought me to voluntarily undertake a conversational relationship to you in the first place.

It is in this sense, then, that the mode of obligation to the other to which I find myself bound in a conversational relationship is unconditional. Not that I do not have my own reasons for entering into such a relation that condition and limit my interest in it, but that every interest I bring with me may be called into question in that relationship. Of course, it is always my option to end a conversational relationship with the other when it is no longer expedient to my interests. But that is not an option consistent with the obligation I have undertaken in conversing with another person. It is, rather, a betrayal of that obligation. Our voluntary commitment to relate to the other person as an interlocutor is always a conditional commitment. But the sense of obligation to which I thereby find myself committed always threatens to explode the conditional parameters of that commitment, to call them into question in a way I am bound to consider insofar as I remain related to the other as my interlocutor. This is what it means to relate to another person as my interlocutor. It is to recognize in the other "a *right* over (one's) egoism"[50] that cannot be conditioned or limited by the interests that bring you to the point of that recognition.

Hence, the asymmetry that precludes any essentially conditional, contractual understanding of my conversationally grounded sense of obligation to the other. It is always the other who has the upper hand in any genuinely conversational relationship, as it is always the other who reserves the right to call into question whatever interests may have brought me into the relation. A sense of reciprocity with the other is established, for Levinas, only with the emergence of what he dubs "the third party" (*tiers*), other others to whom I also find myself responsible. In the presence of multiple interlocutors, multiple others who command my consideration in potentially conflicting ways, I must weigh and evaluate the significance of their different claims in order to know how to appropriately respond. Here the need for impartiality arises, a consideration of every other as, in principle, equally deserving of my consideration and, finally, a sense of reciprocity as I grasp my own claims as worthy of consideration as the claims of one other among others.[51] Emerging in this way on the basis of my originally asymmetrical sense of responsibility to the other, as a complication of that responsibility in the presence of multiple responsibilities, reciprocity is able to take a morally delimited form as the assertion of my rights as an other among others deserving equal consideration. More than a contractual tit for tat that would condition the assumption of my responsibilities, that would leave me free of my responsibilities should the other fail to reciprocate in a way that was in my interests, reciprocity in this context always takes place within the horizon of an unconditional demand for justice as an impartial consideration for all.[52]

Seen in this light, however, it is not clear why Levinas should object to the sense of reciprocity Habermas's theory of meaning requires in my relation to the other. The assertion of my capacity to judge the other, to evaluate the validity of what the other says, is not a product of a tit for tat contract with the other in which I agree to defer to you only if I you agree to return the favor. It is a moment in what is, for Habermas as well as Levinas, an unconditional obligation I undertake in being communicatively rational to consider whatever the other, indeed, any other has to say concerning my claims. It is, hence, a judgment carried out in service to the other as a part of what must be done to understand what the other means to say to me, a condition for the possibility of a meaningful response to the other. As I have analyzed it, the conversational demand for deference to the other is, at bottom, a demand for a response to the other that is genuine, that takes what the other says into account in what I say. But this deferential response is just not possible without my critical evaluation of the validity of what the other says. Otherwise I could not understand what is said to me so as to be able to respond to it.

Even Abraham, to this extent, must judge God's command to sacrifice his son in order to meaningfully respond to it, to obey it. He must anticipate the sort of reasons God could give for his command, critically distinguishing them from reasons that could not be sound, in order to understand God's command *as* a command. He must anticipate God's authority to command even this degree of sacrifice as entitling him to issue such a command and, in this spirit, be prepared to critically distinguish this potentially valid inferential appeal from invalid ones, such as an appeal to a blemish on Issac's knee or the nearby presence of a cricket, which could not, at least on their own, serve as good reasons for it. To understand himself as commanded and so be able to respond to that command, even Abraham must exercise at least this degree of judgment. Any meaningful response to any other demands this much reciprocity.

In fact, though it is not much emphasized in his work, Levinas himself seems to acknowledge much the same point. In a passage from *Otherwise than Being* devoted to clarifying his observations on reciprocity and "the third party," he distinguishes "the entry of a third party" from the occurrence of "an empirical fact." It is not the factual presence of another other that would bring with it the need of reciprocity and judgment, as if the fundamentals of our moral relation to the other would change merely as people come and go from the room. Reiterating a point made in his earlier analysis of this issue in *Totality and Infinity*, Levinas concludes that my proximity to any other always already involves me in a relation to other others and so to a need for judgment and reciprocity. "In the proximity of the other, all the others than the other obsess me, and already this obsession cries out for justice, demands measure and knowing, is consciousness."[53]

To a great extent, this point depends on Levinas's recognition of the way a conversational relationship to another person opens me up to a sense of obligation to any other insofar as they are also capable of becoming my interlocutor, as well as, no doubt, an appreciation of the way any actual relation to a singular other is always contextualized in terms of my relations with other singular others. I am never simply by myself with the other. There are always other others to whom I also find myself obliged. But Levinas may also be recognizing here the impossibility of meaningfully responding to any other as a completely unique and singular other. Though my proximity to the other is, for Levinas, always a call to be for *this* other in particular, responding to this other demands understanding the claims s/he makes. But, as Habermas's theory of language makes clear, this is not possible without evaluating the validity of the reasons the other could offer for her/his claims, a process that brings to bear standards of validity, models of valid inference that are applicable to anyone's utterances. To do so, then, in a conscientious attempt to respond to this unique other is necessarily to treat this unique other as *any* other, subject to the same standards of evaluation as anyone else. To this extent, the third party is virtually present even here in my attempt to muster a meaningful response to the singular other who addresses me, present precisely in my appeal to standards of evaluation that refer not merely to this other but to any other.

Though this point is sometimes overlooked by readers of Levinas,[54] it is clear that Levinas believes the third party is present in every relation to any other and, to that extent, there is a need for judgement and a sense of reciprocity in service to the other. His emphasis on the asymmetrical character of my relation to the other needs, then, to be taken not as a global characterization of my moral experience including my attempts to meaningfully respond to the other but, rather, as a specific characterization of the nature of the appeal that solicits that response. Understanding judgment and reciprocity as necessary for a meaningful response to the other, as in service to the other in that way, is consistent with understanding the demand for deference to the other as asymmetrical, as an unconditional demand incapable of being adequately understood in voluntaristic or contractual terms that would set the conditions, the limits, of that deference.

1.4.2 Communicative Action as a Mode of Social Coordination

The integral presence of reciprocity in Habermas's account of communicative action should not, therefore, discourage us from drawing a strong parallel between communicative action and what I have been calling Levinas's account of conversational deference. To the contrary, it should encourage us to recognize the role of reciprocity, the presence of the third party, in Levinas's own account of our relation to the other even in the singular. But there is another difference between their two accounts in the way the concept of communicative action plays an important role in Habermas's social theory that has no parallel in Levinas's account of conversational deference. For Habermas, the distinction between communicative and strategic action is a distinction between two modes of coordinating action between different agents, the first achieving this end through mutual understanding and consensus and the latter achieving it through the exercise of influence. The coordination of action through communicative action is an inherently cooperative endeavor in a way that is not true of strategic action that merely draws on an individual agent's capacity to influence the behavior of other agents in the same way that s/he is capable of causally influencing other events in the world. This implies, however, that communicative action is always understood, like strategic modes of action, as goal directed. Communicative action aims to realize the goal of coordinating social interaction.[55]

Conversation, on the other hand, though a form of language used to reach understanding, is not inherently in service to the goal of coordinating social interaction. As Habermas notes, "There are contexts of action that do not *primarily* serve the carrying out of communicatively harmonized plans of action . . . but make communication possible and stabilize it—for instance, chatting, conversing, (*Unterhaltungen*) and arguing—in general conversation (*Gespräch*) that becomes an end in itself. In such cases the process of reaching understanding is detached from the instrumental role of serving as a mechanism for coordinating individual actions."[56] Though Habermas identifies conversation as a type of communicative action,[57] it is not clear that he should, given his social theoretic concerns with the coordination of interaction that frame his broadest understanding of communicative action. Or, to put this point in another way, it *is* clear that we should be careful in the parallels we draw between them inasmuch as the sense of conversation Levinas evokes in his work as the basis for our ethical proximity to the other is clearly not subordinated to social theoretic concerns with the coordination of interaction. When Levinas speaks of entering into a conversational relation with another person there is no suggestion of any overarching social purpose beyond the sharing of speech itself. Though, equally, there is no suggestion that there could not be such a purpose. The best way to put the relation might be to say that the sense of conversation that Levinas evokes in his work is a broader concept than Habermas's concept of communicative action. It represents a model of language used to achieve mutual understanding that may or may not fulfill the role of coordinating social interaction.

For this very reason, however, we are right to discern an important parallel between Habermas's and Levinas's accounts of communicative action and conversational deference. As Habermas notes, argumentation is a form of "conversation that becomes an end in itself," and, as we know, argumentation, communicative reason, plays a constitutive role in the achievement of mutual understanding that communicative action utilizes to coordinate social interaction. The conversational sense of deference to the other that Levinas analyzes is, therefore, a constitutive moment in what Habermas understands as communicative action, the moment whereby mutual understanding is achieved through a deference to the other, which, as Levinas argues, takes the form of a call to justify myself. Not every instance of what we might describe, with Levinas, as a practice of conversation is an instance of what Habermas would describe in specifically social theoretic terms as communicative action. But every instance of communicative action essentially involves the conversational deference to the other Levinas evokes in his work.

1.4.3 Procedural and Substantive Dimensions of Language

We come upon a genuine divide between their two perspectives only as we begin to consider the way Habermas and Levinas differ in their accounts of the significance of the sense of obligation opened up within language. This point is initially discernible in the different roles reason plays in their arguments. For Habermas, reason is the ground of the moral point of view. It is in the procedural constraints of the practice of communicative reason, the demand for impartial modes of justification, open to challenge from any corner, that the basis for the principle of universalization is to be found. Indeed, the principle of universalization is itself merely a particular expression of these rational procedures as applied to the specific case of the justification of practical norms. In consequence, as Habermas has stressed, his "discourse ethics" is a procedural ethics, offering only a rational procedure for the determination of valid moral norms that is not itself committed to any substantive values.[58]

For Levinas, on the other hand, our commitment to reason is itself only fully intelligible as a product of our ethical proximity to the other. My deference to the other in accord with rational procedures is only partially explicated by making reference to those procedures. There is also what Levinas characterizes as the "always positive value"[59] of the face of the other, my recognition of my interlocutor as worthy of the impartial consideration demanded of me by reason. As opposed to the procedural ethics Habermas advances in the light of his account of communicative action, Levinas's analysis of our conversational deference to the other leads him to stress the substantive worth of the other person with whom I speak as the ground of a moral point of view onto life. Here we have a significant difference between them that constitutes, or so I argue, a basis for a constructive reflection on their respective contributions to our understanding of moral obligation and its relation to our capacity for language. I devote the next four chapters to a detailed examination of the implications of this divergence in their accounts as it forms the heart of my critical concerns with Habermas and Levinas.

But for now, I want to stress the substantial ways in which Habermas's and Levinas's accounts converge in a shared conceptual terrain emphasizing the important role of a conversational or communicative sense of language in the constitution of our most fundamental sense of moral obligation. And by arguing that this particular sense of language is an inescapable presupposition of our capacity for a meaningful use of language generally, for "all recourse to words," they give us reason to suppose that all human beings, indeed, every being capable of a meaningful use of language, shares in that sense of obligation. How we must articulate that sense of obligation, however, in terms of a commitment to rational procedures or as a recognition of the substantive value of the "face of the other," remains an open question.

Notes

1. See Aristotle, *Politics*, bk. I, ch. 1, 1253.
2. Emmanuel Levinas, *Totality and Infinity*, trans. Alphonso Lingis (Pittsburgh: Duquesne University Press, 1969), 40, and Levinas, *Totalité et Infini* (La Haye: Martinus Nijhoff, 1961), 10. Lingis's translation of *"discours"* as "conversation" in this context seems apt, as it is clear from context of the book as a whole, in which Levinas stresses *discours* as a form of speech undertaken with the other as interlocutor, that he is speaking of a distinctively conversational use of language. Also see *Totalité et Infini*, 68, where Levinas characterizes *discours* as *"un entre-tien."*

On a more substantive note, I should mention that I base my examination of Levinas's conception of language as a ground for our sense of moral obligation in this chapter principally on his account in *Totality and Infinity*. In my estimation, it is the most argumentatively developed account of how our capacity for language opens us up to an ethical sense of obligation to the other. Though his account of the "saying" and the "said" in his later work, *Otherwise than Being or Beyond Essence* (trans. Alphonso Lingis [The Hague: Martinus Nijhoff, 1981]), is of tremendous importance for many aspects of his thought, it largely presupposes what I am interested in examining in this chapter, Levinas's case for why we should believe our capacity for language opens us up to a sense of moral obligation to the other. (See, in particular, page 46 of *Otherwise than Being*, where after a careful and insightful analysis of *what* is said, he simply states without argument that the saying of what is said is always said *to the other*, in an ethical sense of proximity to the other—the principal point he struggles to establish in *Totality and Infinity* and with which I am concerned in this chapter.)

3. Levinas, *Totality and Infinity*, 195. Levinas, *Totalité et Infini*, 169.
4. See Levinas, *Totality and Infinity*, 69, "The interpellated one is called upon to speak; his speech consists in 'coming to the assistance' of his word—in being *present*."
5. Levinas, *Totality and Infinity*, 69.
6. Levinas relates conversation to teaching—"To approach the Other in conversation is to welcome his expression . . . to be taught." (*Totality and Infinity*, 51)—and this teaching/mastery of the other to an "appeal addressed to my attention" (*Totality and Infinity*, 99).
7. See Levinas, *Totality and Infinity*, 40.
8. See, for example, Levinas, *Totality and Infinity*, 195. "For the ethical relationship which subtends discourse . . . puts the I in question."
9. Levinas, *Otherwise than Being*, 56.
10. Levinas, *Totality and Infinity*, 206. Levinas, *Totalité et Infini*, 181.
11. See, in particular, Jacques Derrida, "Signature, Event, Context," in *Limited Inc.*, ed. Gerald Graff (Evanston, Ill.: Northwestern University Press, 1988), and J. L. Austin, *How to Do Things with Words* (Cambridge, Mass.: Harvard University Press, 1962).
12. Adriaan Peperzak, "Presentation," in *Re-Reading Levinas*, ed. Robert Bernasconi and Simon Critchley (Bloomington: Indiana University Press, 1991), 52 & 59.

13. For Levinas's distinction between the "saying" and the "said," see, in particular, his *Otherwise than Being*, 5-7 & 45-51. I will be elaborating more on this distinction as it becomes relevant in chapter 3.

14. Levinas, *Totality and Infinity*, 205 & 207.

15. This is not to say that his criticisms beg the question against Heidegger and Merleau-Ponty. To the contrary, Levinas has some interesting points to make against their views that merit examination in their own right. In particular, I am thinking of his argument against the Heideggerian conception of language as grounded in our practical capacity to make use of the world, the "ready-to-hand" structure of our "being-in-the-world," as Heidegger puts it. Levinas argues that this practical comprehension of things *as* useful in some way or another and, therefore, *as* meaningful presupposes propositional language that posits the world in an objective rather than practical manner. "In the perspective of finality and enjoyment signification appears only in labor, which implies enjoyment impeded. But enjoyment impeded would by itself engender no signification but only suffering did it not occur in a world of objects, that is, in a world where speech has already resounded" (Levinas, *Totality and Infinity*, 97). But this still does not make his point that propositional language presupposes a conversational relation to the other. In fact, the point he is trying to make may not even be necessary to his project, as we could still recognize the Heideggerian point and insist with Levinas that propositional language, though it presupposes a practical comprehension of the world, *also* presupposes a conversational relation to the other in a way our practical comprehension of the world may not. In fact, I am inclined to think that this is a more reasonable position to take.

16. Levinas, *Totality and Infinity*, 96.

17. Levinas, *Totality and Infinity*, 96.

18. Levinas, *Totality and Infinity*, 98. Levinas also emphasizes this connection elsewhere in *Totality and Infinity*. See page 99, where he characterizes the teaching the other brings to me in a conversational relationship by virtue of her/his ability to come to the assistance of her/his word as "the end of equivocation or confusion." Also see pages 93-94, where he describes the signs that would be delivered by someone who "declines the assistance he would have to bring to the signs he delivers" as consequently delivered "in equivocation."

19. See, for example, Derrida, "Signature, Event, Context."

20. As in the deference shown to another when I allow her/him to go before me, saying "After you." See Levinas, *Otherwise than Being*, 117.

21. By referring to a "minimal" meaning, I intend to refer to basic elements of plot, character, and the like—of what took place in the novel—that would allow us to recognize what everyone read *as* the same book despite the usual disagreements as to the deeper meaning of the book as a whole or of some of its dimensions; a minimal meaning that would allow us to understand that when we are debating the significance of, say, *Hamlet*, we are debating the significance of the same play.

22. I have been thinking here of Derrida's example in "Signature, Event, Context" of citing or "grafting" part of a text out of its "internal semiotic context." As Derrida notes, this does not prevent the cited text from signifying something. But, as he also argues, it only continues to signify something insofar as it is grafted onto another discursive chain of signs that provide a new context for it. And this only exacerbates the polysemy of the fragment of the text that is cited. Levinas's point, as I take it so far, is not that this sort of reading strategy is not possible but only that attempting to overcome this polysemy to establish a shared meaning for language among a linguistic community entails the kind of conversational attitude he discusses

23. See Emmanuel Levinas, "Meaning and Sense," in *Collected Philosophical Papers*, trans. Alphonso Lingis, (Dordrecht: Martinus Nijhoff Publishers, 1987), 88-89.

24. See Levinas, "Meaning and Sense," 87, trans. note # 37.

25. Jürgen Habermas, *The Theory of Communicative Action,* Vol. 1, *Reason and the Rationalization of Society*, trans. Thomas McCarthy (Boston: Beacon Press, 1984), 297.

26. By the expression "properly moral" I mean to refer to Habermas's distinction between moral norms that have universal validity and ethical norms that are only valid for specific cultures or forms of life. As Habermas is generally consistent in his use of these terms (with the glaring exception of the term "discourse ethics," which should, given his use of the term, be rendered discourse *morality* to be consistent—a point he has recognized) I will be consistent as well when using these terms in relation to Habermas. But as this use is not widely accepted outside Habermasian quarters, I will not adopt Habermas's distinctive sense of these terms throughout this study. In particular, it would be awkward to rephrase every Levinasian reference to ethics as a reference to morality to make it consistent with Habermas's sense of these terms.

27. Habermas, "Discourse Ethics: Notes on a Program of Philosophical Justification," in *Moral Consciousness and Communicative Action*, ed. Christian Lenhardt and Shierry Weber Nicholsen (Cambridge, Mass.: The MIT Press, 1990), 65.

28. See Habermas, "Discourse Ethics: Notes on a Program of Philosophical Justification," 86-94.

29. This phrase is Robert Brandom's who gets it from Wilfred Sellars. See Brandom's *Making It Explicit: Reasoning, Representing, and Discursive Commitment* (Cambridge, Mass.: Harvard University Press, 1994). I mention Brandom's work here principally because it seems a more adequate inferentialist approach to language than we find in Habermas. Habermas's theory of meaning emphasizes only one inferential role a speech act can play in the "practice of giving and asking for reasons," its role as an inference from another speech act or appropriate set of circumstances that serve as a reason for it. But a speech act can also serve as a reason for other speech acts or practical consequences that follow as an inference from it. To take an example from Brandom, a part of what is involved in grasping the meaning of "That's red" is not merely a knowledge of what could serve as a reason for it, what could lead someone to believe her/himself justifiably entitled to assert it as true, as Habermas emphasizes, but also what follows inferentially from it—"That's colored," for example (see pages 88-89 for this example). But as important as this expansion of our understanding of the inferential roles a speech act may play in the constitution of its meaning may be for the philosophy of language, it is not a terribly pressing point in our context of concerns. For my point here is only that Habermas's inferentialist theory of meaning can be seen as giving further precision to Levinas's ideas concerning the constitution of linguistic meaning in an "outstretched field of questions and answers," that Habermas is developing an insight about language that is also crucial to Levinas. If, as I believe, Brandom's theory of language corrects important inadequacies in Habermas's theory, this only goes to show that at least some of the problems we could observe with Habermas's theory can be corrected without going beyond the parameters of an inferentialist account that preserves the basic insight that Habermas's theory of meaning is developing.

30. For Habermas's understanding and appropriation of Dummett's work, see Habermas, "Toward a Critique of the Theory of Meaning," in *Postmetaphysical Thinking: Philosophical Essays*, trans. William Mark Hohengarten (Cambridge, Mass.: The MIT Press, 1992), in particular, 68 &77. The most important text of Dummett for Habermas is "What Is a Theory of Meaning? (II)," in *Truth and Meaning: Essays in Semantics*, ed. Gareth Evans

and John McDowell (Oxford: Clarendon Press, 1976), 67-137.

31. For J. L. Austin's theory of language as speech acts see his *How to Do Things with Words*.

32. For this example, see Austin, *How to Do Things with Words*, 98.

33. Habermas himself does not, however, merely argue for an expansion of our appreciation of the sorts of validity claims we can make in a speech act beyond that of a claim to truth. He also lays great stress on the way every speech act raises, if only implicitly, *three* validity claims to truth, normative rightness, and truthfulness or sincerity. I only stress the idea of an expansion of our appreciation of validity claims beyond that of a claim to truth because this seems to me to be the crucial point in his theory of meaning. I agree with Maeve Cooke's conclusion in *Language and Reason: A Study of Habermas's Pragmatics* (Cambridge, Mass.: The MIT Press, 1994) that the success or failure of his project in no way turns on his position regarding precisely three validity claims. If anything, as Cooke argues, Habermas's position "seems to point toward a genuinely multi-dimensional as opposed to merely three-dimensional conception of reason" (*Language and Reason*, 94).

34. For Habermas's evolving discussion of this problem, see *The Theory of Communicative Action*, vol. 1, 305 & 329; "Reply to Skjei," *Inquiry* 28 (1985): 111-113; "A Reply" in *Communicative Action: Essays on Jürgen Habermas's The Theory of Communicative Action*, ed. Axel Honneth and Hans Joas (Cambridge, Mass.: The MIT Press, 1991), 239; and "Toward a Critique of the Theory of Meaning," 83-84.

35. Habermas, "Toward a Critique of the Theory of Meaning," 83.

36. See, in particular, Habermas, "A Reply," 239.

37. See, in particular, Thomas McCarthy, "Reflections on Rationalization in *The Theory of Communicative Action*," in *Habermas and Modernity*, ed. Richard Bernstein (Polity Press, 1985).

38. Habermas, "A Reply," 229.

39. Habermas, "A Reply," 230.

40. Perhaps it is like the no smoking regulation that was in effect for bars in California for a while, where the owners were only authorized to advise their customers of the law but not to enforce it.

41. Habermas, *The Theory of Communicative Action*, vol. 1, 287 & 288.

42. I say "rough" as Habermas's critics have led him to refine and reformulate his distinction since its initial articulation in *The Theory of Communicative Action*. For his later formulation of the distinction, see Habermas, "A Reply," 239-240. Also see Cooke, *Language and Reason*, 22-24, for an especially clear synopsis of Habermas's mature position. I do not go into these developments here, however, as I do not believe the basic point of his position in *The Theory of Communicative Action* has changed.

43. Austin, *How to Do Things with Words*, 117.

44. Focusing on Habermas's preoccupation in *The Theory of Communicative Action* with latently strategic uses of language where the strategic objectives of the agent must remain concealed in order to be effective, as with my example of the false promise that could not be strategically successful if my strategic objectives were to become manifest, Cooke argues that Habermas's argument is not generalizable to manifestly strategic uses of language such as a bank robber's "Hand's up!" or "certain kinds of insult" where the agent's strategic objectives need not be concealed to be effective. Habermas's point with latently strategic uses of language is, Cooke argues, "tautological." "The latently strategic use of language is *per definition* a use of language that simulates the communicative use. Its success depends on the success of the pretense, it is thus by its very nature parasitic." But

with regard to manifestly strategic uses of language, Cooke insists that "there is no evidence that Habermas has adequately addressed this issue" (Cooke, *Language and Reason*, 24). It is difficult to see Cooke's point, however, as Habermas's basic insight seems immediately applicable to both manifestly as well as latently strategic uses of language: the strategic success of false promises as well as insults depends on securing their uptake. See "Toward a Critique of the Theory of Meaning," 84, where Habermas reiterates this point in relation to manifestly strategic uses of language (in particular, the bank robber's "Hand's up!"): "They remain parasitic insofar as their comprehensibility must be derived from the employment conditions for illocutionary acts."

45. Habermas, *The Theory of Communicative Action*, vol. 1, 293.

46. See Cooke, *Language and Reason*, 25, where she argues that Habermas merely succeeds in establishing what Cooke calls the "conceptual" dependence of a communicative use of language on its strategic use, which refers to the way one must be learned prior to the former and not a "functional" dependence that would concern its use. Cooke is right that Habermas's argument does not entail "what proportion" of a communicative use of language is necessary to "the functioning of a given linguistic community." But this is not to say that there is no functional point entailed about the way a strategic use of language depends (not merely genetically, but structurally) on a communicative use.

47. Levinas, *Otherwise than Being*, 138. Levinas, *Autrement qu'être ou au-delà de l'essence* (La Haye: Martinus Nijhoff, 1974), 177. Also see *Totality and Infinity*, 215-216.

48. The metaphor is Levinas's. See, for example, Levinas, "Language and Proximity," in *Collected Philosophical Papers*, 123, and Levinas, *Otherwise than Being*, 6-7.

49. See Levinas, *Otherwise than Being*, 102.

50. See above and Levinas, *Totality and Infinity*, 40.

51. For Levinas's treatment of the "third party," see *Totality and Infinity*, 212-214 (Levinas, *Totalité et Infini*, 188), and Levinas, *Otherwise than Being*, 157-161.

52. For Levinas's understanding of justice as impartial consideration of every other (including myself) see *Otherwise than Being*, 157-161 and below, ch. 3.

53. Levinas, *Otherwise than Being*, 158. For the reference to *Totality and Infinity*, see page 213.

54. In this regard see George Trey, "Communicative Ethics in the Face of Alterity: Habermas, Levinas and the Problem of Post-Conventional Universalism," *Praxis International* 11 (January 1992): 412-427. Dealing exclusively with the asymmetrical dimension of my relation to the other apart from a consideration of the role of the third party in Levinas's work, Trey concludes that conceptualization and rational discourse with the other, even letting the other have "a say," are modes of domination of the other (see, in particular, pages 418 and 422). Here he seems to be following Jean-François Lyotard's interpretation of Levinas which, in an equally one-sided reading, stresses that "ethics prohibits dialogue." (See Lyotard, *The Differend*, 111, "Levinas Notice." Also see Trey's reference to Lyotard on page 422 of his article.) This interpretation fails to appreciate the way the presence of the third party demands judgment and reciprocity and is present even in my response to any singular other. It is a good example of the absurdities one quickly becomes entangled with in basing one's reading of Levinas exclusively on his, admittedly dominant, observations of the asymmetrical character of my proximity to the other.

55. See Habermas, "A Reply," 249 & 241-242.

56. Habermas, *The Theory of Communicative Action*, vol. 1, 327. Jürgen Habermas, *Theorie des kommunikativen Handelns, Band I* (Frankfurt am Main: Suhukamp Verlag, 1981), 438.

57. Habermas, *The Theory of Communicative Action*, vol. 1, 328.

58. See, in particular, Habermas, "Discourse Ethics: Notes on a Program of Philosophical Justification," 103-104. For a more general statement of Habermas's concerns with a procedural conception of reason and morality, see his "Themes in Postmetaphysical Thinking," in *Postmetaphysical Thinking*, 28-56.

59. Levinas, *Totality and Infinity*, 74.

Chapter 2

Care, Justice, and the Face of the Other

Though Habermas and Levinas both trace the roots of a moral point of view onto life to our capacity for language and share conceptions of language that are, as I argued in the preceding chapter, convergent in many important respects, their full accounts of language are not identical. In a nutshell, Habermas emphasizes a conception of language as a rule-governed practice while Levinas stresses the relation to the other person that occurs in and through that practice. For Levinas, the center of gravity of our sense of moral obligation does not lie, as it does with Habermas, in the procedures of communicative action but in what he refers to as "the face of the other" to whom communicative action is addressed.

The face of the other, for Levinas, is the face of my interlocutor, this unique person who approaches me with a sense of moral authority, what Levinas speaks of as a form of "authority par excellence,"[1] that is revealed precisely in her/his vulnerability. The other as a unique, singular interlocutor is one who is exposed to my powers, vulnerable to my strength, and yet resists that power in the way s/he calls it into question *as* interlocutor. Herein lies what Levinas characterizes as the "ethical resistance" of the other, not the resistance of another power to mine, but "the resistance of what has no resistance," a mode of resistance constituted in the very exposure of the face of the other to my power.[2] Levinas speaks of this sense of authority without power as the "height" of the other, the sense in which the other comes to me in her/his "destitution" not as my servant or my equal but, paradoxically, as my master, the one who commands me to be concerned with her/his fate.[3]

The question I want to pose for Levinas boils down to a question concerning the need for this reference to the face of the other in his account. Why do we need to refer to anything beyond the procedures of communicative action to understand the grounds of our sense of moral obligation? If Habermas is successful in explicating the grounds of our sense of obligation in language conceived along the lines of a rule-governed practice, then is not Levinas's understanding of conversational deference involving a reference to the face of the other superfluous, at best a poetic amplification of the sense of obligation we already find operative in communicative procedures, but something with which moral theory, strictly speaking, need not concern itself? Or does Levinas's account of the face of the other capture an important dimension of our moral experience for which a procedural understanding of language as a rule-governed practice is simply insufficient? I believe we may best gauge both the effective significance of Levinas's reference to the face of the other as well as provide evidence for its validity by pursuing this last question.

As such, I undertake in this and the next three chapters what might be characterized as an indirect investigation of the validity of Levinas's invocation of the face of the other by way of an examination of some of the problems that haunt Habermas's discourse ethics that Levinas places us, or so I argue, in a better position to productively resolve. In particular, I aim to show how Levinas's understanding of language as a substantive relation to the other can be seen to supplement and correct some of the shortcomings of Habermas's procedural understanding of language as a rule-governed practice and to make a case for how their accounts may be productively brought together to provide a more adequate understanding of the way the moral point of view is established within language understood, with Habermas, as a rule-governed practice responsive, as Levinas argues, to the appeal of the face of the other.

2.1 Care as a Presupposition of Moral Discourse

The issue I examine in this chapter concerns the place of care for the other in our understanding of the moral point of view and its relation to the imperatives of justice. This issue has been most forcefully raised in the work of Carol Gilligan. Based in her critique of Lawrence Kohlberg's theories of moral development, Gilligan's notion of care pulls together a number of related aspects of moral life that she argues have been ignored in the Kantian-based tradition of ethics that Kohlberg adopts in his work. Emphasizing the grounding of moral experience in our sense of connection with others as opposed to the abstract sense of distance required of an attitude of impartiality, care has come to mean in her work an attitude in which moral questions are dealt with primarily in terms of the well-being of particular others in particular contexts in a predominately narrative fashion. As opposed to judgments informed by an appreciation of abstract principles and rights, care centers on one's sense of responsibility as it arises in response to an affective, empathetic appreciation of the concrete needs of others.[4]

For Habermas, all of these themes revolve around the question of the concrete and generalized other. Care seems to focus our attention on the other in her/his concreteness, as a particular person with distinctive needs, while the sense of impartiality demanded by the principle of universalization draws our attention to others generally, to anyone who would be subject to a norm we are seeking to justify. Inasmuch as we are committed to taking the interests of everyone into account in our justification of moral principles we are committed to a conception of justice responsive to only the most generalized interests of others. Seemingly lost in the impartiality demanded by such a universalistic conception of justice, the question of care emerges for Habermas as the question of the significance and place of the concrete other in a moral theory that otherwise privileges the perspective of the generalized other.

Attempting to come to terms with this dichotomy in his work, Habermas has formulated at least two accounts that approach the question in different ways. The first is based on the distinction he draws between morality and ethics. A properly moral point of view first appears, Habermas emphasizes, when a critical distance is taken from the normative assumptions of one's inherited culture, when one begins to critically assess the universal validity of those assumptions, as is demanded by the principle of universalization. But with this, one naturally discovers that while some of one's inherited values can serve as the basis for a universal consensus, representing not merely the particular interests of this or that person or culture but arguably the generalized interests of humanity, some cannot. In some, perhaps most, cases, it is the limits of the validity of one's normative ideals that are revealed. They are shown to be ideals and aspirations, conceptions of a good life that are valid only for certain modes of life but not others—ethical concerns, as Habermas characterizes them, distinct from the moral concerns that articulate generalized interests and are, in this way, a fit basis for a universally valid conception of justice.[5]

Properly moral principles are formed, therefore, only by a process that abstracts from the particularity of one's culture and its specific ethical ideals. Our concern for the concrete other, with a caring appreciation of her/his unique concerns and aspirations, necessarily disappears at this level of abstraction. But there are still roles for care to play on the margins of this highly abstract level of deliberation. To begin, there is a place for our care for the concrete other in our ethical life where we are drawn to fashion our lives according to particular ideals that need not be shared by everyone. Habermas argues that many of the concerns grouped under the rubric of care belong here. He notes how some of Gilligan's subjects discussing the issue of abortion bring in contextually specific concerns with the repercussion of abortion on relations with friends, family, or career in this spirit. Taking for granted the morally permissible character of abortion, their care,

Habermas claims, is for the ethical character of their lives, how to fashion a more personally fulfilling life in the light of their particular aspirations for themselves.[6]

There is also a need for care in appropriately applying moral norms to specific situations. Norms are only justified as morally valid, as universally compelling for all subject to them, in a process that must abstract from the particularities of life. As a consequence, the determination of appropriate applications of moral norms to the unanticipated specifics of any given situation becomes a problem. For the appropriate application of a norm demands a cognitive sensitivity to the particular concerns of those affected by a norm's application, which presupposes, Habermas suggests, a sense of "empathy" or "*agape*," care for the other in her/his concreteness, in other words.[7] Only our care for the other as a concrete person can move us to adequately take into account the potential moral relevance of the other's unique interests and situation. Care is the affective-motivational prerequisite for the cognitive demands made on us in determining the appropriate application of a moral norm.

In this way, a moral as opposed to merely ethical significance emerges for care. As William Rehg argues, discourses of application cannot be understood as external to the principles whose application they concern, with no bearing on their moral content. They help to determine the meaning of our moral principles as they specify the limits and extent of their applicability. To make his case, Rehg refers to a hypothetical scenario in which a philosophy department observes a norm requiring tenure-track positions to be awarded on the basis of "nationwide merit searches." He assumes that the department has adopted the norm out of an impartial concern with fairness, "not simply in view of what is best for the department itself," so that it is a properly moral norm concerned with generalized, not particular, interests. Upon the discovery, however, that the strict observance of the norm would result in passing over a colleague who has taught for years in the department on annual contracts with the hope of eventually being offered a tenure-track position, some members of the department object to the norm's appropriateness in this case, arguing that they would have never agreed to such a norm had they been able to foresee the harm it would bring to their relationship with their non-tenure-track colleague. Such an objection goes right to the heart of the validity of the norm itself, proposing what is effectively a redefinition of its meaning by clarifying the interests that are relevant to its validity. Rehg writes, "The objection is that, under these concrete circumstances, the norm's observance is *not* 'equally good for all'—hence not moral—in view of the disproportionate damage it would wreak on a particular person. Such a move in effect amends, or further specifies, the consideration of interests affected by a norm's general observance, only now in light of a closer consideration of exactly what interests are at stake in a concrete situation."[8] Insofar as our care for the concrete other is a presupposition of such a discourse, an affective prerequisite for cognitively identifying and appreciating the moral relevance of the particular harm that is done to our non-tenure-track colleague in this example, its properly moral significance is established for discourse ethics.

2.1.1 Benhabib's Reassessment of the Moral Domain

Far from excluding our care for the concrete other, Habermas's discourse ethics would appear, then, to acknowledge both an ethical significance to care as an important aspect of our pursuit of a personally or culturally specific sense of a good life and a moral significance insofar as it is an important affective presupposition of the cognitive demands made on us by discourses that concern the application of moral principles. And yet, even these approaches may not exhaust the potential of a Habermasian treatment of the issue of care. Seyla Benhabib, in particular, has contributed to what is, arguably, the most expansive approach to this issue situated firmly within the parameters of Habermas's discourse ethics. Taking Habermas to task for what she argues is a needless restriction of his understanding of the "moral domain" to issues that concern generalized interests with justice, Benhabib argues that there are times when our care for another is a properly moral concern without it being a universal concern of justice. As an example, she considers the hypothetical case of a family of three brothers where the youngest is "struggling financially" and his elders are considering a possible obligation to help. Insofar as the two elder brothers have earned their success through their own work, not through "helping (them)selves to a family inheritance and leaving the younger brother destitute," she argues that there is nothing unjust in ignoring the welfare of their younger brother. But "there would be," she writes, "something morally 'callous,' lacking in generosity and concern in their actions. Unlike Habermas," she concludes, "I am not ready to say that 'callousness, lack of generosity and concern,' are (ethically) evaluative but not moral categories." Though the generosity and concern of family members for one another may not be a matter of justice, it does not follow that they must be ethical matters pertaining only to "the quality of our lives together."[9] There seems to be a properly moral issue raised in the question of our obligations to one another in this case, despite the fact that it does not appear to have direct bearing on the justification or application of a universally valid principle of justice.

This problem has less to do, however, with a theoretical limitation of Habermas's discourse ethics than it does with Habermas's own limited interpretation of it. In substantial agreement with Habermas concerning the grounds of ethics in the procedures of communicative reason, Benhabib only takes issue with his attempt to restrict properly moral concerns to universalizable questions of what is right or just for everyone. As she puts it, Habermas "conflate(s) the standpoint of a universalist morality with a narrow definition of the moral domain as being centered around 'issues of justice.' . . . The universalizability procedure in ethics specifies a model of individual and collective deliberation and imposes constraints upon the kinds of justification leading to certain conclusions rather than specifying the moral domain itself."[10] And so a commitment to communicatively rational procedures need not lead us, on Benhabib's account, to exclude the issues raised in the example of the brothers from the moral domain merely because they do not concern generalized interests that could be the basis for a universally valid conception of justice. Rather, it leads us to expect the brothers to "engage in a discourse about the needs of the one and the responsibilities and expectations of the others."[11] It is the commitment to an impartial discourse concerning normative questions that is the hallmark of a properly moral point of view, for Benhabib. And this commitment is as germane in contexts that raise specific questions about the needs of a concrete other as it is in contexts that raise questions about the generalized interests of humanity.

The commitment to discourse does not, therefore, privilege the generalized over the concrete other. In some contexts, such as Benhabib's example with the brothers, it is a direct commitment to deliberate with the concrete other concerning the moral relevance of her/his particular needs and interests. But where, one might ask, does *care* for the concrete other enter into such a discourse? Benhabib is not as clear on this point as one might like. The most immediate demands of discourse are cognitive, that we take the other's relevant concerns into account in an impartial way in our attempt to draw conclusions regarding normative questions. It may be that in the context of deliberations concerning the particular needs of the concrete other these cognitive demands can only be adequately realized on the basis of caring for the other. But this is only the case because, as Habermas emphasizes, care for the other serves as an affective-motivational prerequisite for the realization of these cognitive demands. Without a caring appreciation for the importance of the other's distinctive needs, an empathetic understanding of how significant, for example, financial difficulties can be in the course of a life project, it is difficult, if not impossible, to deliberate adequately concerning those needs.

In the final analysis, then, Benhabib's expanded account of the role of care in discourse ethics is not that different from Habermas's. Though she expands the ways in which care may have a genuinely moral significance, going beyond Habermas's account of its role in discourses that concern the application of principles of justice, her account agrees with Habermas on the way care gains moral significance as a presupposition of discourse. Both Habermas and Benhabib recognize that it is morally important that we care for the concrete other but only as a necessary condition of adequately approximating the procedural requirements of an impartial discourse, be it a discourse of application of moral principles, as Habermas emphasizes, or a discourse construed more broadly to deal with the justification of more particular, contextualized responses to the needs of the concrete other, as Benhabib stresses. The point they share is the unsurprising one that discourse ethics can only make sense of the moral significance of care insofar as it subordinates our concerns with care to our procedural concerns with discourse, with being communicatively rational with normative questions.

2.1.2 The Subordination of Care to Procedural Concerns with Discourse

Is this subordination of care to procedural concerns with discourse a problem? Perhaps not. Though Habermas and Benhabib are both committed to acknowledging the moral significance of care, neither of their efforts are meant as a wholesale endorsement of an ethic of care against a more traditional deontological concern with justice. In particular, they both stress a regulative priority for our concerns with justice. The claims of care have moral validity but only within the constraints set by justice. As Benhabib points out, we would not want to affirm the sort of care exercised by the Mafia for its extended family inasmuch as it is based on an unjust relation to those outside the family.[12] Perhaps, then, care *should* be subordinated to procedural concerns with discourse as an expression of its justifiable subordination to the impartial perspective of justice that is intimated in the principle of universalization that informs our discourse.

Without questioning this specific point concerning the regulative priority of the claims of justice to care, there are still significant problems with subordinating the moral significance of care to procedural concerns with discourse in such an unqualified way. Take Benhabib's case of the two elder brothers's concern for their younger brother's financial difficulties, for example. It may be true that their care for their brother as a concrete other is a necessary condition for engaging in an adequate moral discourse with him that takes his concerns and interests seriously. But this does not mean that the moral significance of the elder brothers's concern is exhausted in serving as a presupposition for such a discourse. Quite the contrary, it puts the cart before the horse to consider the significance of their care only in the context of the discourse it makes possible as it is their care for their brother that establishes what Benhabib refers to as the "moral sense" that their brother's situation is morally relevant in the first place,[13] that his unique needs as a unique individual deserve their impartial consideration.

Only insofar as they are moved in their care for their brother to see him as deserving of their concrete aid and support do we have what Charles Taylor would call the "point" of the obligation to discourse in the situation, why discourse is called for, what's "uniquely valuable" in speaking with the younger brother in such a way.[14] One's care for a brother is more than an emotional upheaval. It is, in this case, an affectively circumscribed recognition that he ought not to suffer as he does. The discourse in which they engage with him is a way of beginning to respond to that recognition in a way that respects the integrity of their younger brother's point of view on the situation as well as the complexity of the possible consequences of any response. As Benhabib notes, it is not clear that simply giving financial assistance would be an appropriate response if it encourages dependency and the like. Discourse is called to weigh and consider in an impartial spirit the pros and cons of different lines of response. But far from the procedures of discourse providing the context for the moral significance of the brother's care, it would seem that it is their care that discloses the moral relevance of the situation that calls forth discourse.

Much the same could be said of discourses of application. In Rehg's example, it is true that a caring appreciation of the plight of their non-tenure-track colleague is necessary for an adequate consideration of the appropriateness of the norm for awarding tenure-track positions. But the moral significance of that care cannot be reduced to its role as a necessary condition for living up to the cognitive demands of such a discourse as it is their care for the plight of their colleague that establishes the point of such a discourse, their recognition of their colleague's plight as morally significant, as deserving a form of consideration that would not be forthcoming with a merely mechanical application of the norm to the case. It is their caring appreciation of the plight of their colleague which establishes why they see it as morally important to question the norm's appropriate applicability to this situation. More generally, it is true that we must care for the concrete other in order to be discursively responsive to her/his particular concerns and situation. But this is so only because our care for the concrete other is what discloses those particular concerns and situations as morally significant for us in the first place, as deserving of our discursive consideration. The moral significance of care cannot, therefore, be reduced to its role as a presupposition of moral discourse as this overlooks the significance of its role in establishing the point of such a discourse.

Perhaps, though, what we should say here is that care is itself already a form of discourse. Quite apart from any actual deliberation, it embodies that "enlarged mentality" of which Arendt speaks, a capacity "to see things not only from one's own point of view but in the perspective of all those who happen to be present,"[15] an appreciation of the need for an impartial perspective that takes the other's interests into account as much as one's own. To be concerned for another is already to take into account the other's perspective, to recognize that the point of view of the other is important, and so ought to matter in the formation of one's judgment. But to take it as discourse in this sense is to significantly expand the procedural understanding of discourse we receive from Habermas's discourse ethics. The sense in which I recognize an obligation to take the perspective of the other into account in my caring appreciation of the importance of the other is not itself a consequence of my procedural understanding of what must be done to be communicatively rational with moral questions. It is not based on my pragmatic relation to the communicative practice in which I am engaged but, rather, on my relation to the other that that practice establishes. Care involves a substantive recognition of the concrete other as one who deserves my support, a vulnerable person whose suffering is not or should not be tolerable. It is an appreciation of why the other deserves the kind of deference demanded by communicative procedures. As one of Gilligan's subjects brings out so well in her response to "Heinz's dilemma,"[16] the focus of care does not center on formal rights and procedural responsibilities but on the substantive recognition that there "is another human being who needs help."[17] It is the moral significance of this substantive relation to the other that is constitutive of care and that establishes the point of my engagement to discursive procedures with the vulnerable other that gets lost in Habermas's and Benhabib's accounts.

2.2 Justice, Care, and Solidarity

Habermas's second approach to the question of care takes a somewhat different tack than the strategy we have just considered, arguing for the interdependence of care and justice.[18] Based in Mead's idea that "persons, as subjects capable of speech and action, can be individuated only via the route of socialization," Habermas argues,

> The farther individuation progresses, the more the individual subject is caught up in an ever denser and at the same time ever more subtle network of reciprocal dependencies and explicit needs for protection. Thus, the person forms an inner center only to the extent to which she simultaneously externalizes herself in communicatively produced interpersonal relationships. This explains the danger to, and the chronic susceptibility of, a vulnerable identity. Furthermore, moralities are designed to shelter this vulnerable identity.[19]

It is in terms of this idea that morality exists to shelter vulnerable identities, formed through a complex network of communicative interactions, that Habermas constructs his argument for the interdependence of justice and care, understood now as a form of solidarity among reciprocally dependent selves. The protection of a socially vulnerable identity requires both justice, in its liberal version as equal respect for the rights of the individual as an autonomous subject, and solidarity with one another as the necessary conditions for the preservation of the social network or life-world upon which the identity of the individual depends. "Justice conceived deontologically," Habermas concludes, "requires solidarity as its reverse side. . . . Moral norms cannot protect one without the other: they cannot protect the equal rights and freedoms of the individual without protecting the welfare of one's fellow man and of the community to which the individuals belong."[20]

Taken on its own this is a valid point—and it is important to emphasize in order to distinguish Habermas's discourse ethics, grounded in a thoroughly socialized conception of the self, from more traditional social contract theories that have only emphasized a sense of justice as equal treatment. Lacking a socialized conception of the self, these deontological predecessors of discourse ethics fail to grasp the importance of solidarity as a function of our mutual dependence on one another.[21] But there are still problems that tell against it as an adequate account of the question of care. To begin, there is a problem noted by Max Pensky concerning the specific subject of care on this account. As the vulnerability that morality is meant to shelter emerges from the way in which the self is formed through social interactions, "the care for the other, demanded by solidarity, is in fact a care for the fragile networks of reciprocal relationships that constitute the self: care for the other, in other words, is in fact care for a form of interaction for which the injurable other is, so to speak, the ambassador. What is necessarily missing is a substantive conception of the injurability of another person."[22] There is clearly a point to this sense of solidarity inasmuch as we *do* depend on "fragile networks of reciprocal relationships" that demand our care. But it cannot substitute for the sense in which the vulnerability of another person, in and of itself, solicits our concern.

This problem is closely connected to another. Though Habermas's account of solidarity does provide a reasonably convincing justification of caring for the welfare of one's fellow human beings as a function of caring for the networks of interaction in which one's identity is embedded, it appears to succeed only at the cost of sacrificing an understanding of care as an unconditional mode of responsibility for the other to what is, essentially, a teleological understanding. We ought to care for others, we are told, as an extension of caring for ourselves because others are important to our sense of self. Admittedly, this understanding has the virtue of paralleling the sense of "connectedness" that Gilligan emphasizes in her work as a crucial dimension of care. Characterizing one of her subject's responses to "Heinz's dilemma," she notes how the perspective of care "leads her to see the actors in the dilemma arrayed not as opponents in a contest of rights but as members of a network of relationships on whose continuation they all depend."[23] But it is questionable as to precisely what role this sense of mutual dependence plays in the phenomenon of care. It clearly plays a role in its intelligent articulation and implementation. We fail to adequately care for another person insofar as we neglect the larger context of relationships upon which we all depend. Hence, the necessity for Gilligan's subjects to concern themselves not with the claims of concrete others in isolation but with "a network of relationships" in which everyone is implicated. This seems to be the primary way it functions for the subject mentioned above who, in responding to "Heinz's dilemma," rejects the option of the husband stealing the drug needed by his wife on the grounds that he could go to jail and his wife would be deprived of his continuing support.[24] Here, the point is not that their mutual dependence is what justifies the husband's responsibility to care for his wife. It only enters into the respondent's judgment as an important qualification in determining precisely what should be done.

But when mutual dependence is invoked in a justificatory way we come close to losing the unconditional character of the other's appeal in care. For example, another of Gilligan's subjects identifies dependence as a primary reason for care, but it is only the dependence of the other to be cared for on the one in a position to give care. As she puts it, again responding to "Heinz's dilemma," "the wife needed him at this point to do it (steal the drug); she couldn't have done it, and it's up to him to do for her what she needs." Gilligan then concludes, "the moral injunction to act stems not from Heinz's feelings about his wife but from his awareness of her need." Hence, it is not the importance of the other for my concerns with myself, for my sense of identity or whatever, that is the basis of my responsibility to care for the other. It is only my "awareness of her need," my recognition of the substantive vulnerability of the other. The relevant sense of connection to the other seems primarily to lie only in my practical proximity to the other, my being "in a position to help," which makes me uniquely responsible for her. Both of Gilligan's subjects cited here "equate responsibility with the need for response that arises from the recognition that others are counting on you and that you are in a position to help."[25]

These remarks do not, of course, conclusively resolve the question.[26] But they do, at least, suggest the presence of an irreducibly unconditional dimension to our lived experience of care in the way the vulnerability of the concrete other appears to appeal to us unconditionally, contingent only on our practical proximity to the other. It does not, therefore, appear descriptively adequate to characterize care for the other as merely an extension of my care for myself. Even as part of a larger argument that would appropriately identify solidarity with each other as a *generalized* interest (because of the way everyone's identity depends on such interpersonal networks) and so, in this way, a principle of justice having deontological validity—a larger strategy Habermas could and may intend for this argument—it appears insufficient. As a teleological basis for my deontological duty to care for the welfare of the other as a matter of justice, the stress is still laid on my care for the welfare of the other as an extension of my care for myself to the neglect of the way I find myself called to attend to the needs of the other in her/his own right; the way, to paraphrase Gilligan, the moral injunction to act stems only from awareness of the other's need.

This is not to say, of course, that in caring for the other I do not, in an indirect way, *also* care for myself. Insofar as my sense of identity *is* involved with that of the other, my care for the other proves to be mutually beneficial. As such, there is a legitimate role for a teleological understanding of care as a confirmation of the teleological rationality of a response already consolidated deontologically—as an argument for how care enhances the well-being of all parties involved. And this could, in turn, be the basis for recognizing the need to foster a universal mutual concern for one another's welfare as a question of justice, a question of fostering a form of mutual solidarity in which we all have a generalized interest. But to miss the unconditional character of the appeal of the concrete other in care prior to this recognition of our duty to care for the welfare of others generally as a matter of justice, as a form of solidarity that is the "reverse side" of justice, is to miss the way in which the substantive vulnerability of the concrete other appeals to us in care contingent only upon our proximity, our ability to respond.

The problem with both of Habermas's approaches to care is that they attempt to derive its significance from an understanding of communicative action abstracted from a substantive relation to the vulnerability of the concrete other. But care *is* essentially a substantive response to the other's vulnerability. If we understand care as either a presupposition of approximating the demanding cognitive requirements of discourse or a product of our vulnerable dependence on networks of communicative interaction, we miss what Pensky refers to as "the injurability of another person" and the way that injurability makes a directly unconditional claim upon us. We miss the way care is constituted not in communicative action, per se, as a rule-governed social practice or even in our concern for our own vulnerable identities formed on the basis of that practice, but only in response to the vulnerability of the concrete other to whom our communicative action is addressed. We miss, in other words, what Levinas calls the face of the other.

2.3 Care and the Face of the Other

2.3.1 Kohlberg's Approach to Care

Before proceeding to a Levinasian approach to the problem, however, it may be useful to examine one of the latter attempts of Lawrence Kohlberg to deal with this issue. Kohlberg anticipates the broad parameters of what Levinas can bring to this question, providing something of an independent corroboration of his insights. In his essay, "The Return of Stage 6," Kohlberg draws on a distinctive idea of respect that is invoked in a subject's response to "Heinz's dilemma." Agreeing that the husband should steal the drug his wife needs, the subject relates this obligation to "a recognition of dignity, integrity on the part of . . . persons." Kohlberg notes the way this idea of respect for persons goes beyond "avoidance of violating the rights of another person in a negative sense" to embrace "a sense of positive responsibility for the needs and welfare of another person." This insight then allows him to link this sense of respect to both benevolence and justice, giving benevolence a form of priority over justice but one that is still linked to justice by way of the need to resolve conflicting obligations. As he puts it,

> The way of regarding the other that we are calling benevolence views the other and human interaction through the lens of intending to promote good and prevent harm to the other. It is an attitude that presupposes and expresses one's identification and empathic connection with others. . . . Thus . . . benevolence is logically and psychologically prior to what we are calling justice. On the other hand, justice views the other and human interaction through the lens of intending to adjudicate interests, that is, of intending to resolve conflicts of differing and incompatible claims among individuals.[27]

Benevolence and justice are, in other words, merely two different modes of respecting the integrity and dignity of another person, neither of which are reducible to the other but both of which are connected in terms of a basic sense of respect they each actualize in their own way.

Criticizing this approach, Habermas has argued that Kohlberg must equivocate in his understanding of respect for persons in order to derive both benevolence and justice from it. Equal respect for each person means quite different things, Habermas insists, depending on whether we are talking about each person *in general* or each person *as an individual*. Only the second sense involves what we would ordinarily think of as care or benevolence. The first sense merely involves a traditionally liberal sense of formal or equal treatment. Thus, "it does not follow from *respect* for the integrity of a vulnerable person that one *cares* for her well-being."[28] But this argument, correct as far as it goes, seems to miss the point of Kohlberg's analysis. Habermas is right that care does not follow from respect as it has been ordinarily understood in the deontological tradition as a formal respect for generalized others. It does not, however, follow that Kohlberg is equivocating when he speaks of respect for the integrity of persons as a basis for both care and justice. Rather, given his comment on the priority of benevolence as "an attitude that presupposes and expresses one's identification and empathic connection with others," it would appear that he presupposes a sense of respect more closely connected to Habermas's second sense of the term directed toward persons as unique individuals. The key to Kohlberg's approach lies not in equivocating between these two senses of respect but in showing how the sense of respect connected with benevolence leads to the sense of respect connected to justice, how a caring recognition of the dignity and integrity of the concrete other leads to an impartial perspective in which every other is accorded the equal treatment demanded by a formal sense of justice.

For Kohlberg, the mediation between benevolence and justice lies in the requirements of coming to terms with conflicting claims and obligations. "Given this adjudicatory lens, justice presupposes a momentary separation of individual wills and cognitively organizes this separation in the service of achieving a fair adjudication through a recognition of equality and reciprocal role-taking."[29] Justice, in other words, *is* care appropriately transformed by the requirements of conflict. It is a distance we take from a more empathic connection to the other in order to come to terms with a problem that empathic connection is unprepared to deal with—the problem that I recognize the dignity and integrity not only of *this* concrete other but of *many* concrete others and must find a way of balancing their competing claims, of supporting the claims of one without, as far as is possible, coming up short in terms of my obligation to another. Insofar as I am alone with *a* concrete other there is no need for the impartiality of justice. But insofar as I am in society with many others, that sense of impartiality becomes required of me as a complication and transformation of a sense of care insufficient to the demands of the situation.

2.3.2 A Levinasian Approach to Care

With this idea, however, we are encroaching on the thought of Levinas, who also considers the conflicting claims of others to be the context in which an impartial discourse concerning justice arises as a complication of a prior sense of obligation centered on the other in her/his singularity. For Levinas, ethics is grounded, as it is for Habermas, in communicative action, but understood more broadly as the establishment of a relationship to the face of the other: the concrete other soliciting my consideration in her/his vulnerability or destitution as a being exposed to suffering.[30] And the sense of obligation that arises from this relation is an appeal to an unconditional mode of care for the vulnerability of the other, "to nourish the hunger of another with one's own fasting." My proximity to the face of the other is what Levinas frequently describes as a vulnerability to the vulnerable other, an exposure to her/his vulnerability in which one is called from one's concern with oneself toward a concern with the other.[31] In this way, he stresses the sensible character of our lived sense of obligation to the other, the way we are moved by the appeal of the other at an affective level. Our exposure to the vulnerability of the other is not a mode of knowledge. It is not a way of presenting or representing the other but of being affected by the other in her/his singularity, "a passion," as Levinas puts it.[32] To be called by the other in her/his exposure to suffering to alleviate that suffering is to find oneself moved, torn from one's complacency toward the appeal of the other for aid. For this reason, Levinas rejects the role of principles in mediating my sense of responsibility at this level.[33] My sense of responsibility for the other is not founded in my knowledge of principles that can be universally defended in accord with the procedural constraints of a communicatively rational discourse. It stems, rather, from the way in which I find myself moved by the appeal of the other as a singular being. Though Levinas's idiom is distinctive, it would appear that he is describing an experience that is, at the very least, convergent with the sense of care we have characterized as a substantive recognition of the intolerable character of the suffering of the concrete other, an affective exposure to the unconditional demand that that suffering makes upon us.

The extent of this convergence is contestable, however. I am thinking in particular here of the way Roger Gottlieb, in his essay on Levinas and feminism, goes so far as to draw a sharp distinction between the two perspectives. There he identifies care with a feminine sense of "connection" and "emotional kinship" with the other, formed in an "actually existing relation" with the other, while he relegates Levinas's sense of responsibility to a typically masculine sense of distance and "isolation" from the other, based in a relation with the other that is "abstract" and "formal" at best. Care involves an "identification" with the other, while it is the alterity of the other that stands out in Levinas's account.[34] But to sharply distinguish Levinas's understanding of responsibility from a concrete sense of connection to the other in this way is simply mistaken. Though Levinas's phenomenological idiom is extraordinarily abstract, there is nothing abstract in the relation to the face of the other that his idiom attempts to describe. My proximity to the face of the other is not a relation to others generally, which Levinas only takes up with his analysis of the "third party." It is a form of responsibility for the other as a singular being, with singular needs and concerns, that establishes me in a unique relationship, as irreplaceably responsible for the other—what Levinas describes as a sense of "election" through which I may attain a unique sense of myself as one responsible for the other, a morally charged form of identity wrapped up with a unique sense of responsibility for the other, as, for example, the parent of my child or the friend of my friend.[35]

But to have my sense of self formed in this way in terms of a sense of responsibility to the other *is* to have a concrete connection to the other. It is to find the fate of the other important to me. To stress that responsibility is a response to the alterity of the other is not to deny this sense of connection but only to emphasize that it is grounded in meeting the needs of the other in their own right, not in meeting those needs only insofar as they enhance some project of my own. And surely the same must be said for any genuinely caring relationship. There is always the threat that my care for the other may be more a matter of caring for myself through my identification with the other than of genuinely caring for the other. In my relation to my children, for example, I betray my care for them if I care for them primarily in terms of how they fulfill my own sense of identity. If I care for them only insofar as they, say, fulfill my own unfulfilled aspirations for my life, oblivious to their unique aspirations for their own lives, I have, to that degree, ceased to care *for them*. Levinas's sense of responsibility to the alterity of the other captures the way genuine care is oriented to the other. It is a sense of connection in which the other, certainly, becomes important to me. And so, as we have suggested, caring for the other cannot be divorced from caring for oneself. But a genuinely caring connection to the other is a way in which the other becomes important to me in an unconditional sense, leading me beyond my concerns with myself to a concern with the other in her/his own right. It is, so to speak, a centrifugal relation to the other, not a centripetal one. To merely emphasize connection and identification with the other as the content of care, as Gottlieb does, is to miss this distinction.

2.3.3 Care and the Third Party

It is because my sense of responsibility emerges as a unique relationship to a singular other, for Levinas, that it is insufficient to the demands of moral life with others in the plural and justice becomes necessary to order and regulate that singular sense of responsibility. As with Kohlberg, the perspective of justice, that of an impartial concern with universal principles valid for everyone as generalized others, arises as a complication of this singular, foundational mode of responsibility. Levinas gets at this point with his discussion of the problems posed by "the third party." As we have already seen, the basis of my moral obligation to the other is, for Levinas, an asymmetrical relationship with the other. The other comes to me with a sense of authority that prevents me from taking myself in reciprocity as an equal to the other. It is this asymmetry that constitutes the gravity of my moral relation to the other, the sense that there is something unconditionally important at stake in my interpersonal life, more important even than my concerns with myself. As Levinas puts it, "Goodness consists in taking up a position in being such that the Other counts more than myself."[36]

Lived purely in relation to my concern with myself this sense of moral gravity is a rupture with that orientation, the emergence of what would be, in and of itself, an effective sense of devotion to the other. But this devotion is unsustainable in the light of my relations to others in the plural. Here the emergence of a third party, of another other besides the one to whom I already find myself responsible, necessitates the emergence of comparison and deliberation. I must weigh and evaluate the significance of the different claims made on me in relation to one another. But this implies impartiality, what Levinas characterizes as "a copresence on an equal footing as before a court of justice."[37] The gravity of the initial asymmetrical relation is not canceled but is, shall we say, reconfigured, as the moral orientation no longer runs in just one direction but in many competing directions. Reciprocity emerges here as impartiality demands that I take the interests of every other into account, including myself, as an other to the others. The establishment of universal principles regulating and coordinating our obligations to one another becomes necessary. In this way, there is established what Levinas refers to as "the original locus of justice, a terrain common to me and the others where I am counted among them, that is, where subjectivity is a citizen with all the duties and rights measured and measurable."[38]

There are significant qualifications that we should probably make to this account as it stands. I noted in chapter 1, for instance, the way in which Levinas recognizes the presence of the third party already in my relationship to any singular other, how in my proximity to the other, "all the others than the other obsess me, and already this obsession cries out for justice."[39] It is not, therefore, as if we pass from a situation in which considerations of justice are irrelevant to a situation where they suddenly become relevant merely because a third person happens to enter the room. It may also be that Levinas's argument proceeds too quickly to what he calls the "locus of justice," at least in a full-fledged sense. Where the others are those closest to me, my family for example, the direct applicability of the image of citizens with equal rights and duties seems questionable.[40] The more narrative-based, contextual approach of weighing and balancing competing concerns characteristic of Gilligan's articulation of a ethic of care[41] is called for here to take into account the distinctive concerns of those with whom such closeness permits us to approach them in their concreteness. My care for my children (in the plural) is more a matter of evaluating the relative strength and importance of their respective needs and desires in the context of my relationship with them and its requirements than it is of respecting any sort of formal, equal rights they might have to my affection.

Instead of the sudden leap from a devotion to the other in her/his singularity, understood as devoid of a sense of justice, to the principled impartiality of the "court of justice" that Levinas's argument seems to suggest, we ought to recognize something more like a gradient of degrees. To begin with, a sense of impartiality is only implicit in my relationship to the other in the singular, in my need to critically assess the reasons for the claims of the other in order to meaningfully respond to them. With others in the plural with whom we have a personal relationship, such as a family, there is a more pronounced need for impartiality evident, for example, in our concern not to support one child at the expense of another.[42] But the sense of impartiality appropriate here is not yet the rigorously principled sense we find operative in a universally valid conception of justice attentive, as Habermas emphasizes, to the generalized interests of humanity at large, but a more contextually based mode issuing in narrative modes of deliberation. The formal impartiality of a perspective of justice proper emerges only when our concern for others must take into account those for whom distance or sheer numbers prevents us from approaching them as concrete others.

But even with these qualifications Levinas's basic point remains. Much as Kohlberg argues, the need for an impartial perspective characteristic of justice emerges only as we come, by degrees, to take account of our multiple and often conflicting obligations with others in the plural. And in this way justice comes to take on an increasingly regulative priority, much as Habermas stresses. My sense of responsibility to those closest to me must be tempered by the impartial demands of what is right for all. We should not forget Benhabib's point that we not endorse the care the Mafia shows its own at the expense of others. And yet, Levinas is just as clear concerning the need for justice to maintain its connection with the personal sense of responsibility that founds it. As he aptly puts it, "justice remains justice only, in a society where there is no distinction between those close (*proches)* and those far off (*lointains*), but in which there also remains the impossibility of passing by the closest."[43] Justice becomes a mockery of itself when it becomes an empty formalism, a legalism which treats everyone equally but is indifferent to their concrete concerns and needs. And as an empty formalism, it is also probably unsustainable in a community. Apart from everyone's recognition that the injunctions of justice are ultimately in service to the vulnerability of the other for which we find ourselves unconditionally called to care, the demands of justice can only appear as a pointless burden.[44]

The regulative priority of justice is not, therefore, something opposed to the imperative to care, for Levinas. Justice is best conceived as a complication of the perspective that originally opens up in my caring relation to the concrete other. Justice, in other words, *is* care appropriately transformed by the requirements of multiple, competing obligations. We may recognize the regulative priority of justice without losing sight of care as a substantive response to the vulnerability of the concrete other if we understand the moral significance of the procedural requirements of justice as founded on and legitimately complicating the sense of obligation that opens up in our caring proximity to the face of the other. There is a foundational priority to care in this Levinasian account that, far from contradicting the regulative priority of justice, calls it forth.

To conclude, I return to Habermas's comment concerning the role of morality to "shelter" vulnerable identities.[45] Elsewhere, Habermas has identified this as the substantive content of every moral intuition to which discourse procedurally responds by obliging respect for both the autonomy of the individual and the social network upon which that autonomy is dependent.[46] This is a point Levinas could clearly endorse as well. Morality is fundamentally a response to our vulnerability: first and foremost, the vulnerability of the other who solicits me to a sense of responsibility that inaugurates a moral perspective onto life, but also my own vulnerability as the impartial perspective of justice reveals me as an other to the others for whom "it is important to concern oneself and take care."[47] But we do this insight regarding morality and vulnerability an injustice by attempting to understand it exclusively in terms of the procedural demands of our engagement to communicative action. The full extent of the moral significance of our care for the vulnerable other cannot be captured in terms of the pragmatic constraints of communicative procedures. Only through an expanded understanding of communicative action as a relation to the face of the other, an orientation to the other in terms of a substantive sense of the moral worth of my interlocutor as a vulnerable being exposed to suffering, can we make adequate sense of the moral phenomenon of care as the point of an impartial form of discourse with the other.

Notes

1. See Levinas, "Diachrony and Representation," in *Time and the Other*, trans. Richard Cohen (Pittsburgh: Duquesne University Press, 1987), 117.

2. Levinas, *Totality and Infinity*, trans. Alphonso Lingis (Pittsburgh: Duquesne University Press, 1969), 199.

3. See Levinas, *Totality and Infinity*, 75 & 200.

4. See, in particular, Carol Gilligan and John Michael Murphy, "Moral Development in Late Adolescence and Adulthood: A Critique and Reconstruction of Kohlberg's Theory," *Human Development* 23 (1980): 77-104, and Carol Gilligan, *In a Different Voice* (Cambridge, Mass.: Harvard University Press, 1982), especially ch. 2. For a succinct account of the differences between Gilligan's and Kohlberg's approaches, see Lawrence Blum, "Gilligan and Kohlberg: Implications for Moral Theory," *Ethics* (April 1988): 474-477.

5. See Habermas, "Moral Consciousness and Communicative Action," in *Moral Consciousness and Communicative Action*, 176-178.

6. See Habermas, "Moral Consciousness and Communicative Action," trans. Christian Lenhardt and Shierry Weber Nicholson (Cambridge, Mass.: The MIT Press, 1990), 181 and note 60, 193.

7. See Habermas, "Moral Consciousness and Communicative Action," 182. Actually, Habermas makes this point about the need for empathy in applying norms to the case of justifying norms as well. But, as he makes it in the context of specifically discussing "the cognitive problem of application," and as it is the relevance of care for the application of moral norms that has been emphasized in the literature discussing Habermas's position on care, I stress only the first point. Also, I believe an independent consideration of Habermas's understanding of the role of care in discourses of justification is unnecessary as my criticism of his and Benhabib's approach to this issue is aimed at a weakness that informs a discourse ethical understanding of the role of care in either discourses of application or justification.

8. William Rehg, *Insight and Solidarity: A Study in the Discourse Ethics of Jürgen Habermas* (Berkeley: University of California Press, 1994), 198. Also see page 197.

9. Seyla Benhabib, *Situating the Self* (New York: Routledge, 1992), 186.

10. Benhabib, *Situating the Self*, 185. Also see page 9 for her criticism of Habermas's insistence "that the purpose of universalizability procedures in ethics must be the uncovering or discovering of some 'general interest' to which all could consent."

11. Benhabib, *Situating the Self*, 186.

12. See Benhabib, *Situating the Self*, 187.

13. See Benhabib, *Situating the Self*, 186.

14. See Charles Taylor, *Sources of the Self* (Cambridge, Mass.: Harvard University Press, 1989), 87. I return to this idea in greater detail in the next chapter.

15. See Hannah Arendt, *Between Past and Future: Eight Exercises in Political Thought* (New York: Penguin Books, 1954), 220-221.

16. Heinz's dilemma is a hypothetical scenario of moral conflict used by Kohlberg to evaluate moral development. The scenario centers on the question of what a husband should do in a situation where his wife needs a drug in order to live that they cannot afford and their druggist will not give them. In particular, is the husband justified in stealing the drug?

17. See Gilligan, *In a Different Voice*, 54.

18. See Benhabib, *Situating the Self*, 189.

19. Jürgen Habermas, "Justice and Solidarity: On the Discussion Concerning 'Stage 6,'" *The Philosophical Forum* 31 (fall-winter 1989-90): 46.

20. Habermas, "Justice and Solidarity," 47.

21. See Habermas, "Justice and Solidarity," 48, where he makes this point.

22. Pensky, "The Limit of Solidarity," paper presented at the annual meeting of the Society for Phenomenology and Existential Philosophy, October 1994, 18.

23. Gilligan, *In a Different Voice*, 30.

24. See Gilligan, *In a Different Voice*, 28.

25. All quotations in this paragraph are from Gilligan, *In a Different Voice*, 54.

26. Actually, I believe this question of the precise moral significance of connection and interdependence in care is unresolvable on the basis of the current literature on care. The ideas of connection and interdependence have not been analyzed carefully enough. They mainly seem to function as central metaphors in discussions of care, drawn as much from Nancy Chodorow's psychoanalytic work with the origins of gender identity as from the responses of Gilligan's subjects. My only point here is that there is strong evidence of an irreducibly deontological dimension to care that cannot be ignored with an exclusively

teleological account.

27. Lawrence Kohlberg, Dwight R. Boyd, and Charles Levine, "The Return of Stage 6: Its Principle and Moral Point of View," in *The Moral Point of View* (Cambridge, Mass.: The MIT Press, 1990), 156 & 157.

28. Habermas, "Justice and Solidarity," 45.

29. Kohlberg, et al., "The Return of Stage 6," 157.

30. See Levinas, *Totality and Infinity*, 50 & 200.

31. "Exposure" and "vulnerability" are terms Levinas frequently uses to articulate his understanding of the sensible dimensions of our ethical proximity to the other. See, for example, Levinas, *Otherwise than Being*, trans. Alphonso Lingis (The Hague: Martinus Nijhoff, 1981), 14-15.

32. Levinas, *Otherwise than Being*, 128.

33. Levinas, *Otherwise than Being*, 100.

34. See Gottlieb, "Levinas, Feminism, Holocaust, Ecocide," in *Artifacts, Representations, and Social Practice*, ed. Carol Gould and Robert Cohen (Dordrecht: Kluwer Academic Publishers, 1994), especially pages 369-371 and note 8.

35. For his account of "election," see *Totality and Infinity*, 245. The notion of election extends to any relation to another person, even someone we do not and cannot plausibly hope to know, such as the way the suffering of a stranger we might see on T.V. appeals to our sense of personal responsibility despite the fact that there is little chance of establishing a supportive relationship to the other that would take up or institute this sense of election in a stable sense of identity for us. The notion is, therefore, more extensive than the examples given here of understanding oneself as a parent or a friend. I give them only to illustrate some of the concrete ways in which this sense of election to responsibility for the other *can* be taken up and instituted in a stable way in my understanding of myself.

36. Levinas, *Totality and Infinity*, 247.

37. Levinas, *Otherwise than Being*, 157.

38. Levinas, *Otherwise than Being*, 160. Also see 158.

39. Levinas, *Otherwise than Being*, 158. For the reference to *Totality and Infinity*, see 213.

40. See, for example, Michael Sandel's point in his *Liberalism and the Limits of Justice* (New York: Cambridge University Press, 1982) that justice is no substitute for the more spontaneous ethical perspective that informs the life of a well-functioning family (33-34).

41. See, in particular, Gilligan and Murphy, "Moral Development in Late Adolescence and Adulthood."

42. The point I make here is similar, at least, to the point David Wong makes in his "On Care and Justice within the Family," *Contemporary Philosophy* 15, no. 4, 21-24, that there is a role for even a traditionally liberal conception of justice in the life of a family insofar as we are attentive to one another's concerns not as family members but as human beings (22).

43. Levinas, *Otherwise than Being*, 159, and *Autrement qu'être ou au-delà de l'essence* (La Haye: Martinus Nijhoff, 1974), 203.

44. I turn to this issue in much more detail in chapter 5 in connection with the question of community.

45. See Habermas, "Justice and Solidarity," 46.

46. See Habermas, *Moral Consciousness and Communicative Action*, 199-203.

47. Levinas, *Otherwise than Being*, 161.

Chapter 3

The Metaphysical Ground of Moral Authority

Habermas's emphasis on a procedural understanding of ethics is a product of what he discusses as the postmetaphysical character of modern thought. In contrast with earlier understandings of reason that were linked with substantive theoretical insights into the world as a totality, postmetaphysical thought sees the rationality of a proposition purely as a matter of the procedures used in deciding its truth.[1] The rise of proceduralism in modern moral theory is a reflection of this general tendency to decouple our rational insights from overarching, metaphysical views of the world that have, with the rise of empirical science and the increasingly pluralistic character of modern society, become too controversial to serve as a reliable basis for those insights. Taking a moral point of view on a question ceases in this way to be a matter of relating it to some substantive vision of the good, as with Plato, as it is no longer clear that we can rationally agree on any particular vision of what is objectively good in life. Instead, we search for formal procedures for resolving our moral questions that might serve as a basis for rational consensus despite our substantive, metaphysical disagreements. We ask, with Kant, if you could will the maxim of your act as a universal law or, with Rawls, if a public policy is consistent with principles that could be freely agreed to behind a veil of ignorance regarding our social fate or, as Habermas prefers, whether everyone affected by a norm could agree to it in a rational discourse. Taking a moral point of view is not contingent on adopting any particular, contestable vision of what is good in life, but is purely a matter of attending to the fairness or justice of how we approach an issue. Justice or what is right is, as it is often said, prior to or independent of the good.

Habermas's motives for adopting a postmetaphysical perspective onto ethics that eschews controversial, substantive commitments to the good are certainly understandable. One cannot help but be sympathetic with the desire to secure the validity of our most important practical commitments with as little controversy as possible. But the flight from metaphysical controversy has its costs. As we began to see in the last chapter, it is far from clear that a procedural approach to ethics can help us to clarify the significance of the more substantive dimensions of our moral experience, such as our substantive appreciation of the vulnerable, concrete other as deserving of our care. In this chapter, I continue with this line of thought, arguing that the same postmetaphysical emphasis on procedures eclipses the key role a substantive appreciation of the face of the other plays in our ability to make sense of the moral authority of the moral point of view, the way impartial procedures for dealing with moral questions make themselves unconditionally imperative for us. We have already seen how Habermas's account of care as a product of our dependence on networks of communicative interaction loses sight of the unconditional character of the appeal of care. Caring for the other becomes an extension of our care for ourselves rather than a response to an unconditional appeal to shelter the vulnerability of the other. Habermas's difficulty with capturing the unconditional authority of the appeal to care for the other is not, however, an isolated problem but a symptom of a more fundamental difficulty he has with making sense of the unconditional authority of a moral point of view onto life generally. Abstracted from a substantive recognition of what Levinas calls the "always positive value" of the face of the other, the postmetaphysical emphasis Habermas places on moral procedures leaves the moral authority of the moral point of view unintelligible, eclipsing what can only appear from this postmetaphysical perspective as a *metaphysical* ground of moral authority in the face of the other.

3.1 Why Be Moral?

We may best get at this point with the help of Charles Taylor, who raises the question of why anyone should take the moral point of view, as it is constituted in the procedures of discourse, seriously. As Taylor puts it,

> We should endeavor to replace non-rational mechanisms of action coordination by rational forms of reaching understanding. Yet this demand is also confronted by the question of why I should strive for this. Let us accept that such a norm is structurally based in the situation of human speech . . . I nevertheless also have other aims, other interests. Why then should I prefer rational understanding?[2]

It may be true that all communicative action involves an implicit recourse to communicative reason such that no one could be competent with speech without being communicatively rational. But it is also true that the aims of human life are not exhausted in communication. We have what Habermas describes as strategic interests that we may, and often do, prioritize over our communicative aims, as when we lie to achieve our goals irrespective of the damage this does to mutual understanding. But this means that we always have a choice to make between giving greater weight to our communicative or strategic endeavors. And it is here, as Taylor argues, that Habermas's procedural understanding of the moral point of view comes up short. It gives us nothing to say as to why anyone should prefer the moral point of view to other strategic points of view.

This is not to deny Habermas's point that "the possibility of *choosing* between communicative and strategic action exists only abstractly."[3] Socialized individuals must unavoidably engage in communicative endeavors that pay heed to the norms of communicative reason and the principle of universalization. But all Habermas can claim here is that the possibility of a *wholesale* choice between a communicative and strategic attitude toward life is abstract, not that in any given situation there is not a choice to be made between which mode of action to emphasize. And this is the level at which Taylor's question is pitched. When I am speaking with someone I may unavoidably presuppose a commitment to impartiality with my interlocutor as a necessary moment in that communicative endeavor. But when I see a strategic gain for myself to be made by lying, the question is not that of choosing between my strategic and communicative aims but of which to give greater importance. And if I should give greater importance to my strategic aims, the question then is only the practical one of whether I can successfully embed my communicative endeavors in the wider context of my strategic aims, making strategically effective compromises, so to speak, with my communicative objectives for the sake of my more important strategic gains.

It is true, of course, that if I give greater weight to my strategic objectives in this way, going through with a lie, for example, I will find myself in a performative contradiction, both presupposing respect for my interlocutor in the practice of speaking and violating it in the content of the lie. But that is only significant for me if I am *already* committed to giving greater importance to my communicative endeavors and the sense of rationality they presuppose. If I give greater weight to my strategic objectives, a performative contradiction has significance only if it entails the practical incoherence of my strategic project. But this is rarely if ever the case. Lies do not usually self-destruct. Depending on the form and degree of misunderstanding to which they give rise, I may tolerate most any inconvenience a lie may cause me in coordinating action with my interlocutor as the price to be paid for a greater strategic gain.

Confronted with the conflicting exigencies of communicative and strategic action, a far from abstract scenario that surely arises for most of us many times a day, we are confronted with the question of why we should prioritize our communicative aims and their normative constraints. Why, in other words, should we be moral? Establishing the unavoidability of communicative action and its procedural presuppositions is insufficient to address this question. We have nothing to say about what Taylor calls the "point of our moral code . . . what's uniquely valuable in cleaving to these injunctions. . . . We can wax rhetorical and propagandize," as Taylor notes, "but we can't say what's good or valuable about them, or why they command assent."[4] For Taylor, it is with this question that Habermas's proceduralism comes up short in failing to give any account of the importance of the moral point of view in our lives. To establish this, he argues, we need a substantive account of the moral sources upon which our sense of justice draws, the "constitutive goods" that establish its value, the "strong sense that human beings are eminently *worth* helping or treating with justice, a sense of their dignity or value."[5]

In response to Taylor, Habermas readily accepts the charge that his proceduralism makes it impossible to address the question, "Why be moral?" But this, he argues, only reflects a recognition of the pluralistic character of modern life. "In view of the morally justified pluralism of life projects and life-forms," Habermas writes, "philosophers can no longer provide on their own account *generally binding* directives concerning the meaning of life."[6] A substantive account of the good would sacrifice the neutrality that a philosophically adequate theory of justice must preserve for itself if it is to respect the pluralism of modern life. As important as it is, therefore, that we see the value of justice in some way or other, this concern must be understood as relevant to our motivation in taking up a moral point of view onto life rather than its justification.[7] It is a task for the socialization of individuals into modes of life that can foster and support morally informed conduct rather than the philosophical clarification and justification of the moral point of view.[8] Accepting this division of labor, Habermas aspires to answer only what he characterizes as a purely "epistemic" question concerning the content and universality of the moral point of view. "Moral theory is competent," Habermas concludes, "to clarify the moral point of view and justify its universality, but it can contribute nothing to answering the question 'why be moral?' (*'Warum überhaupt moralisch sein?'*)."[9]

There are several issues that deserve comment in Habermas's response to Taylor. To begin, I focus on his characterization of Taylor's question as one of motivation rather than justification. There are certainly grounds for doing so. Taylor frames his account of the sources of our moral intuitions in terms of "that the love of which moves us to good action."[10] But in asking for what "moves" us to be moral Taylor is not asking for a sense of motivation that would be sharply distinct from a reason to be moral, such as considerations that would be extrinsic to our understanding of what morality is about. A bribe *could* move us to be moral in this sense without constituting a convincing reason as to why anyone *ought* to be moral. Taylor's concern with the point of morality, however, is irreducible to such appeals to self-interest that fail to establish why morality as such deserves our assent.[11] Establishing the point of a moral code is a matter of making sense of our response to it *as* moral, as a code with the authority to command that distinctive sense of respect. As he puts it, "'making sense' here means articulating what makes these responses appropriate."[12] In the question, "Why be moral?" we are not merely asking for what could move us, as a matter of fact, to be moral, but what *ought* to move anyone, in principle, to be moral; why assent is the appropriate response to the moral point of view. We are, therefore, asking for a *reason* why the moral point of view deserves to be prioritized, where the possession of such a reason is not independent of what moves us to prioritize it.

In failing to address the question, "Why be moral?" Habermas leaves us, then, not merely without a motive but without a reason for the priority of the moral point of view. But without a reason we find ourselves unable to make sense of the properly moral authority of the moral point of view to command our assent. Confronted with the conflicting exigencies of communicative and strategic modes of action, the authority of the moral point of view can reasonably appear as only hypothetical, conditional upon our preference for the success of our communicative endeavors. But an account that can only make sense of the hypothetical authority of the moral point of view is one that fails to capture the sense in which the moral point of view is a *moral* point of view. As Kant argued, the moral character of an imperative is found only in its categorical or unconditional authority to command our assent. This is not to say that Habermas fails to recognize that we are unconditionally bound to take up and act in terms of the moral point of view. Far from it. But his proceduralism prevents him from showing how this sort of unconditional response is appropriate. Why should the procedures of any specific mode of action, even one that is unavoidable, deserve our unconditional assent? The authority of any procedure, taken on its own, is always conditional upon our acceptance of the goals of the practice it regulates.

In narrowing the proper limits of moral theory to epistemic concerns with the universality or unavoidability of pragmatic procedures it would seem that Habermas saves us from relativism only at the cost of delivering us over to a radical form of subjectivism. He can only make sense of the authority of the moral point of view in a hypothetical way, contingent upon an arbitrary preference for our communicative as opposed to strategic endeavors. In this way, he undercuts his own better deontological insights. What Habermas presents as a reasonable division of labor between philosophical questions of justification and life-world questions of motivation can be seen to conceal a critical inability on the part of his moral theory to make sense of the very moral authority it attempts to justify. We may be able to justify the universality of procedures we recognize as unconditionally authoritative with Habermas's discourse ethics but only by sacrificing our sense of why that moral authority is appropriate to them. We are left with the universality of procedures that have, at best, the status of an unavoidable language game. But to show that we must play by a particular game is not to show that we ought always to play on its terms, that we should never cheat, in other words, that it has the authority to command that sort of unconditional assent.

3.2 The "Always Positive Value" of the Face
of the Other as the Point of Morality

3.2.1 The Historical Articulation of Taylor's Moral Sources

Locked into a procedural understanding of communicative action, Habermas loses sight of the substantive sources of the moral authority of our communicative procedures. When it comes to articulating those sources, however, Taylor's account comes up short as well. Stressing the importance of the substantive, disclosive dimensions of language in contrast to Habermas's emphasis on its pragmatic, procedural dimensions[13], Taylor argues that the goods that move us to be moral "only exist through *some* articulation."[14] And these articulations are always grounded in the particular languages of historical communities, the unique evaluative perspectives onto life they provide. In particular, Taylor locates three competing articulations of the moral sources at work today in the West: a theistic account of the worth of human beings as children of God, a naturalistic account of the value of a particularly "disengaged" understanding of human reason, and a Romantic account of the importance of human expression.[15] In differing ways, Taylor argues, they provide the point to our contemporary moral intuitions.

But, as Taylor documents in his remarkable historical survey, *Sources of the Self*, all of these articulations are in different ways problematic today. And none, certainly, are immune to the challenge that they constitute historically relative expressions of the good that cannot hope to support the universalism that is also an important aspect of our modern moral sensibilities. The very care with which Taylor documents the specificity of their historical emergence only serves to exacerbate this challenge. Though Taylor's work is not meant to propose any particular articulation as a workable source for modernity's moral intuitions, but only to clear the ground for our renewed attention to the problem of our moral sources, one cannot help but wonder if it does not provide a complementary trade-off to that of Habermas's discourse ethics. Instead of grounding the universality of our moral intuitions at the cost of our ability to make sense of why they deserve our assent, Taylor's work seems to risk retrieving a sense of their distinctive importance and authority at the cost of their universality.

Of course, these *may* be the costs we must pay for a coherent moral theory. It may be that the demands of universalism and unconditional authority at work in our contemporary moral intuitions are simply at odds with one another, the one requiring a procedural account abstracted from the particularity of substantive visions of the good while the other needs a substantive vision of the good unable to sever its links with the historical specificity of particular life-worlds. Perhaps the options Habermas and Taylor present us form an insurmountable dilemma for modernity in which we can salvage one aspect or the other of our moral sensibilities but not both. Before we prematurely accept the terms of this dilemma, however, we should return to Levinas's work, which appears to forge a path between its horns in a way that is sensitive to both Habermas's universalistic aspirations and Taylor's concerns for substantive moral sources.

3.2.2 The Face of the Other and the Priority of the Right to the Good

Like Habermas, Levinas is attentive to the grounds of our moral experience in the very act of speaking with another person. But, unlike Habermas, he does not see the normative dimensions of that act constituted exclusively in the procedures that are presupposed in its coherent realization but, rather, in the relation to the face of the other that is established in that act. It is in this reference to the face of the other that we find what Taylor would characterize as the point of the moral point of view for Levinas. As we saw in chapter 2, it is in our care for the vulnerable other that we come to see the point of an impartial discourse with the other, why it is unconditionally important to address the other. In our care for the other we see her/him as unconditionally deserving of that kind of consideration. There is a sense of the good, to speak with Taylor, that opens up in the face of another person who commands my caring consideration in this way, a sense of the authority of the other to command me to take her/his concerns into account in my life, a sense of goodness Levinas also evokes as a kind of "glory" and "inspiration."[16] It is this substantive appreciation of the moral worth of the other that makes sense of our intuition that the unconditional imperatives of the moral point of view as it is constituted procedurally in communicative action ought to be unconditionally respected, not subordinated to my other strategic interests. It is my substantive relation to the face of the other that occurs in and through communicative action that is capable of establishing what makes such an unconditional form of response to its procedures appropriate, a form of "height" equivalent to a form of authority that no mere procedure can possess, a sense of the "always positive value" of the other sufficient to command, at first, my care and, in the context of my relations with others in the plural, my impartial consideration. Why should we be moral? Why should we take the moral point of view seriously? Because, Levinas urges quite simply, of the "always positive value" of the face of the other to which I find myself exposed in my communicative proximity to the other.

Levinas's account may in this way be usefully assimilated to Taylor's account of moral sources, to that which establishes the point—the importance, the authority —of our moral intuitions. But in doing so we should note two points of divergence that draw Levinas away from Taylor and back toward Habermas. First, there is their understandings of the good that constitutes these sources. Taylor's understanding of the good is certainly not reducible to any form of self-interest. Akin to Levinas in this respect, his understanding of the good harks back to a Platonic account insofar as it implies a relation to something nonsubjective, beyond the self and its interests, which establishes criteria for what is important in life in a way that is irreducible to our subjective desires—what Taylor refers to as "strong evaluations."[17] But his regulative vision of a life capable of balancing the demands of all the goods that constitute our modern sense of self, a life able to "live this identity more fully," as he says, ultimately appears to fall back on an Aristotelian vision of the highest good as a fulfilling life "which somehow combines to the greatest possible degree all the goods we seek."[18]

Levinas's understanding of the goodness that occurs in my responsibility for the other cannot be captured within such an Aristotelian perspective. As he puts it, "Goodness consists in taking up a position in being such that the Other counts more than myself,"[19] in which I realize that there is something more important at stake in my life than myself and my own fulfillment—the fulfillment of my obligations to the other. As such, it is a sense of goodness that calls into question every aspect of my pursuit of a fulfilled life for myself, a sense of goodness that calls me decisively beyond my concern for myself. Levinas stresses this point in emphasizing, perhaps more radically than he needs, the "liturgical" character of the work of goodness, requiring "on the part of him who exercises it a putting out of funds at a loss," a service without promise of happiness.[20] Though, in the final analysis, Levinas recognizes the moral importance of caring for oneself in the context of an impartial appreciation of the concerns of others,[21] there can be no doubt concerning the priority of the goodness of my responsibility to the other over any sense of a good or fulfilled life I might pursue for myself. It may be viewed as what Taylor would call a "hypergood," establishing the perspective from which the relative worth of other goods may be evaluated,[22] circumscribing the limits within which they may legitimately be pursued.

This hypergoodness of my responsibility for the other converges, therefore, with an important sense of the deontological idea of the priority of the right to the good that Taylor rejects: "that what is important in ethical life is the obligation we have to others, e.g., to fair dealing and benevolence, and that these are incomparably more weighty than the requirements of a good, or fulfilled, or valuable, or worthwhile life."[23] As such, there are grounds to separate it from our concerns with the goods of a fulfilled life by referring to it specifically as what is right as long as we do not lose sight of the substantive vision of goodness that constitutes it. In this way we can begin to address Habermas's concerns with the abandonment of moral proceduralism and the pluralistic character of modern life. A part of what we are called to in the face of the other is to respect and, indeed, support the other's distinctive conception of what goes to make up a fulfilled life, whether or not we can see it as good for ourselves. Having our pursuit of the good life called into question by the other entails recognizing the limits of its validity in this way, the lack of justification for imposing it arbitrarily on the other.

It is only when a particular vision of the good life conflicts with the goodness of one's responsibility to the other that this pluralism is itself called into question. As Levinas says, the only "intolerance" entailed here "is directed not against doctrines but against the immorality that can disfigure the human face of my neighbor."[24] It is this sense of the good, of the unconditional importance of one's responsibility to the other, that is the condition for the possibility of a pluralism that would not degenerate into mutual indifference. It is a sense of goodness that must be fostered in society in order to underwrite the solidarity that is, as Habermas recognizes, the condition for any responsible exercise of freedom. For this reason, Levinas's perspective finds itself at odds with the atomistic vision of pluralism that has tended to dominate modern liberal societies. Based in the image of the citizen as consumer liberated by the market for her/his personal consumption without regard for collective responsibilities, this pluralism of indifference has proved itself inconsistent with the requirements of a mutually supportive community that would foster not only the personal freedom we demand for ourselves but also the justice and material solidarity commanded of us in the face of the other. As such, we can recognize the validity of much of the socialist and communitarian critiques of this market-dominated liberalism.[25] But to oppose one particularly detrimental form of pluralism is not to oppose pluralism per se. Quite the contrary, the goodness of responsibility demands a pluralism of mutual respect and solidarity as part and parcel of what it means to be responsible for the other.[26]

3.2.3 The Saying and the Said

The other major point of divergence with Taylor concerns Levinas's apparent agreement with Habermas that the moral dimensions of language lie in the very act of speaking with another person or, as Levinas puts it, in language as saying as opposed to what is said. In every communicative action there is, in addition to what is said in the expression, in the signs that the communicative agent gives forth, the giving forth of those signs to the other. It is here, in this saying of what is said, that we find ourselves in proximity to the face of the other. Prior to the significance of what is said in my expression to the other there is a moral significance to the very act of speaking with the other. But, for this very reason, this significance cannot be of the same order as a theme or content conveyed by what is said. It is merely what Levinas sometimes characterizes as an "orientation" to my speech, the simple "Here I am" (*Me voici*) of my exposure to the claims of the other, the sense of "gravity" or "urgency" of my relationship to the other.[27] It is, as such, a significance that necessarily falls short of an articulate understanding of why this or any other person should deserve my unconditional consideration. It is, as Levinas has it, citing a novel by Vasily Grossman, "instinctive and blind . . . the kindness of an old lady who gives a piece of bread to a convict along the roadside . . . the kindness of a soldier who holds his canteen out to a wounded enemy . . . goodness without ideology . . . goodness without thought. The goodness of men outside the religious or social good."[28] This "goodness without ideology" is, for Levinas, a form of solidarity with the other that is irreducible to any distinctive, culturally shared understanding of what we owe to one another, any historically articulate sense of what is "said" about the importance of the other. It is a form of "kindness" that subtends my proximity to any other person as someone who could speak to me and, in that gesture, command my unconditional consideration.

But to speak in such an unqualified way of a "goodness without ideology" is, I believe, misleading insofar as it suggests the possibility of a sense of the moral worth of the other that would somehow have no need of articulation, a saying that would not need to be said. Levinas's work is, unfortunately, virtually silent on this aspect of the relation between the saying and the said. Because Levinas devotes the lion's share of his attention to the inevitable betrayal of the saying within the said, a point we will come to shortly, one cannot help, however, but get the impression that he conceives of the significance of saying as sufficient unto itself apart from anything said, something that can only be compromised as it is put into words. It is important, however, that we distinguish these two points—the question of the need of saying to be said and the betrayal of the saying within the said. Just because Levinas endorses the second point, it does not follow that he should conclude that the saying has no need of the said. Indeed, such a conclusion would not square easily with the great emphasis he places elsewhere in his work on the importance of Judaism as a "privileged civilization," "the unique means to preserve the humanity and the personality of man,"[29] which suggests that the moral orientation of saying needs to be said, articulated in historically distinctive accounts of the substantive worth of the other such as we find in Judaism. But *why* it needs to be said remains unclear. What does an articulate account of the moral worth of the other bring to our "orientation" to the other in speech?

It is here that it may prove useful to return briefly to Taylor and his analysis of the importance of articulation for our substantive insights into the good. The key to his analysis is that we cannot grasp something as important or significant without an account as to why it is significant. Making this point against forms of moral subjectivism that would reduce our sense of what is important in life to what we decide or feel to be important, his insight has relevance for Levinas's account of the saying and the said as well. "I couldn't just *decide* that the most significant action is wiggling my toes in warm mud," Taylor writes. "Without a special explanation, this is not an intelligible claim. . . . So I wouldn't know what sense to attribute to someone allegedly *feeling* that this was so. What could someone *mean* who said this. Perhaps," as he continues playing with his example, "mud is the element of the world spirit, which you contact with your toes." But then it is the account of the special relation between mud and the world spirit that enables me to see it as significant, not my feeling that way.[30]

If Taylor is right here, then it simply does not make sense to speak of a sense of the moral worth, the moral *importance*, of the other person achieved wholly apart from what can be said about that importance, about why the other is important. But this quite valid point should not lead us to reject Levinas's understanding of the moral significance of saying out of hand. Just because our substantive recognition of the moral worth of the other person needs articulation, it does not follow that it is grounded exclusively in that articulation or that that articulation is itself groundless. What is said about the substantive importance of the other can be understood as responsive to a need that is established at the level of speech itself, as an answer to a call that is constitutive of saying anything at all to another. We have already seen how we cannot make sense of the authority of the moral point of view to command an unconditional sense of deference to the other without a substantive recognition of the unconditional worth of the other person. But insofar as it is in the act of speech itself that I find myself unconditionally bound to consider the point of view of the other, this entails that I cannot make sense of what I am committed to in the very act of speech without a sense of the unconditional worth of the other with whom I speak. As hermeneutic animals, creatures who must make sense or, at least, try to make sense of our experience, we cannot but find ourselves impelled to recognize the unconditional worth of our interlocutors as a condition for making sense of how we are bound in speech to an unconditional mode of deference to them.

Levinas's account of the moral significance of saying may best be redeemed, I believe, as a phenomenological account of the way in which we find ourselves drawn in the very act of speech to a sense of the unconditional worth of the other. Whereas Habermas's analysis of communicative action is limited to a pragmatic analysis of the formal procedures that are presupposed in speech, Levinas attempts to articulate our lived experience of speech, our lived appropriation of communicative endeavors whose distinctive demands pose unique problems for our efforts to make some kind of sense of our experience. In speaking with another person we find ourselves bound to a mode of deference to the other capable of calling into question any strategic reasons we might have for entering into a communicative relationship with that person. As such, we find ourselves committed to a mode of deference that must be strategically unintelligible insofar as it exceeds what is required by any of our strategic objectives with speech. Making sense of such a strategically unintelligible yet also unavoidable commitment demands a substantive recognition of the unconditional worth of the other as the point of such a commitment, the reason why we might regard that commitment as appropriate despite its lack of strategic utility.

Communicative action can only, therefore, be lived intelligibly by communicative agents as a demand, a persistent solicitation or call to consider the other as unconditionally worthy of the consideration demanded of them by their communicative commitments. To be *called* to a sense of the unconditional worth of the other is not yet, however, to have an understanding of the worth of the other that answers that call. An understanding of the substantive worth of the other can only be worked out, as Taylor would stress, at the level of the said in terms of our accounts of why the other deserves our unconditional consideration. But what is said about the other must be understood as responsive to a call that emerges in our lived appropriation of speech, our attempts to make sense of the commitments we find ourselves unavoidably undertaking in saying anything at all to another person.

It is in this way that we can speak of an as yet inarticulate moral significance to the very act of speech. In speaking with another person I find myself bound to defer to the other *as if* s/he were unconditionally worthy of my consideration. But to relate to my interlocutor *as if* s/he were unconditionally worthy in this way is to make what amounts to a presumption of her/his worth, a presumption that can only be cashed out in terms of an account of why the other deserves my consideration. Apart from such an account this presumption can be lived, of course, as little more than an affective tone to my relationship to the other, perhaps no more than a feeling of being well-disposed toward the other or of finding myself affected with a sense of the gravity or urgency of what is said to me. This is, undoubtedly, at least part of the reason why Levinas emphasizes the affective dimensions of our ethical proximity to the other, as we saw in chapter 2. We are vulnerable to the other at an affective level if only because the other appeals to us not merely at the level of what is said, but prior to that, in the saying of what is said. In finding ourselves bound to an unconditional mode of deference to the other in the very act of speech, we find ourselves moved to understand the other as unconditionally worthy of that deference, called to such an understanding as a way of cashing out the presumption of her/his worth we make in speaking to her/him *as if* s/he mattered, as a way of making sense of the strategically unintelligible mode of deference to the other to which we find ourselves unavoidably bound.

It is always conceivable, of course, that I might not be able to cash out my lived presumption of the other's worth, that I might never find the words to articulate it. Perhaps, to imagine an extreme case, I have come to hold a completely misanthropic understanding of humanity as vile and unworthy of anything but my strategically motivated consideration. I will still ineluctably find myself relating to the other *as if* s/he were significant in a way that belies my misanthropy and moves me to call it into question. Though I will not be able to make sense of the peculiar way in which in speaking with the other I am drawn to relate to the other with a form of deference that transcends my strategic interests, I cannot but be affected by it, haunted by it, moved to an inarticulate form of "goodness without ideology," modes of kindness that transcend my ideology, "the kindness of an old lady who gives a piece of bread to a convict along the roadside . . . the kindness of a soldier who holds his canteen out to a wounded enemy." This does not entail, of course, that I will abandon my misanthropy. It is difficult to understate the power of our ideological commitments. But no ideology can completely drown out this countervailing current that emerges in our speaking with other people, a call of the saying for a said that would contest every ideology, that would understand the other as having the unconditional authority to call into question any of our ideological commitments.

It is in this sense that Levinas is justified in speaking of the irreducibility of the saying to the said, the way in which what is said can never adequately capture the moral significance of saying. Every attempt to make the significance of saying said is capable of being called into question by the other. The moral importance of the other as interlocutor to which we find ourselves called in speaking with the other cannot, to this extent, be reduced to any theme insofar as that importance exhibits itself as a right to call any theme into question, including the theme that attempts to articulate why the other possesses this right. The face of the other, it is important to recall, is always the face of my interlocutor, not "the word that bears on the Other as a theme," as Levinas notes, but the one to whom that word is said. And as interlocutor, as the one to whom the word is said, the other "has quit the theme that encompassed him, and upsurges inevitably behind the said" as the one who maintains an absolute right to question what is said. It is because of this "divergence that inevitably opens between the Other as my theme and the Other as my interlocutor" that we must speak of the transcendence of the "height" of the other to any thematic account, the irreducibility of the significance of saying to anything that can be said.[31] It is for this reason that Levinas speaks as he does of the need to unsay the said that attempts to say the significance of saying, to deny the limitations of the themes that would otherwise attempt to present it in order to draw attention to the way, as an orientation to the other, the significance of saying always exceeds what is said.[32]

It is important to note here that we are speaking of a distinctive way in which the significance of saying exceeds what is said, a specific sense in which what is said betrays the face of the other to which it is in service, not a wholesale irrelevance of what is said that would make only mute silence adequate to the call of the face of the other in speech. Levinas's point regarding the transcendence of the saying to the said should not be understood to undermine the need to make saying said, to come to an articulate understanding of the moral worth of the other that answers the call to recognize the other as worthy of our unconditional deference. It is only to insist that every articulate understanding of the worth of the other at our disposal is, at best, a more or less inadequate attempt to gesture at a sense of importance that ultimately defies thematic presentation, to recognize the limitations of every thematic account of the moral worth of the other in relation to the face of the other who always reserves, as interlocutor, the right to call those thematic accounts into question. Taylor's point about the need for the articulation of our sense of what is morally important, our ability to say why something is important in order to be able to understand it as important, remains.

But in understanding our discursive accounts of the moral worth of the other person as responsive to a call that is knit into the very fabric of speech itself, of our attempts to make sense of the commitments we unavoidably undertake in taking up speech with the other, we are able to wed Taylor's insight into the need for a substantive sense of the point of a moral point of view onto life with Habermas's insights into the universal ground of the moral point of view in language itself. If we understand language as Levinas leads us to, as a practice in which we find ourselves called to a substantive sense of the moral worth of the other, we can see how the moral point of view is constituted in language not merely in terms of procedures that bind us to impartial forms of consideration of the other but also in terms of a substantive sense of the worth of the other to that consideration to which we are called in intelligibly taking up language. Insofar as our substantive understandings of the worth of the other person are responsive to a call constitutive of our intelligible appropriation of language itself, we have no reason to dismiss them as merely ethical considerations that can have no bearing on the universally valid content of the moral point of view. To the contrary, we have reason to suppose that no one who is intelligibly committed to communicative endeavors can be blind to the substantive moral worth of what Levinas refers to as the face of the other. Though every attempt to articulate that worth will necessarily be limited and colored by the discursive resources of one's particular social-historical tradition and so will be, to this extent, historically distinctive, we must recognize them as historically distinctive attempts to articulate a moral point of view that is itself grounded universally in our attempts to make sense of the modes of deference to which we find ourselves bound in speaking with one another. We need not choose, therefore, between a moral proceduralism that would capture our intuitions about the universal validity of the moral point of view but sacrifice the intelligibility of our intuitions about its unconditional authority and a substantive morality that would preserve the latter while sacrificing the former. Though communicative action *is* a rule-governed social practice, accessible to a procedural analysis, we cannot make the moral significance of that practice intelligible at the level of the rules that govern it but only in terms of the substantive significance of our interlocutor to which we are called in that practice. The key, it would seem, lies in an expanded understanding of communicative action that would grasp it not merely in its procedural but in its substantive dimensions as well, as an orientation or form of proximity to the face of the other.

3.3 The Moral Point of View as a Substantive *and* Procedural Point of View

The moral point of view, understood as unconditionally authoritative for us, cannot be limited to a perspective that emerges exclusively from the adoption of communicative procedures. It is, rather, a perspective that only fully emerges in our substantive orientation to the face of the other that is established on the basis of those procedures. Grasping the moral point of view in its fullness involves holding both of these perspectives together, the procedural as well as the substantive. Thus far, however, I have only emphasized the way Habermas's procedural perspective needs the substantive vision of the face of the other invoked in Levinas's work. Grasping both the procedural and substantive aspects of the moral point of view together, however, requires that we also pay attention to the way in which the substantive vision of the face of the other evoked by Levinas is dependent on the procedural perspective emphasized by Habermas.

3.3.1 Impartiality and the Articulation of the Humanity of the Other

This is a concern we can observe in James Marsh's work. Much as Levinas does, Marsh attempts to expand on Habermas's conception of communicative action with a phenomenological account of the embodied subject of that action, the lived experience it implies.[33] Attempting to be phenomenologically faithful to our ethical experience of the "suffering," "marginalized other," Marsh comes to endorse Levinas's most basic position that "the call of the other is the original ethical 'fact' from which theorizing proceeds and to which it leads." Coming very close to the position I have been defending here, he speaks of "the face-to-face relationship" where the "other speaks to me and I to him" as what "grounds" and "gives rise to ethical reflection." But he is careful to qualify these observations by stressing the way in which the ethical import of the face of the other is apparent only to those already "informed by the notions of right, morality, and justice."[34]

What is the motivation and significance of this qualification? Marsh's comments on the "call of the other" are not extensive and are made in the context of a different set of questions from our own. They are, therefore, difficult to pin down in this context. It is possible, however, to see his point about the dependence of the ethical significance of the face of the other on "notions of right, morality, and justice" as gesturing in one of two directions. On the one hand, it could attest to a refusal to break with the most basic insight of Habermas's ethics, that the moral point of view is constituted in terms of communicative *procedures*. Cognizant of the phenomenological importance of the "suffering other" in ethical experience, the way in which most ethical practice is motivated not principally by theoretical reflections on ethical principles but by a concrete encounter with the suffering of those who are oppressed, Marsh may be trying to acknowledge this point while still insisting that the ethical character of this experience is a consequence of commitments to principles of "right, morality, and justice" stemming from our unavoidable commitments to the procedures of communicative reason. Taken in this way, it is our procedural commitment to a rational sense of impartiality that obliges us to consider the suffering of the other as ethically significant, a derivative implication, so to speak, of our commitment to those procedures. But in this case we come back to the problem of the intelligibility of the moral authority of those procedures. If we recognize a duty to heed the concerns of the other only as a consequence of communicative procedures that demand an attitude of impartiality of me, then we cannot make reference to the face of the other as the point of those procedures, what justifies their unconditional observance. The question of why the other deserves that mode of consideration remains unaddressed. Only a substantive grasp of the "height"or goodness of the other in a way that goes beyond a procedurally grounded understanding of my duties toward the other can allow us to recognize the "call of the other" as what "gives rise to ethical reflection," *why* we find ourselves bound to take our procedural duties as unconditionally important.

On the other hand, Marsh could be getting at a point I want to stress as well concerning the way the "call of the other," though irreducible to procedural commitments, is, nevertheless, as unintelligible apart from communicative procedures as the moral authority of those procedures are apart from that substantive call. On one occasion, for example, he makes his point as a matter of our inability to "fully articulate" the "appeal of the other" "without linguistic communication leading to the principles of right, morality, and justice."[35] Stressing the dependence of the *full articulation* of the significance of the face of the other on impartial moral principles does not reduce that significance to what can be derived from procedural commitments. It simply stresses the importance of those procedures, or principles derived from them, for our capacity to comprehend that significance. And this is a point well taken by Levinas. The significance of saying is, as Levinas insists, not said. The significance of my orientation to the other in speech is only an inarticulate presumption of the importance of the other, a way of relating to the other as if s/he mattered. An articulate understanding of the worth of the other able to cash out that presumption obviously requires more.

That it requires, in particular, a grasp of "principles of right, morality, and justice" may be seen from a reexamination of Levinas's account of the third party, where he is concerned with just this problem of the relation between the sense of obligation that opens up in my proximity to the other and the sense of justice demanded of me in the presence of many others. In his account of the third party, as we have seen, Levinas conceives of my awareness of impartial principles of justice as founded on my relationship to the other in the singular, a complication of that primary sense of obligation in the presence of other others. But, as I have already tried to show in other ways, this story may be misleading if taken without qualification. Of particular note here is the way in which the account only works insofar as it is the face of the other in its pure human vulnerability that moves us to a sense of responsibility. Though it is always the concrete other to whom I find myself obliged in my proximity to the other, there is nothing in what calls me to this responsibility that I do not find as well in my proximity to any concrete other. As he puts it, it is "in the nakedness of the face," the face of the other as "abstract man, disengaged from all culture," that we find "the birth of morality."[36]

With this idea of the abstract humanity of the face we have something of a mediating notion between the concrete and generalized other. The abstract humanity of the other is, for Levinas, the humanity of a concrete other, soliciting me to care not for humanity at large but for the humanity of this specific person. Most simply, Levinas is claiming that the moral authority of the face of a concrete other is not revealed in terms of anything unique to any concrete other but only in what s/he, in each case, uniquely embodies: her/his human vulnerability. It is here, in this universal dimension of the face in its singularity, that the moral worth of the other is found. And it is only for this reason that the third party can emerge, merely insofar as s/he is human, as another other equally soliciting my responsibility and, so, impelling me to a sense of justice.

An articulate grasp of the face of the other in its abstract humanity is impossible, however, outside of a context in which I grasp the importance of an impartial sense of justice, the context of the third party. In speaking with another person I find myself moved to take the other seriously, as if s/he mattered. But this is not to have an articulate idea of the abstract humanity of the other as the basis for my presumption of the other's importance. Indeed, the structure of Levinas's analysis of our proximity to the other entails that this dimension of the face must be occluded in favor of the specificity of the other. The abstract humanity of the other solicits our concern not for others generally but for this other in her/his specificity. It is not, in other words, humanity that becomes important to me in my speaking with the other but the concrete other I am addressing. The gravity of speech is always a specific gravity, so to speak, oriented toward the face of the concrete other to whom speech is addressed. The abstract humanity of the other cannot emerge in any articulate way as the subject of that gravity until I have weighed and compared the competing claims of many concrete others and come to the conclusion that it is nothing unique to any of them that claims my concern, but something they each uniquely embody. But to have done this is already to have taken up the perspective of justice, the vantage point of impartiality that the claims of the third party bring in their wake.

The idea of the abstract humanity of the other as the basis of her/his moral worth cannot exist, therefore, apart from a principled sense of impartiality. Prior to that, my sense of obligation is always a partiality for the concrete other or others to whom I am closest, toward whom I have gained a specific sense of responsibility or taken up a sense of election, as the parent of this child, that person's friend, these people's neighbor, etc. Prior to the articulate emergence of a sense of impartiality, my idea of the worth of the other must be inclined toward particularity and exclusivity, focused on the importance of others as my family, friends, neighbors, etc.—understandings whose significance we should not be too quick to dismiss, however, as it is always the other in her/his specificity who appeals to me. It is only in the particularity of a sense of election to or responsibility for the concrete other that s/he becomes important to me, as I find myself uniquely responsible as a parent of this child or as friend or neighbor of this person. It is not so much wrong, then, to understand the worth of the other in terms of one's particular relationship to her/him as it is limiting in relation to the gravity of one's relations to those who fall outside those parameters. It is not wrong to understand the importance of one's child in terms of her/his specificity as one's child. But it misses the way other children may also lay claim to one's concern.

In this way we can see the emergence of an inevitable tension and potential conflict between my sense of responsibility to "those close" to me and a sense of justice toward "those far off." Transcending the limitations of overly particular and exclusive conceptions of moral worth cannot simply be a matter of forgetting the unique importance of my children, friends, and neighbors but, more a matter of realizing that their unique importance as *my* children, friends, and neighbors lies in the way I have made them uniquely important to me *as human beings* in my specific relationship to and sense of responsibility for them. But gaining such an articulate understanding can only be a matter of a fallible process in which one is exposed to the claims of others beyond the parameters of one's more exclusive understandings and comes to find those understandings increasingly inadequate to one's moral experience—a learning process, as Habermas correctly emphasizes,[37] with social and historical as well as personal dimensions. And it is only at the end of such a dynamic developmental process, in the attainment of an impartial sense of justice to others in general, that one can vouchsafe the idea of the humanity of the other as the basis for her/his moral worth, as what it is about the face of the other that solicits and deserves one's care and consideration.

Thus, there is an important sense in which the face of the other, as Levinas understands it, as the face of "abstract man," cannot emerge for us as an articulate subject of moral obligation prior to the emergence of a sense of impartiality and justice, much as Marsh argues. In the final analysis, we must recognize that the moral point of view is constituted structurally between the two poles of a procedural impartiality and a substantive concern for the face of the other and dynamically or developmentally between increasingly particular and increasingly universal conceptions of the moral worth of the other. It is to such a structurally and dynamically complex understanding of the moral point of view that we must have recourse if we are to account for the interdependencies as well as the tensions between the formal and substantive aspects of our moral experience, the impartiality of justice toward others generally and the partiality of care for the concrete other, the grounding of morality in personal relationships and a sense of moral maturity that must transcend this grounding but may never uproot itself.[38]

3.3.2 Ethical Proximity to the Other as a Communicative Proximity

We may, therefore, no more abstract the substantive dimension of the moral point of view that Levinas helps us to discern from its procedural dimension that Habermas highlights than we may abstract the procedural from the substantive. Both are required for an adequate grasp of what it means to have a moral point of view onto life. But the dependence of the substantive dimension on the procedural that I have been stressing thus far in terms of the need for articulation runs deeper still. It is not as if one could have even an inarticulate presumption of the worth of the other person apart from the possibility of a communicative relation with the other. The face of the other is the face of my interlocutor. It is my conversational relationship to the other *as* interlocutor that is, for Levinas, the basis of my ethical sense of deference to the other. As emphasized in chapter 1, this is a point Levinas shares with Habermas concerning the importance of our capacity for language for a sense of moral obligation. Without my commitment to communicative modes of endeavor that establish, by virtue of the procedures which are essential for their successful adoption, a relation to the other, an impartial perspective onto the other that unconditionally obliges me to consider her/his perspective as well as my own, it is difficult to imagine how a genuinely ethical or even a genuinely human sense of the other could emerge for us. My proximity to the face of the other, in Levinas's ethically loaded sense of this phrase, is not the perceptual presence of a face that, as merely another kind of object in my perceptual field, intrinsically commands no more of my attention than any other object. This is, undoubtedly, at least a part of why Levinas stresses our inability to make the face of the other present as an object that could be known.[39] As ethically significant, the face of the other is always *more* than the face to which I am perceptually present. It is the face of my interlocutor, the one who speaks to me and, in that way, commands my attention in a way no object can.

As such, we should not be too quick to dismiss Marsh's comment that the ethical import of the face of the other would be inaccessible to one who was not "informed by the notions of right, morality, and justice." Inasmuch as these notions are already implicit in our commitment to communicatively rational procedures and the impartiality they demand of us, they are implicit in the communicative endeavors that establish an ethically significant relation to the other. But, to return to our earlier critical point, we cannot recognize our substantive appreciation of the face of the other as the point of those communicative procedures, as what enables us to grasp them as unconditionally important, if we reduce the moral significance of our awareness of the other to a consequence of procedural demands, a sense of the other as important only insofar as communicative procedures require us to consider her/his point of view. Taken by themselves, these procedures cannot establish the moral importance of anything. They simply make pragmatic demands of us to adopt a perspective of impartiality as a condition of successful communication that, presumably, we may value for strategic reasons of our own. They can be seen as *morally* important only if they are conjoined with a substantive recognition of the unconditional worth of the other, my interlocutor, that allows me to make sense of why the other might deserve the unconditional mode of consideration these procedures demand of me. My substantive sense of the "always positive value" of the other, though inaccessible apart from a commitment to procedures of communicative rationality, must go beyond what is strictly entailed in merely following those procedures if I am to intelligibly understand how or why I could be morally bound to them.

3.4 The Metaphysical Ground of Moral Authority?

As we come to recognize the limitations of a postmetaphysical perspective in ethics, acknowledging both procedural and substantive dimensions of the moral point of view, it would appear that we must acknowledge an inescapably metaphysical dimension to our moral experience. But in what sense is the face of the other a *metaphysical* ground of moral authority? To begin, there is simply the way in which our substantive sense of the "always positive value" of the face of the other transgresses the postmetaphysical parameters of Habermas's discourse ethics. Rather than limiting our understanding of what is involved in taking a moral point of view onto life to our understanding of the way we are unavoidably bound to pragmatic procedures of communicative action that oblige us to attend impartially to the point of view of the other, Levinas seeks to articulate the substantive good to which our adherence to those procedures is in service. Beyond this largely polemical sense, however, it is unclear how the appeal to the face of the other could be construed as metaphysical in any of the other ways in which Habermas understands it. In particular, Levinas's account of face of the other does not appear to entail any totalizing vision of the world as a whole, nor does it place either ideas or self-consciousness at the foundation of such a totalizing vision or privilege theoretical over practical life—three hallmarks of traditionally metaphysical thought according to Habermas.[40] If the appeal to the face of the other constitutes a return to metaphysics, then, it would appear to be a particularly thin, even benign sense of metaphysics to which we return, one consistent with and supportive of most of the other objectives that fuel Habermas's postmetaphysical project.

Though subject to diverse and competing modes of historical articulation, it is a substantive sense of the good that in some form or other must be recognized by anyone intelligibly committed to modes of communicative action, as a condition for making sense of the unconditional character of the demands posed to them by that commitment. In this way, it dovetails with Habermas's moral universalism, offering us a phenomenological understanding of what is involved in intelligibly undertaking the sorts of communicative commitments Habermas stresses in his work. Though it is certainly possible that someone might lack the discursive resources to articulate an understanding of the moral worth of the other or might even stubbornly refuse to do so out of a deeply entrenched misanthropic perspective onto life, it is not plausible to suppose that someone might not find themselves *called* to such an understanding. Inasmuch as we are hermeneutic animals, creatures who are bound to at least try to make sense of our experience, we are also creatures who find ourselves impelled to recognize the other as worthy of the deference we are bound to show her/him in our communicative endeavors. Working out the interpretive frameworks in which we can articulate the worthiness of the other to our unconditional deference is a historical project that we cannot anticipate from culture to culture. But there is nothing historically variable in the way every communicative agent, regardless of her/his culture, must find her/himself called to work out such interpretive frameworks as part and parcel of an intelligible appropriation of her/his communicative commitments. Hence, we have good reason to anticipate the universal validity of this substantive understanding of the good for anyone who is *intelligibly* committed to communicative modes of action, assured that the price of complete insensitivity to this good, the price of a consistent misanthropy, is the loss of the ability to make sense of a significant and unavoidable dimension of human experience.

Moreover, as a good that calls into question every sense of the good we may project *for ourselves*, it enjoys a priority over every other sense of the good that is identical with what Habermas recognizes as the priority of the right to the good. The "always positive value" of the face of the other is not, therefore, a good that is inconsistent with Habermas's deontological insights but, on the contrary, is convergent with and supportive of those insights, establishing the point of that priority, why we believe it is important to give priority to considerations of justice over the pursuit of what we understand as good for ourselves. In his own consideration of these questions, William Rehg comes to similar conclusions regarding the need for what he calls, with Taylor, the "constitutive good" of discourse ethics, the point of our commitment to procedures of impartial deliberation. In particular, he argues that one would have no reason to accept discourse ethics without a prior acceptance of what he characterizes as the good of "rational or autonomous cooperation" in which we attempt to secure the cooperation of others in a way that respects everyone's freedom and integrity.[41] But he also suggests that this is a point to which Habermas need not object, as it concerns what Rehg argues is "a good with such unique status vis-à-vis other goods that its priority simply *is* the priority of the right to these other goods," "a unique sort of metavalue that one cannot rationally reject except in an abstract fashion."[42] The key to Habermas's concerns, on this reading, is not the postmetaphysical disavowal of a substantive sense of the good that he stresses himself, but the character of the good to which we have recourse in fully articulating the moral point of view. If the good that we presuppose in endorsing the moral importance of procedures of impartial deliberation with others is a good that is supportive of moral universalism and the priority of the right to the good, then it is not a sense of the good that discourse ethics need disavow.

To this extent, it may be misleading to characterize Levinas's appeal to the face of the other as metaphysical. As it is consistent with concerns with moral universalism and the priority of the right to the good that lead Habermas to his postmetaphysical disavowal of the importance of substantive goods for the moral point of view, what we learn from Levinas may be less a matter of the need for a return to metaphysics as the need to clarify the postmetaphysical project Habermas undertakes. Perhaps the appeal to the face of the other is metaphysical only in relation to Habermas's misunderstanding of the requirements of his own postmetaphysical concerns. But, interestingly, Levinas is led for reasons of his own to characterize the appeal to the face of the other as metaphysical, understanding metaphysics as a relation "toward an alien outside-of-oneself (*hors-de-soi étranger*), toward a yonder."[43] What Levinas means to stress here is the exteriority of the face of the other, the way in which it involves a relation to a sense of alterity that cannot be assimilated into the sphere of one's concerns with one's own life, a sense of the infinite that defies presence and transcends conceptual comprehension, a sense of what is absolutely other that hints at what is wholly other, God.[44] This sense of metaphysics touches on what has been, undoubtedly, the most troubling dimension of Levinas's work for many readers involving him in what Jacques Derrida, among others, has criticized as an internally incoherent attempt to present what, by his own account, cannot be presented, to say what cannot be said.[45] Here is another sense in which the appeal to the face of the other may be characterized as metaphysical, though perhaps in a less benign way than the polemical sense we have examined so far. I turn to the issues raised by Levinas's own understanding of the metaphysical character of his work in chapter 6, as I take up an array of questions that all turn on the general issue of the epistemic viability of Levinas's account of the face of the other.

But for now, I want to conclude by stressing the limitations of Habermas's postmetaphysical perspective onto ethics, the need to be open to the face of the other as a metaphysical ground of moral authority if only in the way it transcends that postmetphysical perspective. Though laudable in its intent to avoid substantive normative commitments that have become increasingly controversial, Habermas's postmetaphysical project blinds us to the substantive point of undertaking a moral point of view onto life and leaves the unconditional authority of the moral point of view unintelligible. In that way it fails to adequately clarify the moral point of view, a key, if not *the* definitive task of moral theory. Though an adequate explication of the moral point of view must attend to its procedural dimensions, as Habermas does so well, it must also seek to articulate the "always positive value" of the face of the other as the substantive point of our commitment to those procedures. As Habermas himself has recognized,

> Each must be able to recognize him- or herself in all that wears a human face. To keep this sense of humanity alive and to clarify it—not, to be sure, through direct intervention, but through unceasing, indirect theoretical efforts—is certainly a task from which philosophers should not feel themselves wholly excused.[46]

Notes

1. See Jürgen Habermas, *Postmetaphysical Thinking*, trans. William Mark Hohengarten (Cambridge, Mass.: The MIT Press, 1992), 6 & 33-35. Also see Seyla Benhabib's succinct characterization of postmetaphysical thought in her *Situating the Self* (New York: Routledge, 1992), 4-5.

2. Charles Taylor, "Language and Society," in *Communicative Action: Essays on Jürgen Habermas's Theory of Communication*, ed. Axel Honneth and Hans Joas (Cambridge, Mass.: The MIT Press, 1991), 30-31.

3. Habermas, *Moral Consciousness and Communicative Action*, trans. Christian Lenhardt and Shierry Weber Nicholson (Cambridge, Mass.: The MIT Press, 1990), 102.

4. Charles Taylor, *Sources of the Self* (Cambridge, Mass.: Harvard University Press, 1989), 87.

5. Taylor, *Sources of the Self*, 515.

6. Jürgen Habermas, *Justification and Application: Remarks on Discourse Ethics*, trans. Ciaran Cronin (Cambridge, Mass.: The MIT Press, 1993), 75.This is only one aspect of his response to Taylor. I take up his concerns with the philosophical status of Taylor's invocation of substantive goods when I turn to a consideration of the philosophical status of Levinas's appeal to the face of the other in chapter 6.

7. Habermas, *Justification and Application*, 75.

8. Habermas, *Justification and Application*, 79.

9. Habermas, *Justification and Application*, 77 & 76 and *Erläuterungen zur Diskusethik* (Frankfurt am Main: Suhrkamp Verlag, 1991), 185.

10. Taylor, *Sources of the Self*, 93.

11. See his dismissal of Hare in *Sources of the Self*, 87.

12. See Taylor, *Sources of the Self*, 8 & 77.

13. See Taylor, "Language and Society," 34.

14. Taylor, *Sources of the Self*, 91

15. See Taylor, *Sources of the Self*, 495.

16. See Levinas, *Otherwise than Being*, trans. Alphonso Lingis (The Hague: Martinus Nijhoff, 1981), 140-145.

17. See *Sources of the Self*, 4. For Taylor's Platonic reference, see his account of "constitutive goods," 92-93. Levinas also evokes Plato in emphasizing the transcendence of the good to the self. See in particular his "Philosophy and the Idea of Infinity," in *Collected Philosophical Papers*, trans. Alphonso Lingis (Dordrecht: Martinus Nijhoff, 1987), 47, 53, & 57.

18. Taylor, *Sources of the Self*, 504 & 66.

19. Levinas, *Totality and Infinity*, trans. Alphonso Lingis (Pittsburgh: Duquesne University Press, 1969), 247. Also see page 215 for a discussion of the asymmetry of our relation with the Other.

20. See Levinas, "Meaning and Sense," in *Collected Philosophical Papers*, 92-93 & 107 and "Diachrony and Representation," in *Time and the Other*, trans. Richard A. Cohen (Pittsburgh: Duquesne University Press, 1987), 118-120. I note that he may stress this point more radically than he needs for there does seem to be a promise of, at least, a *meaningful* life in our relation with the other and, especially, our children. See *Time and the Other*, 80-94, and *Totality and Infinity*, 267-269, 274-277, & 281-285. But this promise only emerges on the condition of having one's self-interested desire for happiness called into question. It is, therefore, consistent with the point I am trying to make in this paragraph.

21. See Levinas, *Otherwise than Being*, 160-161. For more on this point see my discussion of Levinas's idea of "the third party" in chapters 1 and 3.

22. Taylor, *Sources of the Self*, 63.

23. Taylor, *Sources of the Self*, 533, n. 66. Taylor rejects this as "self-destructive," involving "a forgetfulness of self which aspires beyond human powers." This is a criticism to which Levinas often seems to open himself up, especially in his "liturgical"

characterization of moral life. But I believe it is misguided and fails to take into account the appropriate place for a concern with a fulfilled life in the context of a responsible relation with others. The right, in this sense, takes priority over one's own good. But it need not demolish one's concern with it.

24. Emmanuel Levinas, *Difficult Freedom*, trans. Seàn Hand (Baltimore: The Johns Hopkins University Press, 1990), 174.

25. I am thinking here of the work of several people. See, for example, Charles Taylor, "Cross-Purposes: The Liberal-Communitarian Debate," in *Liberalism and the Moral Life*, ed. Nancy Rosenblum (Cambridge, Mass.: Harvard University Press, 1989) 159-182; Michael Walzer, *Spheres of Justice: A Defense of Pluralism and Equality* (New York: Basic Books, 1983), and "The Communitarian Critique of Liberalism," *Political Theory* 18, no. 1 (February 1990): 6-23; and finally, Michael Sandel, "The Procedural Republic and the Unencumbered Self," *Political Theory* 12 (1984): 81-96.

26. For more on this sense of pluralism, see my "Liberalism, Communitarianism, and the Conflictual Grounds of Democratic Pluralism," *Philosophy and Social Criticism* 19 (1993): 293-316.

27. See Levinas, *Totality and Infinity*, 98, *Otherwise than Being*, 149 & 6-7, *Autrement qu'être ou au-delà de l'essence* (La Haye: Martinus Nijhoff, 1974), 190, and "Language and Proximity," in *Collected Philosophical Papers*, 123 & 120.

28. Levinas, *In the Time of the Nations*, trans. Michael B. Smith (Indianapolis: Indiana University Press, 1994), 91.

29. Levinas, *Difficult Freedom*, 137 & 286. Also see chapter 5, "The Moral Relevance of Judaism to Modernity."

30. Charles Taylor, *The Ethics of Authenticity* (Cambridge, Mass.: Harvard University Press, 1991), 36-37.

31. All references to Levinas here are to *Totality and Infinity*, 195.

32. Levinas speaks of unsaying in *Otherwise than Being*, 181. An example of such unsaying can be found in his description of "ethical resistance" as "the resistance of what has no resistance" (*Totality and Infinity*, 199), where the point is to stress the way the sense of resistance being invoked exceeds any sense of objective resistance to which the theme of resistance would be adequate. I take up Levinas's thesis on the irreducibility of the saying to the said in more detail in chapter 6.

33. See his claim on page 11 of his book *Critique, Action, and Liberation* that "communicative praxis . . . meaningfully presupposes and implies subjectivity."

34. See *Critique, Action, and Liberation*, (Albany: State University of New York Press, 1995), 180-183 & 244-245.

35. Marsh, *Critique, Action, and Liberation*, 245.

36. Levinas, "Meaning and Sense," in *Collected Philosophical Papers*, 101.

37. See Jürgen Habermas, "Historical Materialism and the Development of Normative Structures," in *Communication and the Evolution of Society*, trans. Thomas McCarthy (Boston: Beacon Press, 1979), 95-129.

38. This also points toward the need, in political theory, for a pluralistic account of civil society as a network of, more or less, personal associations and solidarities in which a universal idea of justice is made meaningful—given a point—and in which my network of face-to-face relations gestures beyond itself to the point of calling forth an impartial idea of justice. I turn to a more detailed examination of this idea in chapter 5.

39. A particularly controversial point for many readers of Levinas I examine in more detail in chapter 6.

40. Habermas gives this account of metaphysical thought in *Postmetaphysical Thinking*, 29-33.

41. See Rehg, *Insight and Solidarity* (Berkeley: University of California Press, 1994), 138.

42. See Rehg, *Insight and Solidarity*, 140 & 147. Rehg's position on this issue is, therefore, formally identical to the Levinasian position I am advancing here. I believe that he does not push far enough, however, with a clarification of the content of the constitutive good that discourse ethics presupposes. For example, in speaking of the good of rational cooperation, it is important to know in what sense it is valued. Is it valued merely as one important aspect of the good life I project for myself? But then it is unclear how it could have the kind of priority over other goods that Rehg claims for it. If, on the other hand, we take its unconditional value seriously, the articulation of what is at stake in this good would probably converge with what Levinas refers to as the "always positive value" of the face of the other as what commands me to seek modes of cooperation with the other that take the concerns and interests of the other into account, even if it should entail the sacrifice of some aspect of the good for myself.

43. Levinas, *Totality and Infinity*, 33, and *Totalité et Infini* (La Haye: Martinus Nijhoff, 1961), 3.

44. See Levinas, *Totality and Infinity*, 48-52 & 34. "It is understood as the alterity of the Other and of the Most-High."

45. See Jacques Derrida, "Violence and Metaphysics: An Essay on the Thought of Emmanuel Levinas," in *Writing and Difference*, trans. Alan Bass (Chicago: The University of Chicago Press, 1978).

46. Habermas, *Postmetaphysical Thinking*, 15.

Chapter 4

The Liberties of the Ancients and Moderns

In chapters 2 and 3, I attempted to establish the relevance of Levinas's reference to the face of the other with respect to two deficits in Habermas's moral theory. Grounding the moral point of view exclusively in communicative procedures leaves Habermas unable to adequately account for the place of care in our moral lives and unable to make sense of the unconditional or properly moral authority of the moral point of view. Both of these deficits may be overcome, however, with an expanded account of communicative action that takes into account the face of the other as the moral point of our commitment to communicative procedures. Put most simply, my aim in chapters 2 and 3 has been to begin an argument to the effect that Habermas's postmetaphysical commitment to proceduralism in moral theory is more trouble than it is worth, that in excluding a Levinasian appeal to the face of the other we create more problems than we resolve.

In this chapter, I extend that argument into political theory with a consideration of the relevance of Levinas's account of the other to a balanced understanding of the relation between our rights to public and private autonomy, the liberties of the ancients and moderns. In particular, I take up Habermas's treatment of this issue in his review of John Rawls's political liberalism, where the charge that Rawls privileges the liberties of the moderns over the ancients stands out. Offering his own procedural approach to the legitimation of liberal-democratic principles as an alternative, Habermas argues that his approach is better suited to balancing the two liberties, to showing how they are derived, as he puts it, from the "same root."[1] By examining Habermas's criticisms of Rawls as well as Rawls's response, however, it should become clear that though Habermas is correct in his criticism of Rawls, his own approach to the question of the liberties of the ancients and moderns fails to solve the problem. Both Rawls and Habermas offer convincing reasons to balance our appreciation of the liberties of the ancients and moderns. But in pursuing an exclusively procedural approach to the problem, Habermas only manages to reverse it, privileging now public over private autonomy.

4.1 Privileging Private over Public Autonomy

4.1.1 Habermas's Critique of Rawls

Habermas bases his criticism of Rawls on what he characterizes as "the two-stage character of his theory."[2] Firmly embedded in the social contract tradition, Rawls's theory of justice begins with the idea that justice is a matter of which principles could be fairly agreed to by all subject to them—hence, his characterization of justice as fairness. But it is not, of course, the case that every actual agreement is fair, as some, if not most, real agreements are marked by inequalities that permit some to take advantage of others, to get others to agree to terms of cooperation they would not agree to if they were in a position of equality. To correct for this "arbitrariness of the world," Rawls proceeds with the idea of a hypothetical contractual situation, what he dubs "the original position," in which we are to imagine parties who are behind a "veil of ignorance," unaware of their place in society or their particular conception of a good life. In this way, the parties to the original position are denied any knowledge of arbitrary circumstances that could allow them to gain an advantage over their fellow citizens and so are constrained to come to an agreement as equals in a way that could not be questioned as unfair.[3] It is only after this first stage of his theory of justice in which we have clarified the basic principles of a just society that would be agreed to in a position of initial equality that we can move, by degrees, to consider the actual circumstances of real citizens who must apply those principles to their specific situations.

Habermas grants that Rawls "proceeds from the idea of political autonomy and models it at the level of the original position" in the way the parties there must come to an agreement on principles of justice as equals. He goes on to argue, however, that political autonomy is only given a "virtual existence in the original position . . . (which) does not fully unfold in the heart of the justly constituted society." Constrained as they are by the principles of justice decided by the hypothetical parties of the original position, real citizens "cannot reignite the radical democratic embers of the original position in the civic life of their society." They "cannot conceive of the constitution as a *project*" that must remain "open and incomplete" as "shifting historical circumstances" demand. Instead of recognizing the way the citizens of a just social order must be *essentially* involved in public life, exercising their public autonomy in reconsidering the nature and extent of their private liberties and public responsibilities in the light of changing historical exigencies and insights, Rawls's theory of justice establishes "a priority of liberal rights which demotes the democratic process to an inferior status . . . that constrain(s) democratic self-legislation . . . prior to all political will formation."[4]

Moving to his own position, Habermas tries to show how an emphasis on democratic procedures for real political will formation can lead to a more balanced account of private and public autonomy, one in which they "*mutually* presuppose each other."[5] For Habermas, democratic procedures of collective self-determination derive their legitimacy, as one might expect, from the unavoidable validity of the procedures of communicative rationality operative in communicative action. They are merely the institutionalization of those communicative procedures for a community constituted through law, a specification of the form an impartial discourse must take when applied to principles having the force of law. As he puts it, "the democratic principle states that only those statutes may claim legitimacy that can meet with the assent of all citizens in a discursive process of legislation that has been legally constituted."[6] The idea of a democratic society *is* the idea of a communicatively rational society, of a society that accepts that its conflicts should be resolved through rational debate that permits everyone's interests to be impartially taken into account.

When adequately understood, however, this ideal of democratic self-determination through law requires private as much as public autonomy. A community can only legitimately determine its public life through laws if all, as free and equal, are entitled to participate. It is only in this way that everyone can, as the social contract tradition has stressed, understand themselves as the authors of the laws to which they are subject. But this democratic process of self-determination must presuppose the personal autonomy of citizens who, as Habermas stresses, cannot even "assume the status of legal subjects without subjective private rights." That is, citizens cannot stand in relation to one another as free and equal in a process of democratic lawmaking without equal rights to personal autonomy that guarantee their integrity as free and equal in that process. Rights to personal autonomy are a prerequisite for any real exercise of public autonomy on the part of citizens. In this way, the liberties of the moderns need not be construed as external constraints placed on the liberties of the ancients, as Habermas claims Rawls does, but rather as the necessary "enabling conditions" of the latter, a constitutive dimension of what it means for a community to seek to legitimately determine its affairs for itself.[7]

4.1.2 Rawls's Response

Rawls responds with three points meant to clarify the status of political autonomy in his work. First, he seeks to correct what he claims is a misunderstanding on Habermas's part of the status of the stages in his account, which are meant to describe "neither an actual political process, nor a purely theoretical one." Rather, they are meant as a clarification of the types of "norms and information" that real citizens in civil society may consider relevant to their political judgments, "depending on the subject and the context." Habermas's criticism overlooks what for Rawls is the "crucial point," that his account of justice is subject to "our reflective considered judgments." The idea of the original position is, after all, only intended as a theoretical aid to the reflections of actual citizens attempting to determine for themselves what could be fairly endorsed by all. It is not, therefore, as if the principles of justice determined in the original position would constrain the democratic self-determination of an actual political community or demote the democratic process to an inferior status. They are merely recommendations as to how such a self-determining community ought to proceed with its political life, considering foundational questions from the hypothetical point of view of what all could agree to under artificial conditions that would guarantee equality and impartiality. The final court of appeal for the account of justice remains *our* considered judgments, the democratic deliberations of citizens in civil society.[8]

Next, he questions Habermas's charge that citizens under a just constitution "cannot reignite the radical democratic embers of the original position in the civic life of their society," that they cannot experience their constitution as a historical "project." In "any actual society that is more or less unjust . . . the ideal of a just constitution is always something to be worked toward." Indeed, the challenge under such circumstances is precisely, as Habermas himself puts it, "a delicate and above all a fallible and revisable undertaking, whose purpose is to realize the system of rights *anew* in changing circumstances." But even under an ideally just constitution where there is no such work left to be done, citizens are not deprived of their public autonomy simply because they have the good fortune of inheriting a just constitution that needs no further work. "Are the citizens of Rousseau's society of *The Social Contract*," Rawls asks, "never fully autonomous because the Legislator originally gave them the just constitution under which they grow up?" Only exceptional historical circumstances make it necessary for a community to determine for itself the fundamentals of its constitutional system. This does not deprive others under less exceptional circumstances of their public autonomy, however, as long as they have appropriated for themselves the insights embodied in their otherwise just constitutions.[9]

Finally, Rawls takes issue with Habermas's claim that "basic liberal rights" in his theory "constrain democratic self-legislation . . . prior to all political will formation." To the contrary, Rawls emphasizes that his account "allows—but does not require—the basic liberties to be incorporated into the constitution and protected as constitutional rights on the basis of citizens's deliberations and judgments over time." Far from constraining democratic will formation, basic liberal rights may only emerge *as* basic through an exercise of popular sovereignty.[10]

Concluding his replies on this topic, Rawls draws attention to the way justice as fairness understands public and private autonomy as "co-original and of equal weight" in the way they are listed together in the first principle of justice, which Rawls argues would be agreed to in an "original position" of equality among citizens, a principle guaranteeing the "most extensive" public and private liberties "compatible with a similar liberty for others." This balanced emphasis on both liberties reflects their roots in what Rawls conceives as the two "moral powers" of citizens that his theory of justice seeks to model and safeguard: our "capacity for a sense of justice," for a public mode of life to which all can agree, and "a conception of the good," a private understanding of what constitutes, for us, a fulfilling life. Grounded in a respect for these moral powers, Rawls's theory seeks to give equal expression to the importance of both the public as well as the private liberties in which they may be realized, our political capacities to be involved in the fair consolidation of public life as well as our private capacities to pursue what is, by our own lights, a good life.[11]

But where Rawls's theory of justice pays the liberties of the ancients and moderns equal respect in the way it pays respect to the two moral powers of the citizen in which they are rooted, Habermas's account, Rawls argues, fails to recognize their equality. Despite his intentions, Habermas privileges political over private autonomy in the way he derives the normative significance of private autonomy from its role as a necessary presupposition of our ability to exercise a legitimate political practice of self-determination through law. While granting Habermas's point, Rawls insists, nevertheless, that it is one-sided. We can only recognize the equal status of political and private autonomy by granting the independent basis of the worth of the latter in our respect for the moral power of citizens to have and pursue their own conception of the good—as Rawls's account does but Habermas's does not.[12]

4.1.3 Public Autonomy as a "Primary Good"

At first glance, it would appear that Rawls adequately defends himself against Habermas's criticisms. His theory is not intended as an end run around democratic sovereignty but as only a system of claims to be evaluated in and through the deliberations of real citizens in civil society. It is not exempt from but embedded in a larger context of democratic deliberation. That Rawls leaves the constitutional status of liberal rights unresolved in the original position is even further evidence of the important role of popular sovereignty for his theory of justice. But, on reflection, both of these points finally underscore the way Rawls's account is vulnerable to Habermas's criticism. We need to remember that the thrust of Habermas's criticism is not that Rawls does not intend to acknowledge the equal importance of political autonomy but only that his theoretical model fails to live up to that intention. Rawls's remarks on the way his theory is subject to "our reflective considered judgments" only confirms this point, however, as it places the role of democratic deliberation outside the theoretical model proper in the reception of the theory by a community that would consider accepting it. This is consistent with Habermas's point that democratic self-determination is only given a "virtual existence" in the model itself. It is a point *we* who are considering the theory take for granted and must seek to embody in our deliberations but not one that is effectively modeled in the theory that presents the basic principles of justice as derived independently of any real democratic process.

It is for this reason that the analogy Rawls draws between himself and Habermas on understanding the constitution as an open-ended "project" is a limited one. For Rawls, the constitution can only be a project in the sense that, under any plausibly realistic circumstances, there will still be much work to be done in bringing society up to the standards of justice and in applying those standards to that still, more or less, unjust situation. The possibility is left open, however, for Rousseau's wise legislator to simply give people a wholly just constitution—a possibility that does not really make sense for Habermas, as the legitimacy of any legal norm depends on the real democratic process that permits those adopting it to understand themselves as authors of the law to which they are subject.[13] What insights we have into justice can only be gained in and through such an open-ended, fallible process, not handed down to us, even as an ideal possibility, from a purportedly wise legislator. It is this centrality of public autonomy in Habermas's theory of justice that makes the constitution *essentially* a project for him in a way that it is not with Rawls.

This point is further highlighted by the role assumed by popular sovereignty in Rawls's model for the determination of the constitutional status of liberal rights. Though Rawls comes as close here as anywhere to meeting Habermas's objection, he finally comes up short in the way his theory constrains popular sovereignty at this constitutional stage to the implementation of basic rights that not only have been decided previously in the original position but also have been interpreted there as "primary goods" whose value lies in their importance for each individual's pursuit of a conception of the good.[14] This is a problem Habermas gets at in another part of his critique of Rawls, where he draws attention to how Rawls's model "assimilate(s) the deontological meaning of obligatory norms to the teleological meaning of preferred values."[15] Once again, this is an unintended artifact of Rawls's theoretical model, arising in the way it represents the parties to the original position as rational but not reasonable. By a "rational" agent, Rawls means someone with "the powers of judgment and deliberation in seeking ends and interests peculiarly (her/his) own," a capacity to choose effective means for our ends and to critically combine those ends into a coherent whole. By "reasonable" he means to refer to our readiness "to propose principles and standards as fair terms of cooperation and to abide by them willingly, given the assurance that others will likewise do so." The two terms refer, in other words, to the two moral powers of citizens for a conception of the good and a sense of justice.[16]

Rawls's theory of justice attempts to pay respect to each of these powers by representing them both in the original position that gives rise to the principles of justice. But only the first is modeled in terms of its participants, who are understood as rational agents in that sense. Though they are denied a knowledge of their specific conception of the good by the veil of ignorance, the parties to the original position are understood to want to advance their own conceptions of the good, whatever it might be. The second power, our sense of justice, is modeled only in the structural constraints of the original position, which, by virtue of the veil of ignorance, situates all parties as equals, bound, therefore, to adopt principles that are fair to everyone as equals.[17] This means, however, that the parties to the original position can only understand basic rights as primary goods it would be rational for them to want in order to advance their own conceptions of the good, whatever it might turn out to be.[18] An equal distribution of these rights is decided on only because, as equally situated in relation to one another, there is no rational basis in this situation for anyone to agree to anything less or to expect anything more.[19] Hence, our rights to political autonomy, in particular, are judged solely in terms of how they stand to enhance our capacity to pursue our own good, our capacity for personal autonomy, in other words. This can be seen most clearly in Rawls's arguments for the "priority" of our basic rights to political autonomy, by which he means the way they are not subject to qualification for the sake of greater social or economic opportunities, which, consistent with the constraints of his model, all subordinate their importance to their functional significance in our pursuit of our own personal good.[20] In the final analysis, therefore, Rawls's account can only give voice to reasons for political autonomy that grant it an instrumental value in relation to personal autonomy, to reasons that regard it as "a means to a person's good."[21]

4.2 Privileging Public over Private Autonomy

So it would appear that Habermas's criticism remains valid. But what of Rawls's countercharge? Does Habermas prioritize pubic autonomy in a way that also belies his own intentions? Our first inclination, once again, may be to say no. Habermas himself warns us against "functionalizing *all* basic rights for the democratic process, since negative liberties also have an intrinsic value."[22] Furthermore, in formally deriving a system of basic rights from the idea of democratic self-determination he begins with a "right to the greatest possible measure of equal individual liberties," which, because it is a necessary presupposition of individuals being able to address one another as free and equal legal subjects, must be prior to rights of political autonomy that recognize our capacity to then shape the law as its authors.[23]

Both of these responses miss the point, however. Though Habermas does grant a kind of priority to rights of personal autonomy in his formal derivation of basic rights, this sense of priority is ultimately secondary to the priority enjoyed by the idea of democratic self-determination from which the basic rights are derived. To exercise the kind of public autonomy that the ideal of democratic self-determination embodies one must enjoy private autonomy. One must be free to think and act for oneself to be in a position to make an independent, autonomous contribution to public life. The priority of private autonomy is, in this way, only the priority of an instrumentally necessary condition to what it conditions and, hence, a priority that actually subordinates the importance of private autonomy to the public autonomy it serves. We can only grasp the importance of private autonomy in this account as a function of its instrumental importance to public autonomy. Though Habermas may intend to affirm the intrinsic value of personal autonomy, his procedural understanding of democracy leaves him no basis for such an affirmation. It establishes an evaluative perspective that only makes room for the worth of what could contribute to the successful enactment of democratic procedures. Hence, he is only able to assert *that* personal autonomy has an "intrinsic value," but is unable to say *why*. His admonition against "functionalizing *all* basic rights for the democratic process" comes as something of an afterthought with no clarification as to its grounds.

This is not to deny what Habermas has accomplished here. He does convincingly show that public and private autonomy "mutually presuppose" one another. Without public autonomy there could be no legitimate enactment of our rights to private autonomy in law. And without private autonomy there could be no free and equal individuals capable of exercising their public autonomy. Both private and public autonomy are, as such, integral components of the principle of democracy. But the roles they play in this principle, the contributions they make to the legitimacy of the rule of law, are not equivalent. Our rights to public autonomy make a direct contribution, as it is only through their exercise that a political order may enjoy "the assent of all citizens in a discursive process" that constitutes its legitimacy. Our rights to private autonomy only make an indirect contribution insofar as they create the conditions for the possibility of public autonomy whose realization, in turn, makes it possible for a political order to enjoy legitimacy.[24] As Habermas stresses, "the *democratic process* bears the entire burden of legitimation."[25] And, as bearing the "entire burden," it also constitutes our rights to public autonomy as the center of gravity, so to speak, in that process of legitimation.

Habermas may, however, have other resources with which to deal with this issue. Drawing from the more sociohistorical perspective provided by Habermas's theory of modernity, William Rehg has argued that Habermas could acknowledge an intrinsic value to private autonomy that would not subordinate its importance to public autonomy in two ways: First, he could stress its functional significance in the role it plays in the constitution of a functionally differentiated social order, in particular, the economic subsystem, which only operates effectively through the free play it grants to individuals to pursue their own good in their own way. To the extent that we value this functional achievement of modernity we should value the private autonomy that makes it possible independent of its contribution to practices of democratic will formation. Second, in a culture that has, by and large, become postmetaphysically disenchanted with any vision of the world that would pre-determine our purposes with our lives in traditional ways, sketching in advance a vision of the good life to which we would be expected to live up, we have come to define the good life increasingly in terms of individual fulfillment, being free to pursue our own conception of the good in our own way. This provides a "normative significance" to private autonomy that is, once again, independent of its contribution to practices of public autonomy.[26]

These points are well taken. There are, no doubt, many reasons for the value we attach to private autonomy, and these two are, in particular, consistent with Habermas's reflections on modernity. But in appealing to these reasons it should be noted that we have gone beyond Habermas's procedural account of democracy. A recognition of the functional and normative significance of private autonomy rests on more than a commitment to impartial discursive procedures that grant everyone an opportunity to assent (or not) to the law. It rests on our shared understandings of the substantive value of a functionally differentiated social order and a life lived authentically in pursuit of the fulfillment of one's unique identity, their contribution to our vision of a good life. And, in this way, they are what Habermas characterizes as ethical reasons for valuing private autonomy, reasons that are only valid for a particularly modern evaluation of life, for people such as ourselves who value a functionally differentiated social order and the authentic development of personalities. As *ethical* reasons, however, they must be subordinate to our instrumental reasons for valuing private autonomy because of the necessary role private autonomy plays in practices of democratic self-determination. These instrumental reasons do not appeal to an ethical sense of the good but only to what is unconditionally right, our communicatively grounded duty to engage in impartial discourses with everyone subject to a norm in order to critically assess its validity. Our reasons for recognizing the instrumental value of private autonomy in relation to democratic self-determination must have priority over our reasons for recognizing its intrinsic value in the way the right has priority over the good.

Habermas fails, then, to offer the kind of balanced treatment of the liberties of the ancients and moderns that he seeks. Though reasons for acknowledging the intrinsic value of personal autonomy are available to him, they are only reasons for considering it as good in an ethical sense. They are not, therefore, at the same level as the reasons we have for understanding the importance of public autonomy or the *instrumental* value of private autonomy that concern what is unconditionally right. Our respect for the private autonomy of our fellow citizens is, undoubtedly, a good for many reasons. But it can only be seen as unconditionally right, in Habermas's account, in terms of the instrumental role it plays in the legitimation of the rule of law through democratic practices of self-determination. Admittedly, this may not be a significant practical problem, as our rights to private autonomy are secured unconditionally insofar as they are instrumental to the exercise of public autonomy. There are no ethical considerations that could trump our reasons for an unconditional sense of respect for the private autonomy of citizens, that could undermine or compromise that basic right.[27] But, then, there was not really a practical problem with Rawls's theory of justice either, as he effectively guarantees our rights to public autonomy without risk of compromise in his first principle of justice. Habermas's concern with Rawls was purely theoretical, a matter of a needlessly truncated theoretical range of vision that prevented Rawls from adequately acknowledging the importance of public autonomy in his theory of justice. My concern with Habermas, in turn, is the same. Without the theoretical resources to understand the intrinsic importance of private autonomy in an unconditional way, Habermas's approach to the issue of the liberties of the ancients and moderns inevitably subordinates the liberties of the moderns to those of the ancients, despite his better intentions. He fails to live up to what he describes as the aspiration of Kant and Rousseau "of deriving both elements from the same root" in such a way that "liberal rights may neither be merely foisted on the practice of self-determination as extrinsic conditions nor be made merely instrumental to its exercise."[28]

4.3 The Common Root of Our Rights to Public and Private Autonomy

Neither Rawls nor Habermas intend to subordinate either public or private autonomy to the other. Both recognize that, as Habermas emphasizes, a *right* to private autonomy may only be instituted legitimately in law through the democratic self-determination of a legal community and, as Rawls reminds us, the value of private autonomy cannot be reduced to its functional significance as a presupposition of public autonomy. Beginning, however, only with a recognition of the foundational importance of democratic procedures for political legitimacy, Habermas is denied grounds for articulating an independent, unconditional basis of worth for our private autonomy, and, working from a theoretical model that grants only a "virtual existence" to public autonomy and constrains us to regard all rights as goods valued in terms of their importance to an individual's projects, Rawls cannot help but subordinate the worth of public autonomy to private autonomy.

Taking a step back from the intricacies of their exchange, however, we may obtain a better perspective onto what prevents a successful resolution of the problem. One of the concerns at work in Habermas's endorsement of a procedural account of law and democracy in his exchange with Rawls is his dissatisfaction with the way Rawls's theory relies on substantive normative concepts, in particular, "the concept of the citizen as a moral person" with a reasonable sense of justice and a rational conception of her/his own good, which Rawls seeks to represent in the original position. Consistent with his postmetaphysical suspicions regarding all substantive values, he argues that Rawls's assumption "stands in need of a *prior* justification" and a demonstration of its "neutrality toward conflicting worldviews."[29] But regardless of what one thinks of Habermas's postmetaphysical orientation, it is not Rawls's invocation of substantive normative assumptions that is the basis for his problems with the liberties of the ancients and the moderns. They stem, rather, from the way his theoretical model only grants a virtual existence to political autonomy and constrains us to understand it as a good in the service of private autonomy. If anything, the problem here is not that Rawls has made controversial substantive normative assumptions but that his model fails to adequately represent one of those assumptions, our capacity for a sense of justice, in which, for Rawls, the value of political autonomy is rooted. Indeed, it would appear that Habermas only succeeds in reversing the problem precisely because he lacks, as Rawls points out, a substantive idea of how the value of private autonomy is grounded in our respect for the other moral power of citizens, their capacity to rationally pursue their own conceptions of the good. Lacking that, Habermas lacks a basis for an unconditional sense of the intrinsic value of private autonomy, a sense of its unconditional worth that would not be derived from the role it plays in democratic procedures of self-determination.

These considerations suggest a different approach to the problem from the proceduralist orientation advanced by Habermas: a theoretical model that can adequately represent political autonomy as the procedural grounds of legitimacy for any legal norm without ignoring the substantive normative assumptions behind our sense of the intrinsic value of private autonomy. Or, in keeping with Habermas's comment concerning a common "root" of our respect for private and public autonomy, they suggest the need to get behind our respect for both democratic procedures and the private autonomy of citizens, to discern the common normative grounds for our unconditional respect for the liberties of the ancients *and* the moderns in a way that would do justice to their interdependence without reducing the value of either to its instrumental importance to the other. In the remainder of this chapter I show how the demands of both of these lines of thought may plausibly be met in acknowledging, with Levinas, the substantive value of the face of the other as the normative basis of our respect for both the private and public autonomy of our fellow citizens, in understanding each as distinct but complementary and interdependent ways of giving the other the unconditional consideration to which we find ourselves bound in our communicative endeavors.

4.3.1 Public and Private Autonomy and Our Infinite Obligation to the Other

It is not that hard to see how Levinas would deal with our rights to private autonomy. Our respect for the private autonomy of the individual is simply an expression of the unconditional mode of consideration of the other to which we find ourselves called in our proximity to the other. It is our substantive sense of the moral worth of the other, of the other's authority to command our consideration of her/his concerns, that obliges us to respect the other's personal concerns with her/his life. Though it is true that personal autonomy becomes morally important as a presupposition of our capacity for democratic self-determination, we have morally compelling reasons to respect the personal autonomy of the other regardless of this. It is the intrinsic moral worth of the other, not as citizen, as a participant in practices of democratic self-determination, but simply as other that is the ground of our sense of the intrinsic unconditional importance of the private autonomy of the other.

Things are not as clear, however, when it comes to public autonomy and its importance for the political legitimacy of legal norms. Levinas is largely silent about the political sphere of life, sketching an outline of the place of the political in his account of the third party that he never really fleshes out. And what little he does say about the political is hardly tailored to a sense of the moral importance of one's role as a citizen. Political life is continually demeaned as a violation of the spirit of ethical life, akin more to the rational pursuit of warring interests than to the genuine peace of an ethical sense of responsibility for the other.[30] But Levinas's decidedly cynical view of politics should not blind us to his need for a conception of political life that would be constituted not in opposition to the ethical claims of the other but in service to them. In particular, it is important to note the indeterminate character of the sense of obligation that emerges for us in our proximity to the face of the other, what Levinas speaks of as its "infinite" character. "The infinity of responsibility," he writes, "denotes not its actual immensity, but a responsibility increasing in the measure to which it is assumed. . . . In this movement my freedom does not have the last word."[31] In proximity to the other, it is always the other who has the last word, calling into question every position I would adopt on my own. My responsibility for the other is ever "increasing" insofar as I can never be done with it, never fulfill it in a way that would free me of my responsibilities. With the fulfillment of one responsibility I am left still in proximity to the other, obliged to defer, yet again, to the other. There is, in this way, no clear end or definition of my responsibility to the other—a mode of responsibility that is essentially a mode of servitude or devotion. We encounter a determinate limit to our responsibilities only with the presence of the third party and the requirements of an impartial sense of justice brought in its wake. It is only here as I find myself encumbered with potentially conflicting responsibilities for others in the plural that I find that those infinite responsibilities demand their own determination, a setting of limits in relation to one another. Weighing the claims of every other equally, including my own claims as an other to the others, I am called to determine the limits and extent of my obligations in terms of impartial principles of justice.

We cannot reasonably expect, however, to make such a determination on our own. Though it is not noted in Levinas's account of justice and the third party, it is an inescapable implication of that account that the determination of impartial principles of justice must involve the participation of all concerned, as any determination I would make for myself may always be called into question by the other. As we noted, it is always the other who has the last word. No determination of my responsibilities to others could, therefore, hope to be responsive to those others without giving them an ongoing role to play in their determination, without giving them a voice. As Levinas says at one point, "Justice is a right to speak,"[32] and, as such, it must surely involve a right of the other to speak on her/his own behalf in the determination of justice, to call into question whatever determination has been made to that point. In this way, the determination of our mutual responsibilities through law must involve a respect for the public autonomy of the other as a basic right, a right to participate in the determination of the principles of justice to which s/he is subject.

Democratic deliberative procedures are, therefore, an absolutely essential requirement for any legitimate determination of principles of justice that would be binding on a community. The legal statutes to which we are subject can only be accorded legitimacy insofar as they have been adopted in a deliberative process that is responsive to the other, to all those who would be subject to them. Our sense of the importance of public autonomy cannot be reduced, as it is inadvertently in Rawls's account, to its value in our pursuit of a good life for ourselves, its instrumental value for our personal autonomy. It is also important, as Habermas stresses, because of its unconditional significance as part and parcel of what is involved in the legitimate determination of our mutual responsibilities through law. As we flesh out Levinas's account of the third party, it is clear that public autonomy must be given more than a "virtual" presence in his account of the political, as its noninstrumental importance in the determination of principles of justice is an inescapable implication of his recognition of the infinite character of our sense of responsibility to the other.

But democratic procedures are not understood, as they are by Habermas, as the exclusive grounds of the legitimacy of law in this account. As with our respect for the personal autonomy of the other, so our respect for her/his public autonomy is grounded in our substantive appreciation of the moral worth of the other, of the other's unconditional authority to command our consideration, in this case, to command our consideration in the process through which our mutual responsibilities are determined. It is because my sense of obligation to the other is infinite that I find myself bound to give the other a voice in the determination of the principles of justice to which we will be subject, bound to give the other "the last word." My appreciation of the right of the other to that last word is as much an expression of my substantive sense of the worthiness of the other to my unconditional consideration as is my appreciation of the right of the other to her/his own pursuit of a good life. It is the "always positive value" of the face of the other that serves, in this way, as the common root of our respect for the liberties of the ancients and the moderns. Viewed from this perspective, they emerge as distinct but complementary modes of deference to the other, the one centered in a deference to the other's concerns for her/his personal life and the other centered in a deference to the other's concerns with the determination of the mutual obligations that are constitutive of our public life.

This is not to deny the interdependence of public and private autonomy that Habermas emphasizes. It remains true that we cannot expect to legitimately institute a right to private autonomy in positive law except through an exercise of public autonomy, and we cannot expect to exercise public autonomy without some measure of private autonomy. But we cannot understand the grounds of our respect for public and private autonomy solely in terms of this interdependence on the Levinasian account developed here, as our sense of the moral importance of each is understood as derived from our more fundamental sense of the substantive moral importance of the other, the authority of the other to command our consideration of her/his public *and* private concerns. My sense of the moral worth of the other, not as citizen or as private individual, but *as other,* constitutes a right of the other to my infinite consideration. My respect for the public autonomy of the other as citizen and the personal autonomy of the other as private individual can, in turn, be seen as finite determinations of that infinite right, specifications of it.

4.3.2 The Heteronomous Grounds of Autonomy

Viewed somewhat differently, we may also understand these complementary modes of deference to the other as citizen and as private individual as *limitations* of our originally infinite sense of obligation to the other. This is an idea Levinas makes use of in his understanding of the role of contracts in the determination of our responsibilities. He tells a story from the Talmud in which a son who has been sent by his father to hire some workers promises them food in return for their service. But upon his return, his father admonishes the boy to return and specify the food to which they will be entitled, telling him, "even if you prepared a meal for them equal to the one King Solomon served, you would not have fulfilled your obligation toward them, for they are the descendants of Abraham, Isaac, and Jacob." As Levinas interprets the story, the father's concern for the unlimited character of their unspecified obligation to the workers is a reflection of our infinite sense of responsibility to the other person, who, just as "the descendants of Abraham," is worthy of an incalculable service. "Everything begins with the right of the other man and with my infinite obligation toward him," writes Levinas. "What is truly human is beyond human strength (*L'humain est au-dessus des forces humaines*). Society according to man's strength is merely the limitation of this right and this obligation toward him. . . . The contract is more concerned with limiting my duties than defending my rights. The descendants of Abraham are capable of perceiving (*d'entendre*) this necessity and of coming to an agreement (*de s'sentendre*): they are ripe for a contract."[33]

It is in this idea of the contract as a limitation of my originally infinite duty to the other rather than as an assertion of my rights against the other that we gain the most succinct and precise insight into a Levinasian understanding of positive law. The determination of our obligations through law, the consolidation of a legally binding social contract between us, is always, for him, a tailoring of our moral obligations to our human strengths, giving determinate and manageable form to what would otherwise be an incalculable duty. By tracing our sense of the legitimacy of law not merely to procedures of democratic self-determination, as Habermas does, but to an infinite sense of obligation to the other, Levinas invites us to a fundamental transformation of our understanding of the grounds of a politically legitimate legal order. For Habermas, the political legitimacy of law is grounded in the autonomy of citizens who are both its subjects and authors. Levinas would not contest this. But his work draws attention to what we could call the heteronomous grounds of that autonomy in our sense of the moral worth of the other person. It is only that fundamentally heteronomous sense of obligation to the other that enables us to make sense of the unconditional importance we attach to our autonomy as an expression not only of what we want for ourselves but also of what we demand as a right for the other.

In proposing a heteronomous understanding of the grounds of political legitimacy, Levinas appears to return, however, to an idea that Habermas rejects as problematic: "the notion of a higher law (*legeshierarchie*)" that would rank "morality above law." Offering his own view of the political legitimacy of law as consistent with and complementary to morality, but not derivable from it, as if a democratically enacted legal order were merely an imperfect approximation of a higher moral law, Habermas argues that positive law is always both narrower and broader than morality: narrower insofar as law is not universally binding on all moral subjects but only on those residing within the boundaries of the nation that has enacted it and broader insofar as law is not the product of moral reasoning alone but also of pragmatic compromises among conflicting interests and the ethical aspirations of particular communities.[34] These points are well taken. But as valid as they are they need not and should not should lead us to dismiss Levinas's insights into the heteronomous grounds of autonomy. To see our infinite responsibility to the face of the other as the ground of political legitimacy is not to understand legitimate positive law as a "mere imitation (*Abbildung*)" or "copy (*Abbild*)" of the moral law.[35] Nor is it to deny that there are any nonmoral purposes to the law, such as our need to work out pragmatically feasible compromises with one another over conflicting interests or to find ways to secure our shared ethical aspirations. It is only to recognize that as we deliberate impartially with our fellow citizens about the scope of law, it is the face of the other that calls us to be fair in our deliberations, that enables us to see why it is morally important to give the other an effective voice in the consolidation of whatever compromises we reach or ethical aspirations we agree to pursue and to respect as far as possible the other's personal concerns with the integrity of her/his life in those compromises and ethical aspirations. The quite valid recognition that law is a human product in service to a variety of human concerns—pragmatic and ethical as well as moral—is consistent with the recognition that as we come to terms with those diverse concerns we are always bound to a "higher law" that obliges us to the other in ways we cannot ignore.

To speak of a "higher law" in this way is only to stress the importance of our sense of the moral point of law, the substantive good to which our respect for the other through law is in service. It is, in the final analysis, not that different from Kant's appeal to the substantive idea "of the *dignity* of a rational being . . . (to which) reason . . . refers every maxim of the will." As Taylor argues, Kant understood the dignity of a rational being, her/his unconditional worth, as a constitutive good, the moral point of the priority we should give to the impartial, universalizable perspective inherent in reason that Kant captures in the categorical imperative. It is the dignity of a rational being that is the end of the good will, what we aim to respect in our willing to be good, in asking whether our practical norms could be willed as universal laws.[36] Levinas's contribution to Kant's thesis lies in his phenomenological reconstruction and amplification of it, his clarification of the sense of dignity to which it pays heed as based not merely in our capacity for reason but in our proximity to the embodied presence of the vulnerable other, who, as interlocutor, calls us into question and, in that way, to an exercise of reason. Apart from this, however, Kant and Levinas are in agreement on the central moral importance of the idea of the dignity of the human person, a substantive value that is, perhaps, the most important casualty of Habermas's otherwise Kantian emphasis on rational procedures.[37]

Arguably, one of the major virtues of Rawls's work, vis-à-vis Habermas, lies in the way he stays closer to Kant's substantive insight with his idea of the two moral powers of the citizen, a conception of the importance of the human person in both the public and private dimensions of her/his life that is at the basis of Rawls's moral and political reflections, the central idea that is modeled in the original position in the way its structure constrains its participants to be reasonable in the midst of their pursuit of their own rational interests. Rawls's principle difficulty, as Habermas correctly sees, lies in the way the original position constrains us to think of our rights to public autonomy in a teleological way, as primary goods a rational agent would want as a condition for the pursuit of anything else s/he might value. This perspective not only clouds the properly deontological status of these rights understood from a moral point of view as, first and foremost, modes of unconditional respect we owe the other rather than as goods we seek for ourselves. It also subordinates the importance of rights of public autonomy to those of private autonomy in the way it conceives those rights as valued by rational agents only insofar as they are instrumentally important for their pursuit of their own good. Levinas's perspective allows us to address this problem, however, by stressing the deontological status of those rights as complementary modes, specifications of the otherwise infinite sense of obligation that is commanded of us by the dignity of the other person. Understood in this way, Rawls's conceptions of the two moral powers of citizens provide an insightful determination of two of the principal ways in which the other can appeal to me, as a public citizen and as a private individual, which serves to articulate and delimit our substantive sense of the moral worth of the other person that is the common root of our respect for the public and private autonomy of the other.

4.3.3 The Democratic Determination of the "Higher Law" of the Other

In articulating, in their own ways, a sense of the substantive moral worth of human beings, Kant, Rawls, and Levinas all make reference to something of a "higher law" beyond positive law, a moral point to law that would enable us to make sense of our respect for law. But even though there is certainly something "higher" about the moral worth of the other, it may be misleading to characterize it as a "law," as there is nothing regulative about the dignity of the other person in any determinate sense. In providing us with a point to our respect for law, it does not provide us with anything like a regulative schema for the organization of that respect in legal statues. We cannot, for example, imagine this substantive idea settling the question of what we owe one another, as it always obliges us to leave that question open to question in the light of the ongoing concerns of the other. As Habermas rightly stresses, the constitution of a just political community is always an open-ended project, permanently subject to reconsideration as we allow the other to call any provisionally settled determination of our rights into question.[38]

As such, we cannot expect to derive any particular legal order or determinate conception of rights and duties directly from our substantive sense of the dignity of the other person, as it must remain an indeterminate notion, open to determination only in terms of the diverse concerns and insights that could be raised in an ongoing and unpredictable deliberative process. In particular, it is important to be sensitive to legitimate cultural diversity in the articulation and implementation of the rights that would give specification to our sense of the dignity of the other. As Habermas notes, the ethical aspirations of a particular community always "permeate" its articulation of constitutional rights because they provide the historical context for the interpretation of those rights.[39] Though every legitimate political community must come to terms with the dignity of the other person, the precise character of the terms they adopt will vary depending on their shared understandings and concerns. Citizens of Quebec, for instance, prohibit what would otherwise be their private liberty to place commercial signs in English and, with the exception of native English-speaking citizens, their right to send their children to non-French-speaking schools. And though the legitimacy of such measures is always debatable, it is arguable that, taken with appropriate consideration of the interests of the English-speaking minority, they not only do not compromise our attempts to secure the dignity of the other person, but also are actually demanded by it in the specific context where a significant portion of the population has legitimate ethical concerns with the continuing viability and integrity of its cultural way of life. Hence, our consideration of the other may require, in certain circumstances, recognition of cultural rights that go beyond and stand in tension with the usual rights of individuals to personal autonomy that we associate with modern liberal-democracies insofar as there are important shared cultural concerns within a political community that can only be effectively addressed in a legal manner.[40]

As the unconditional imperative that appeals to us in the face of the other is indeterminate, our understanding of the constitutional forms capable of being legitimately responsive to that imperative must be equally indeterminate as well, open to redetermination in terms of the specific circumstances and concerns of particular communities. Though the substantive idea of the dignity of the other person is rich enough to, arguably, rule out certain arrangements on the front end—for example, totalitarian regimes that deny their subjects any public presence or libertarian regimes that would fail to guarantee even minimal material conditions for the meaningful exercise of personal autonomy—the line can only continue to be drawn in a politically useful way as we consider the specific cases in question, deliberating in terms of the specific concerns and interests of specific communities. Once again, it is only through genuinely democratic deliberative procedures that meaningfully attempt to consider the point of view of the other, of every other affected by a constitutional regime, that any political community can hope to adequately determine the most appropriate legal measures to shelter the dignity of the other person in both its public and private dimensions.

Without a substantive recognition of that dignity, however, our rights to public and private autonomy lose their moral point and we lose our ability to construct a balanced account of their moral importance. We cannot overlook the importance of what Habermas has done purely in terms of an appeal to the legitimating force of democratic procedures, as it is only from this perspective that we can understand the interdependent character of these rights, the way they presuppose each other in the very act of democratic self-determination. But without a sense of the moral point of those procedures in the face of the other, we lose sight of the moral importance of private autonomy apart from the instrumental role it plays in the exercise of public autonomy. And we forget the common root that obliges us to an unconditional mode of respect for both liberties as complementary determinations of our always infinite responsibility to the other.

Notes

1. Jürgen Habermas, "Reconciliation through the Public Use of Reason: Remarks on John Rawls's Political Liberalism," *The Journal of Philosophy* 92, no. 3 (March 1995): 127.
2. Habermas, "Reconciliation through the Public Use of Reason," 128.
3. For Rawls's original account of the "original position" and the "veil of ignorence," see *A Theory of Justice* (Cambridge, Mass.: Harvard University Press, 1971), in particular, 11-22 & 136-142.
4. See Habermas, "Reconciliation through the Public Use of Reason," 128-129. Also see John Rawls, "Reply to Habermas," *The Journal of Philosophy* 92, no. 3 (March 1995): 151, for his understanding of Habermas's characterization of his theory as "two-stage," which I have adopted here.
5. Habermas, "Reconciliation through the Public Use of Reason," 130.
6. Habermas, *Between Facts and Norms: Contributions to a Discourse Theory of Law and Democracy*, trasn. William Rehg (Cambridge, Mass.: The MIT Press, 1996), 110.
7. See Habermas, "Reconciliation through the Public Use of Reason," 130, and *Between Facts and Norms*, 128. For Habermas's general discussion of the principle of democracy and the derivation of basic rights from it, see *Between Facts and Norms*, 104-111 & 118-131.
8. See Rawls, "Reply," 151-153.
9. See Rawls, "Reply," 153-156. The passage from Habermas cited by Rawls is from *Faktizität und Geltung: Beiträge zur Diskurstheorie des Rechts und des demokratischen Rechtsstaats* (Frankfurt am Main: Suhrkamp, 1992), 464.
10. See Rawls, "Reply," 156-158.
11. See Rawls, "Reply," 163-164. For a statement of his "first principle of justice" see *A Theory of Justice*, 60-61.
12. See Rawls, "Reply," 169. For another statement of the same basic point against Habermas see Amy Gutman and Dennis Thompson, *Democracy and Disagreement* (Cambridge, Mass.: The Belknap Press of Harvard University Press, 1996), 17-18.
13. See, for example, Habermas, *Between Facts and Norms*, 121: "It is only participation in the practice of *politically autonomous* lawmaking that makes it possible for the addressees of law to have a correct understanding of the legal order as created by themselves."
14. Rawls understands "primary goods" to encompass those things that "a rational man wants whatever else he wants" (*A Theory of Justice*, 92), those basic rights, liberties, economic opportunities, and income, and the social bases of self-respect, that are reasonably construed as the prerequisites for our pursuit of any particular conception of a good life we might have. For a more recent statement, see Rawls, *Political Liberalism* (New York: Columbia University Press, 1993), 179-181.
15. Habermas, "Reconciliation through the Public Use of Reason," 114.
16. Rawls, *Political Liberalism*, 49-50.
17. See Rawls, *Political Liberalism*, lecture 2, no. 5-6.
18. See Rawls, *Political Liberalism*, 305 & 315-316.
19. See Rawls, *A Theory of Justice*, 150-151.
20. See Rawls, *Political Liberalism*, Lecture 8, no. 6.

21. Rawls, *Political Liberalism*, 315: "the parties (to the original position) cannot invoke reasons founded on regarding the development and exercise of this capacity (for a sense of justice in which our rights to political autonomy are rooted) as part of a person's determinate conception of the good. They are restricted to reasons founded on regarding it solely as a means to a person's good."

22. Habermas, *Between Facts and Norms*, 418. The end of this sentence, "since negative liberties also have intrinsic value," does not actually appear in this sentence in the German text (See *Faktizität und Geltung*, 504). But as noted in the translator's introduction (xxxvi), "Habermas himself has had a considerable hand in the translation, in some cases adapting and rewriting the text for the Anglo-American audience . . . *adding clarifying phrases* (my emphasis)." As this phrase is consistent with the point of the original sentence I assume it is one of these "clarifying phrases" added by Habermas himself.

23. See Habermas, *Between Facts and Norms*, 121-123.

24. Thanks to Vic Pederson, whose helpful and generous comments on an earlier version of this chapter, presented as a paper at the 1998 Central Division Meeting of the American Philosophical Association, brought me to a clear realization of this point.

25. Habermas, *Between Facts and Norms*, 450. I am grateful to William Rehg, whose commentary on the earlier version of this chapter I presented at the American Philosophical Association noted the significance of this citation in the context of this issue.

26. Professor Rehg made these points in his written commentary on the paper I presented on this issue at the American Philosophical Association. Once again, I am grateful to him for his comments as they provided the impetus for the clarification and extension of many of the points I make in my critique of Habermas here.

27. Though we may have reasons to qualify this point somewhat, as we still have need of democratic legislation to institutionally determine and specify our rights to private autonomy. And this means we must have recourse to the full range of relevant considerations in making reasonable decisions about the appropriate extent of those rights in relation to others. Speaking generally, it is surely the case that our practical deliberations in such cases would be better off including reference to all of the reasons we would have for understanding the importance of private autonomy. And if there are reasons for understanding it to be of intrinsic unconditional importance, then Habermas's failure to appreciate such reasons would be expected to have practical consequences for the deliberations that would determine our rights. But I do not want to stress this point, as I believe Habermas's approach to liberal-democratic rights does, for the most part at least, a good job of guaranteeing the effective institutionalization of those rights. The point I want to stress is principally theoretical.

28. Habermas, "Reconciliation through the Public Use of Reason," 127.

29. See Habermas, "Reconciliation through the Public Use of Reason," 119. Habermas's specific objection to Rawls here dovetails neatly with his arguments elsewhere for proceduralism. At their base is a desire to avoid the sort of substantive assumptions that can only be controversial in an increasingly pluralistic context. See, in particular, Habermas's response to Charles Taylor in his "Remarks on Discourse Ethics," in *Justification and Application*, trans. Ciaran Cronin (Cambridge, Mass.: The MIT Press, 1993), 69-76. For a more general perspective on the way proceduralism fits in with his postmetaphysical understanding of philosophy, see his "Themes in Postmetaphysical Thinking," in *Postmetaphysical Thinking: Philosophical Essays*, trans. William Mark Hohengarten (Cambridge, Mass.: The MIT Press, 1992), 28-53.

30. See, for example, the preface to *Totality and Infinity*, where Levinas defines politics as "the art of foreseeing war and of winning it by every means . . . opposed to morality" (trans. Alphonso Lingis [Pittsburgh: Duquesne University Press, 1969], 21).

31. Levinas, *Totality and Infinity*, 244, & "Philosophy and the Idea of Infinity," in *Collected Philosophical Papers*, trans. Alphonso Lingis (Dordrecht: Martinus Nijhoff, 1987), 58.

32. Levinas, *Totality and Infinity*, 298.

33. Emmanuel Levinas, *Nine Talmudic Readings*, trans. Annette Aronowicz (Indianapolis: Indiana University Press, 1990), 98 & 100 and Levinas, *Du Sacré au Saint: Cinq Nouvelles Lectures Talmudiques* (Paris: Les Éditions de Minuit, 1997), 20-21.

34. For Habermas's discussion of these points, see *Between Facts and Norms*, 104-111.

35. See Habermas, *Between Facts and Norms*, 107, and *Faktizität und Geltung*, 138.

36. See Immanuel Kant, *Fundamental Principles of the Metaphysics of Morals*, trans. T. K. Abbott (Amherst, N.Y.: Prometheus Books, 1988), 63 & 56, and Charles Taylor, *Sources of the Self*, (Cambridge, Mass.: Harvard University Press, 1989), 94 & 365.

37. If by the "dignity" of a person, we simply mean the sense of worth we acquire as subjects of the law, accorded a value only to the degree that the law commands it of us in the respect for persons it institutes, then this sense of dignity is, of course, preserved intact in Habermas's account. But with this sense of dignity, as derivative from our respect for legal or moral procedures, we lose a sense of the dignity of the other that could serve as the point of those procedures, the end of the good will, as Kant speaks of it, that must implicate us in a more substantive sense of the worth of the other, a sense of the dignity of the other that is the reason for our respect for moral and legal procedures, the "intrinsic worth" (see Kant, *Fundamental Principles*, 63) of the other that the law aims to respect.

38. This theme of democracy as an open-ended project has been richly developed in the works of Claude Lefort and Cornelius Castoriadis. For Lefort, see, in particular, "The Image of the Body and Totalitarianism," in *The Political Forms of Modern Society*, ed. John Thompson (Cambridge, Mass.: Polity Press, 1986), and "The Question of Democracy" and "Human Rights and the Welfare State," both in *Democracy and Political Theory*, trans. David Macey (Minneapolis: University of Minnesota Press, 1988). For Castoriadis, see, in particular, "Power, Politics, Autonomy" and "The Greek *Polis* and the Creation of Democracy," both in *Philosophy, Politics, Autonomy: Essays in Political Philosophy*, ed. David Ames Curtis (New York: Oxford Press, 1991). Also see my essays "Reconsidering the Limits of Democracy with Castoriadis and Lefort," in *Reinterpreting the Political: Continental Philosophy and Political Theory*, ed. Lenore Langsdorf and Stephen H. Watson with Karen A. Smith (Albany: State University of NewYork Press, 1998), and "Liberalism, Communitarianism, and the Conflictual Grounds of Democratic Pluralism," *Philosophy and Social Criticism* 19 (1993): 293-316.

39. See Habermas, "Struggles for Recognition in the Democratic Constitutional State," in *Multiculturalism: Examining the Politics of Recognition*, ed. Amy Gutman (Princeton, N.J.: Princeton University Press, 1994) 122-128 & 133-134.

40. See Charles Taylor, "The Politics of Recognition," in *Multiculturalism: Examining the Politics of Recognition*, where he examines the questions posed by Quebec for our understanding of the rights of the individual and comes to a similar conclusion. Also see Will Kymlicka's excellent examination of the issue of cultural rights in his *Liberalism, Community, and Culture* (Oxford: Clarendon Press, 1991), where he argues for the importance of culture in a different way than Taylor does, as the necessary context for the ability of the individual to freely choose to develop her/his life in a particular way (See, in

particular, page 165-166). I do not mean to settle their debate here, only to endorse their shared thesis that we need to be flexible in our interpretation of constitutional rights given specific cultural concerns.

Chapter 5

The Moral Relevance of Judaism to Modernity

In assessing the contribution Levinas's insights can make to moral and political theory in general, and Habermas's discourse theoretical approach to moral and political life in particular, I have continually returned to Taylor's thesis that without a substantive appreciation of the good at stake in our commitment to impartial communicative procedures we fail to grasp their moral point, why our commitment to them is so important. But the concerns behind Taylor's thesis have also surfaced in the context of recent interest in the question of the moral and political importance of community. The recent revival of communitarian lines of thought, directed especially against the shortcomings of liberal political theory, has stressed the importance of a sense of community with one another in marshaling support for a sense of justice, in anchoring a sense of justice in the lives of those who would be subject to it. Sustaining a sense of justice in a political community, it is argued, requires a meaningful sense of community through which its members can come to realize their mutual importance to one another and, consequently, see the point of being just to one another, why it is important to be just. But modern liberalism, it is claimed, has been largely indifferent to concerns with community. Driven by a reasonable though ultimately misplaced commitment to neutrality on the question of what modes of life people ought to be pursuing, liberals have tended to ignore the question of the communal ties we weave with one another as a question that can only legitimately concern the private decisions each individual makes with regard to the mode of life that suits her/him best. Liberating us to pursue our own good in our own way, modern liberalism has, therefore, neglected the communitarian conditions necessary to sustain the sense of justice it advances.

The problem communitarians attribute to liberals is that they frequently work with a sense of justice that presupposes a sense of community they then proceed to either neglect or actually undermine. Preoccupied with political principles and procedures, they lose the point of those principles and procedures in much the way we have seen Habermas lose the point of the moral point of view, by losing sight of the lived ways in which we become important to one another and, in that way, gain a reason to be fair to one another. But the communitarian resolution of this problem typically seems to sacrifice our universalist aspirations with justice. Michael Sandel, for instance, whose criticisms of John Rawls's theory of justice were ground breaking for the recent revival of communitarian thought, offers us a civic-republican ideal of community, grounded in the shared understandings of a self-governing republic as a common good. And though his vision of community may be sufficient to foster a sense of justice in us toward our fellow citizens, those who become important to us as a function of their involvement with us in this collective republican project of importance to us, it is difficult to see why it would necessarily contribute to sustaining a similar sense of justice toward strangers, those who do not share the common good of "our" republic with us. Aware of this problem, Sandel comments, "At their best, local solidarities gesture beyond themselves toward broader horizons of moral concern, including the horizon of our common humanity." But all he offers to support us in this hope is the observation that "in practice . . . it is the savage in his poor hut who welcomes the stranger" before the cosmopolitan.[1] In fact, this may be true. But it leaves the grounds of this "gesture beyond itself" unexamined. Taken on its own, there seems to be no good reason why local solidarities should not gesture only toward themselves, chauvinistically indifferent to the fate of the stranger.

Those of a more liberal stripe who have been wakened from their dogmatic slumbers, so to speak, by the communitarian critique have been more attentive to preserving our universalist concerns with justice. By focusing on a distinctively political conception of community, a sense of community that would be formed in terms of what Habermas has characterized as a shared "constitutional patriotism,"[2] a common attachment to the constitutional principles that are at the basis of liberal democracy, it seems possible to acknowledge communitarian concerns while also preserving, in classically liberal fashion, a sense of neutrality to modes of life, communal or otherwise, that would flourish outside the political domain. And, in this way, by conceiving of our sense of community as formed in terms of a patriotic attachment to principles that endorse human rights understood as universal in nature, rights we guarantee to ourselves in our political institutions but should not, in principle, deny to anyone, we can see how local solidarities can begin to gesture beyond themselves, insofar as they are formed precisely in terms of a shared appreciation of principles that do not turn a blind eye to the stranger.

As promising and as insightful as this strategy has been, however, it seems ultimately to respond to the communitarian challenge in a way that merely displaces it. Seeking to understand how a community might sustain a liberal-universalist sense of justice, liberals advance a mode of constitutional patriotism that would be necessary for such a community. But why a community would sustain such a patriotic attachment to universal principles is left, once again, unexamined. Left only with a patriotic attachment to principles, we are not given adequate resources to see the point of those principles, why we ought to regard them as morally important. And so, the liberal-communitarian debate leaves us stranded between a sense of community that may account for our support of a sense of justice while it sacrifices our understanding of the universal scope of justice and another that salvages our universalist concerns with justice while leaving the moral point of our sense of justice unintelligible.

In this chapter, I come to terms with this apparent dilemma by first reviewing the recent communitarian case for the political significance of a sense of community. In particular, I examine Michael Sandel's argument for this point as he makes it in relation to Rawls's theory of justice, probably the most important liberal theory of justice of our time. Following that, I turn to an examination of the liberal response to this challenge, the articulation of a distinctively liberal sense of community formed around a patriotic attachment to liberal-democratic political principles as it has been worked out, in particular, in the efforts of Rawls and Habermas. Taken together, they are helpful in allowing us to get at the key elements of what is, arguably, the predominant liberal approach to the issue of community. Finally, I turn to Levinas and an examination of the resources he brings to the question of community, most notably, in his understanding of the moral relevance of Judaism to modernity. As I argue, Levinas's account of Judaism as "a way of living that is a ritual and a heartfelt generosity" (*rite et générosité de coeur*)[3] provides a way of moving beyond the dilemma that is posed by the liberal-communitarian debate, a way of appreciating the importance of a sense of community for our ability to grasp the point of being just that, though it is not restricted to the political sphere as liberal conceptions of community are, is still adequate to our liberal-democratic concerns with respecting a plurality of modes of life as well as our universalist understanding of liberal-democratic principles.

5.1 The Case for Community

There are many aspects to the recent communitarian critique of liberalism, but the most important, I believe, centers on the way in which a liberal sense of justice presupposes a sense of community for which it does not allow. Michael Sandel has made this point most succinctly in relation to Rawls with his claim that "we cannot be persons for whom justice is primary, and also be persons for whom the difference principle is a principle of justice."⁴ In speaking of the priority of justice, Sandel means to refer to the liberal principle of the priority of the right to the good, the way in which a liberal social order "seeks not to promote any particular ends, but enables its citizens to pursue their own ends" and, therefore, seeks to "govern by principles that do not presuppose any particular conception of the good," remaining neutral, as it is said, with respect to the competing conceptions of a good life advanced by citizens in their private lives.⁵ In speaking of the difference principle, Sandel refers to one aspect of Rawls's substantive conception of justice concerning the distribution of material resources, income and social and economic opportunity, which asserts that every inequality in the distribution of those resources must be justifiable as advantageous to everyone else and, in particular, to the least advantaged.⁶ Sandel's point, then, is just that this aspect of Rawls's understanding of justice demands more than the prioritization of the right can provide, that if we are able to see the difference principle as valid for us we cannot be neutral with regard to all competing conceptions of the good and vice versa.

Sandel's argument for this claim begins in a consideration of Rawls's argument for the difference principle in which Rawls draws on an intuition about what we can be said to deserve. It is undoubtedly true that a greater range of opportunities opens up for me if I come from a wealthy family or have great natural talents. But the question of whether I deserve these greater opportunities turns, for Rawls, on the question of whether I deserve the assets (my family's wealth or my natural talents) that make these opportunities possible for me. But surely there is nothing about me that makes me especially deserving of being born into a wealthy family or with great natural talent, no more than there is something about a child of a poor family or a child with severe Down's syndrome that makes her/him deserve her/his lack of wealth or talents. And if I cannot say that I deserve the social or natural assets that enable me to enjoy greater opportunities in life then neither can I legitimately claim to deserve those greater opportunities.⁷

A just distribution of resources in society must respect this point, insisting that no one has any greater claim to a good life than anyone else. In this way justice demands that everyone receive an equal share of the resources available in society regardless of their natural or social assets *except*—and this exception constitutes the difference principle—where it can be shown that an unequal distribution would be to the advantage of everyone else, especially the least advantaged. Here the idea behind the difference principle is just that an absolutely egalitarian distribution of resources would not provide the incentive for the most talented in society to develop their talents and, in that way, improve the life prospects of everyone in society. Where it can be shown that the greater rewards of the most advantaged in society are necessary to secure the best life available to even the least advantaged, it becomes rational for even the least advantaged to agree to the inequity.⁸

Turning to Sandel, it is not the difference principle, per se, that he takes issue with but only what he believes is a missing link in the argument Rawls advances for it. As Sandel argues, one could agree that no one deserves the assets they use to pursue a good life for themselves and so do not deserve the greater or lesser chances for a good life they enjoy on the basis of those assets. But to grant that no one deserves their assets is not equivalent to saying that everyone has an equal claim on their development. I could just as well conclude that no one deserves anything at all and that we are all free to grab for what we can in life without, of course, being able to claim that we are entitled to what we obtain in this war of each against all. To get to the difference principle I need also to believe that other people are entitled to have an equal say in the development of my assets and the distribution of what I have been able to make of them, that they are "common assets" in that sense.[9]

But it is precisely this that Sandel argues Rawls fails to provide. With the priority of the right to the good, Rawls's theory of justice only makes provisions at a political level for a society of autonomous individuals whose sense of moral connection to other individuals would be formed on the basis of voluntary agreements, what Sandel refers to as a "cooperative" sense of community.[10] The difference principle requires, however, a deeper sense of connection with others in my community, one that would enable me to recognize their claims on my life as legitimate even as I develop what would otherwise be my own talents and opportunities. But it is unclear why the autonomous individuals who inhabit Rawls's just society should recognize such claims, why those who have secured their own life opportunities should see another's lack of opportunities as relevant to them, even to the point of the sort of sacrifice the difference principle could demand.

Put this bluntly, however, Sandel's point has always seemed to me to overlook what is surely the most basic moral connection we have with others for Rawls, our sense of fairness in which his theory of justice *as* fairness is anchored. Implicit in that sense, as Rawls develops it, is a recognition of our duty to give equal consideration to the concerns and interests of everyone in establishing a just social order, one that could freely and rationally be agreed to by all concerned. If I want, then, to be fair about the distribution of resources available in society I must attend to everyone's legitimate concerns and interests in order to secure their agreement. As no one has any prior natural claims to deserve more resources than anyone else, the question has to be settled completely in terms of what could be fairly agreed to by all. But, in framing this objection in this way, it is possible to see what I believe is the basic insight that animates Sandel's criticism of Rawls. In saying that it is our commitment to fairness that gives us reason to impartially consider the concerns and interests of others, in this case to regard others' claims on the development of my talents and opportunities as equal to my own, I am basically saying that it is our commitment to impartially consider the concerns and interests of others that gives us reason to impartially consider the concerns and interests of others. That is, I am really just begging Sandel's question as it is ultimately about why we should be fair in this way, why we should consider others as deserving of this sense of fairness. Rawls takes this sense of fairness for granted in his work. And he does a very good job of theoretically explicating and clarifying it. But he does not give us a good account as to how it could have a compelling hold on us, why we have any good reasons to respect it.

Sandel's answer is that it is only by belonging to a community in such a way that my membership is constitutive for my sense of who I am that I am able to develop a sense of the importance of other members of that community sufficient to recognize them as deserving of an attitude of fairness and impartiality.[11] To the degree that I understand who I am as a father of these children or a citizen of this republic, these children and my fellow citizens become important to me as an extension of my sense of the importance of my membership in that community. I see my own life wrapped up with the good of this family or this republic and can understand the value of others insofar as they participate in and support this good we all share. Bringing this idea home to Rawls, Sandel wants to argue that we can only be people for whom the difference principle is a principle of justice because we are first people who value the common good of belonging with others in a distinctive community, who recognize the importance of mutual solidarity and support for one another out of an appreciation of the value of that sense of community. In other words, the sense of fairness presupposed in the difference principle has as its ultimate condition a shared appreciation of the value of the communities to which we belong—a shared good toward which we cannot be neutral as liberalism would otherwise prescribe.

Taken at this level, moreover, it seems clear that Sandel's argument is not directed exclusively at Rawls but at any liberal theory of justice that accepts the priority of the right to the good. Any liberal account of justice must include demands for equal consideration and a sense of impartiality toward others for which it cannot account without suspending its neutrality toward the good of a constitutive conception of community. In particular, Sandel's argument is as damaging to a libertarian liberal such as Robert Nozick as it is to Rawls, as the same sorts of questions could be put to Nozick in a slightly different way. Why should the losers in the free market respect the property of the winners? Nozick argues that only a radically free market respects our sense of self-ownership, the idea that we belong only to ourselves in such a way that we ought to be at liberty to determine our own lives for ourselves, to pursue our own good in our own way. But when our loses in the market begin to make our pursuit of a good life impossible why should we refrain from simply taking the property of the wealthy by whatever means we find at our disposal and secure a bit of the good life for ourselves? Nozick's ultimate answer involves his appeal to a sense of justice centered in a respect for everyone's self-ownership.[12] Yet, why should people who value self-ownership but who have been deprived of the material means to make any meaningful use of it respect it in others who have the material resources they need? Once again, without a sense of community that would give us a sense of the importance of these others sufficient to command that kind of respect and consideration, our intuition about justice ceases to make sense. It loses its point.

5.2 Constitutional Patriotism in a Liberal Political Community

In the time since Sandel's critique was initially made, both Rawls and Habermas have acknowledged the need for a distinctively political sense of community centered in what Habermas refers to as a form of "constitutional patriotism." Habermas makes this point in response to Charles Taylor, who raises the same basic issue as Sandel with what he refers to as "the republican thesis," his claim that citizens need a patriotic identification with their historical community in order to sustain the voluntary modes of self-discipline (paying taxes, maintaining national defense, and a general observance of law) necessary to a free society, a form of citizen virtue characterized by Montesquieu as "une préférence continuelle de l'intérêt public au sien propre."[13] Endorsing this communitarian insight, Habermas writes, "the legally constituted status of citizen depends on the *supportive spirit* (*Entgegenkommen*) of a consonant background of legally noncoercible motives and attitudes of a citizenry oriented toward the common good." But he narrows the scope of Taylor's point by insisting that it only implies "that the universalist principles of constitutional democracy need to be somehow anchored in the political culture of each country." A "substantive consensus on values," which he believes inconsistent with modern conditions of pluralism, is unnecessary. Only "a consensus on the procedures for the legitimate enactment of laws and the legitimate exercise of power," a political consensus in support of liberal-democratic constitutional principles, in other words, is required—hence, the idea of a "liberal political culture" characterized by a "constitutional patriotism" sufficient to accommodate the communitarian challenge to liberalism while preserving a liberal sense of neutrality toward nonpolitical cultures that would continue to proliferate through the voluntary efforts of citizens in their private lives.[14]

Rawls makes a similar point with his recent idea of a political community united around shared liberal norms and principles, seemingly the very sort of constitutive community Sandel argued his earlier work lacked, in which all share at least one final end, "the end of supporting just institutions and of giving one another justice accordingly. "[15] The citizens of Rawls's liberal polity are understood to share a sense of the good of this community, with the important qualification that this shared good be political in nature, by which he means that it can be "shared by citizens regarded as free and equal" without presupposing "any particular . . . comprehensive doctrine." By a "comprehensive doctrine," Rawls means an account of "what is of value in human life" meant to "inform our conduct, and in the limit to our life as a whole."[16] The priority of the right to the good can, then, be seen to survive in Rawls's thought in a qualified way in this understanding of the political character of the shared good of a liberal community, a sense of justice that can be supported by citizens with competing and even incommensurable conceptions of what goes to make up a good life generally for a human being. Here the status of justice as a shared good is explicitly recognized while also insisting on its independence from and neutrality toward any comprehensive conception of the good that would embrace nonpolitical dimensions of life.

5.2.1 The Importance of Being Reasonable

It is in this sense that Rawls describes the account of justice that would be shared in a liberal political community as "freestanding," derived only from the "fundamental ideas of a democratic society" and not from any comprehensive doctrine.[17] But, in a move that is crucial for our understanding of both his and Habermas's conceptions of community, Rawls acknowledges that the acceptance of a conception of justice within a community makes presuppositions of the comprehensive doctrines that would flourish therein. In particular, it is crucial that they be "reasonable" in the sense that they "not reject the essentials of a democratic regime," that their adherents be reasonable in the sense that they "desire for its own sake a social world in which they, as free and equal, can cooperate with others on terms all can accept."[18] Only in this way is it conceivable that such a political conception of justice, derived from the "fundamental ideas of a democratic society," might enjoy the support of citizens who, though they hold divergent conceptions of the good, agree on the importance of a democratic sense of cooperation with one another "as free and equal." It is for this reason that Rawls advances the idea of an "overlapping consensus" of reasonable comprehensive doctrines that would serve as the basis for a community's support of a liberal sense of justice, a consensus among those of competing comprehensive doctrines who, because they are all reasonable, are able to find their own, differing reasons within their comprehensive doctrines to support liberal principles.

Habermas likewise emphasizes the need for reasonable comprehensive doctrines in a community capable of sustaining liberal-democratic political practices. Evoking the Salman Rushdie affair, Habermas argues that a liberal political culture demands, at the very least, "not unreasonable comprehensive doctrines (which) allow for a civilized debate among convictions."[19] He endorses the need for what he speaks of as a "democratic *sittlichkeit* . . . which meets (liberal constitutional principles) halfway," a cultural ethos in which citizens have been socialized to be "sensitive to problems affecting society as a whole," to desire, as Rawls puts it, "a social world in which they, as free and equal, can cooperate with others on terms all can accept." A liberal political community held together only by its shared constitutional patriotism presupposes an "enlightened political socialization" in which the cultivation of an impartial concern for the common good of "society as a whole" leads to the support of an impartial ideal of justice that attempts to be fair to all concerned.[20]

Habermas and Rawls are surely right to stress the importance of reasonable comprehensive doctrines in a community capable of being united around a liberal constitutional patriotism. Liberal-democratic principles presuppose a sense of reasonableness, a willingness to privilege fair terms of social cooperation over the unbridled pursuit of one's interests. But it is for just this reason that their account of a liberal political community fails us when we look to it for a response to Sandel's communitarian critique. Just as Rawls's early work takes for granted a sense of fairness whose grounds remains unexamined, leading Sandel to posit a need for a constitutive sense of community as the social basis for our mutual importance to one another, he now takes for granted a sense of reasonableness that amounts to a desire to be fair, to seek terms of social cooperation that could be endorsed by all as free and equal. Rather than giving us an account of the communitarian grounds of the sense of fairness presupposed by liberal principles, the sense of community to which Rawls appeals once again takes it for granted. Why we should be reasonable in the first place, why we should see our fellow citizens as important enough to consider them as equals to ourselves, remains mysterious. And so the ultimate grounds for a community's support of liberal principles of justice based in that sense of fairness remains likewise mysterious.

Much the same could be said of Habermas's account as well. To say that the traditions upon which a liberal political culture is based need to be "not unreasonable," open to "civilized debate among convictions," is, in effect, to say that they must foster or, at least, not preclude the willingness to be open to the perspective of others outside the tradition that an impartial sense of justice demands. This is just to say, though, that a culture that could support an impartial sense of justice must be based on traditions that are not inconsistent with that impartiality. It does not explain how or why the members of those traditions could develop a sense of the importance of being impartial. What is it in a liberal political culture that would bring us to see the point of entering into a "civilized debate" with our fellow citizens characterized by a serious consideration of their interests and concerns? At most we are informed of the need for impartiality within the traditions that would support an impartial sense of justice—a point that is true enough but that fails to address the communitarian question concerning how such a sense of impartiality could be fostered in the first place without a prior sense of community. To say that a liberal political culture needs "enlightened political socialization" is very much like saying a culture capable of supporting an impartial sense of justice needs to be one that supports impartiality—an insight that does not really advance our understanding of the conditions for that support.

5.2.2 Does Being Reasonable Require Explanation? Reciprocity, Mutual Advantage, and the Common Good

It could be objected on Rawls's behalf, however, that my criticism overlooks the way in which he does not understand reasonableness to imply mutuality or solidarity with others, as I have assumed, but only what he characterizes as reciprocity, which, though it is not reducible to seeking mutual advantage does not require us to be "moved by the general good" either. [21] Hence, Rawls may not need to explain the presence of reasonable comprehensive doctrines in the sense I have been stressing as it does not involve an attachment to the common good that Sandel's constitutive sense of community is meant to provide. Indeed, as reciprocity implies an insistence that the terms of social cooperation benefit me as well as others, it is conceivable that being reasonable needs no explanation at all because it is, at least in part, a desire for a social order consistent with my desire for my own personal welfare.

It is not clear, though, that Rawls can maintain his distinction between reciprocity and *both* a commitment to the general good and mutual advantage. The latter distinction makes the former ambiguous in a way that raises once again our concerns with the communitarian grounds of reasonableness. Both reciprocity and mutual advantage require that I benefit from the terms of social cooperation. Only in this way can others expect me to freely and rationally consent to those terms. But from the perspective of mutual advantage all are understood to judge their advantage relative to their "present or expected future situation as things are," whereas with reciprocity that judgment is to be made "with respect to an appropriate benchmark of equality."[22] Assessing my advantage relative to such a "benchmark of equality" means, however, accepting a *fair* judgment as to what will constitute the benchmark for that assessment, accepting a benchmark that is fair to everyone by taking everyone's legitimate interests equally into account. Only in this way, for example, could I judge that a society governed by Rawls's difference principle would benefit me regardless of the loss of expected income should I be someone who could be fabulously successful in a market economy without that principle. Only if I have accepted that my advantages in that non-Rawlsian market economy cannot constitute a fair benchmark because they could not be fairly accepted by everyone as free and equal could I be led to see myself as, nevertheless, benefitted by Rawls's social order despite my real losses. But this implies a commitment to fairness that brings us back directly to our considerations concerning the communitarian grounds of that commitment, the basis of our recognition that others in our community are worthy of the sacrifice to which our sense of fairness commits us in the sense of community we share with them. In short, whatever is left of the distinction between reciprocity and a commitment to the common good after reciprocity has been distinguished from mutual advantage only serves to reinforce our questions of Rawls's work.

5.2.3 A Procedural Account of Reasonableness

On Habermas's behalf, it could also be objected that my criticism overlooks other important aspects of a liberal political culture he highlights in his work that could advance our understanding of the conditions for a reasonable ethos of impartial concern for the common good. He refers, for example, to the need for institutional procedures of democratic deliberation within a political culture, noting, in particular, how the publicity of such a political discourse places constraints on the kinds of reasons that can be given that dispose a political community toward impartiality.

> Under this condition (of publicity), concealing publicly indefensible interests behind pretended moral or ethical reasons necessitates self-bindings that either on the next occasion expose a proponent as inconsistent or, in the interest of maintaining his credibility, lead to the inclusion of others's interests. . . . To the degree that practical reason is implanted in the very forms of communication and institutionalized procedures, it need not be embodied exclusively or even predominantly in the heads of collective or individual actors.[23]

With this line of thought we come upon a meaningful attempt to respond to the communitarian challenge, to offer an account as to why or how a sense of impartiality necessary for a support of a liberal sense of justice could be fostered in a liberal political community. Although, in this case, Habermas offers an alternative to the communitarian account, suggesting that a concern for impartiality may arise not through a sense of community, a sense of our mutual importance to one another through our shared involvement in a historical community, but through the presence of deliberative procedures that can themselves dispose us to increasingly impartial political judgments, if only because of the constraints placed on the sorts of reasons we can get away with in justifying those judgments. This emphasis on the motivating power of procedures is in keeping with Habermas's emphasis on the procedural nature of the consensus that holds together a liberal political community. It enables him to avoid having to appeal to any sort of "substantive consensus on values" he believes would be at odds with the pluralistic conditions of modern society.

It would be a mistake, however, to place too much emphasis on this procedural response. Even Habermas is careful to qualify what we can expect of it by noting how it frees us from having to look for practical reason "exclusively or even predominantly in the heads of collective or individual actors," but not absolutely. Though we should not downplay the importance of such deliberative procedures in encouraging impartiality, neither should we forget the way even the most inclusive and public of deliberative procedures may be rhetorically manipulated. Even the most self-interested action may be dressed up with a facade of impartiality. And though it is eventually vulnerable to exposure, such duplicity is equally prone to encouraging over time the kind of cynicism that dominates today, in which most of us expect little more of political discourse and come to assess the positions of political actors not so much by the reasons they offer as by the self-interested advantages or disadvantages their positions afford us. Only an actively engaged citizenry committed to a genuine pursuit of the common good would be sufficient to resist this devolution of political deliberation into a barely concealed process of interest-based bargaining in which the interested parties manipulate a facade of impartiality to their own advantage. We cannot, therefore, rely exclusively on procedural constraints in accounting for a liberal political culture sufficient to the kind of constitutional patriotism Habermas needs. Procedures that encourage impartiality need a public disposed to impartiality to check the abuse of those procedures.

5.2.4 Constitutional Patriotism in a Self-Governing Republic

Habermas's emphasis on democratic deliberative procedures brings us closer, though, to what may be his most fundamental understanding of a liberal political community, as it points to the importance of political autonomy in his work, of "a population *accustomed* to liberty."[24] Habermas ends *Between Facts and Norms* by emphasizing the centrality of political autonomy for his understanding of law and democracy.[25] Liberal-democratic constitutional principles are, for Habermas, the necessary "medium" in terms of which a community can come to legitimately determine its collective life for itself.[26] The system of basic rights we accord one another in liberal democracies are the rights we must accord one another if we are to understand ourselves as authors of the law to which we are subject. "The substance of human rights," Habermas writes, "resides in the formal conditions for the legal institutionalization of those discursive processes of opinion- and will-formation in which the sovereignty of the people assumes a binding character."[27]

In this way, it is plausible to suppose that a political community committed to the project of determining the conditions of its collective life for itself must come to value liberal-democratic principles as the necessary medium in which that project can be pursued. The grounds of our constitutional patriotism are clarified as we see how an impartial sense of justice can become important to us insofar as it is essential to the success of a collective project of importance to us. As Habermas writes, "The forces of social solidarity can be regenerated in complex societies only in the forms of communicative practices of self-determination."[28] This is, in effect, the republican side of Habermas's understanding of liberal democracy. Though Habermas never backs down from his understanding of the deontological or moral validity of liberal-democratic constitutional principles, he also gives us reason to suppose that they can only become important to us in a teleological or ethical way through their connection with a collective project we share, in this case, a project of collective self-determination.[29] As he notes, the republican model of political community has an advantage over the liberal one in that it "makes it clear that political autonomy is an end in itself that can be realized not by the single individual privately pursuing his own interests but only by all together in an intersubjectively shared practice."[30] Though Habermas remains critical of the republican emphasis on the integration of a political community around shared substantive values or the notion that society as a whole could constitute a "collectively acting citizenry," he does not reject the idea of political autonomy as an "an end in itself" around which society could organize itself but only seeks more plausible, modern conditions for its realization: instead of a consensus on substantive values, a consensus on democratic procedures, and instead of a "collectively acting citizenry," a deliberative democracy. Thus, the formal or procedural grounds for the integration of a liberal political community are laid consistent with the substantive cultural diversity of modern societies at the subpolitical level.[31]

Habermas is undoubtedly correct in seeing a renewed sense of the importance of political autonomy at the heart of a viable liberal political community. As I concluded earlier, only an actively engaged citizenry can check the abuses of otherwise impartial institutional procedures. Unfortunately, this republican dimension of a liberal political community does not provide sufficient support for the kind of constitutional patriotism Habermas seeks. For one, it fails to provide the sort of universalistic support for liberal-democratic principles that he needs given his universalistic understanding of their validity. For Habermas, the basic principles of democratic self-determination are derived from what he characterizes as the "discourse principle," a corollary of the principle of universalization we have already examined, which states that "just those action norms are valid to which all possibly affected could agree as participants in rational discourses."[32] As with the principle of universalization, the discourse principle establishes impartiality as the key criteria for the justification of any norms; *all* affected should be able to rationally assent to the norm. When applied to the specific case of regulation of action by legal statutes within and for a particular community, this imperative takes on a democratic significance with respect to the political institutions a community must sustain in order to understand its laws as legitimate.

Thus, even though liberal-democratic principles may only demand a sense of impartiality toward our fellow citizens who are subject with us to the laws we make for ourselves, they are intrinsically connected to the unrestricted sense of impartiality demanded by the discourse principle. But a republican sense of support for liberal-democratic principles based in a project of political autonomy offers no intrinsic support for this unrestricted, universal sense of impartiality. At most, a constitutional patriotism based on a sense of the importance of those constitutional principles for our political autonomy provides support for the importance of those principles *for us*, but not for others who are irrelevant to our autonomy. As with Sandel's own civic-republican account of community, we are given, at best, a sense of impartiality that is restricted to our fellow citizens. There is no reason, for example, to suppose such a politically autonomous community would concur with Habermas in the judgment that questions of immigration need to be decided from the perspective of all concerned, taking into account the interests of prospective immigrants as well as one's own community.[33] Taken on its own, a support for a sense of impartiality based in a community's republican concerns with its own political autonomy is not inconsistent with a chauvinistic indifference to the concerns of outsiders.

Of more importance, however, is a second problem concerning the way liberal-democratic principles are, as Habermas argues, a necessary medium for self-determination but only for *legitimate* self-determination. "A system of rights that gives equal weight to both the private and the public autonomy of the citizen. . . . should contain precisely the basic rights that citizens must mutually grant one another if they want to *legitimately* regulate their life in common by means of positive law"[34] (emphasis mine). And by "legitimately," we should understand modes of legal regulation consistent with "the procedural conditions for the democratic genesis of legal statutes,"[35] which is to say, consistent with liberal-democratic principles that define the constitutional parameters for any legitimate act of collective self-determination. The problem here is just that Habermas's account of constitutional patriotism is now manifestly circular, taking for granted the very thing it should be explaining. A political community capable of supporting liberal-democratic principles requires a desire on the part of that community to legitimately determine the collective conditions of its life together, which is to say, a desire on the part of the community for the very liberal-democratic principles whose support we are trying to explain.

We may better be able to appreciate this point if we remember the way traditional republican theories of self-government have been perennially haunted by the problem of the tyranny of the majority. There is nothing inherent in the collective aspiration to self-determination that precludes the denial of fundamental rights to minorities. Of course, it can then no longer be said to measure up to the ideal of legitimate self-determination as Habermas correctly articulates it. But *why* should a community aspire to a collective project of self-determination in that precise sense? Why should the legitimacy of their collective actions matter to them, as it has clearly not mattered to many nationalist projects of self-determination we have witnessed in the twentieth century? It is not the collective aspiration to self-determination per se that gives rise to a patriotic attachment to liberal-democratic principles but only an aspiration to legitimate self-determination. But then Habermas's account presupposes the attachment to legitimacy (collective self-determination conducted within liberal-democratic parameters) it would explain.

5.2.5 The Need for a Thicker Sense of Community

Neither Habermas's nor Rawls's conception of a liberal political community appears adequate, therefore, as a response to concerns with the communitarian conditions of a liberal social order. In different ways, they either take the support of that social order for granted or offer accounts that provide insufficient anchorage of liberal-democratic principles within the community. The idea of constitutional patriotism appears, then, to be more of a marker for a set of problems that are left either unaddressed or inadequately addressed than a positive contribution to their solution. But why should this be? At first glance, the idea of a liberal political community formed on the basis of a shared constitutional patriotism appears to give us precisely what Sandel claims we need, an account of a sense of community formed around a shared appreciation of the good of that community, in this case, the shared good of our support for liberal political principles, a sense of community constitutive for at least a part of my identity, in this case, my identity as a citizen who supports liberal principles and, consequently, can develop a sense of solidarity with my fellow citizens who also lend their support to those principles on that basis. The only qualification Habermas and Rawls make to this otherwise communitarian scenario is to limit this sense of community to the political sphere, where it centers on a support for the very principles that would underwrite a liberal respect for our rights to personal autonomy outside the political arena. In this way, we acknowledge the importance of a sense of community in securing liberal principles of justice in a society without sacrificing basic liberal commitments to the right of individuals to pursue their own good in their own ways.

In the light of our considerations here, however, we have reason to suppose that every account of a political community that limits its understanding of what binds us together in a community to this constitutional patriotism must come up short as a response to the communitarian challenge. The communitarians draw our attention to the need for a sense of community to explain how we could become patriotically attached to the principles of a liberal constitution in the first place, or, more generally, how we could come to see ourselves as connected with others in such a way that we see the point of treating them with the kind of respect and impartiality that liberal principles demand of us. Any invocation of a sense of community that is formed in terms of its shared support of liberal principles must, therefore, fail to answer that need, as it takes for granted the very support of those principles for which we want an explanation.

To adequately address this need we must refer to a "thicker" sense of community, one that can enable us to understand how we come to matter to one another in ways that precede and go deeper than our shared support of liberal principles and that therefore can be invoked without begging the question as an account of the communitarian basis of our support for such principles. It must invoke a sense of community among the adherents of competing comprehensive doctrines capable of explaining how they are, as they must be, *reasonable*. It cannot appeal to a sense of community that takes the presence of this liberal political virtue[36] for granted but must articulate the bonds of solidarity between us capable of enabling us to see the point of being reasonable with one another despite our otherwise competing visions of the good. Such an account must, therefore, say something about what draws us to the support of liberal-democratic principles, what is at stake in our support of them. It needs to articulate the goods that are sheltered by liberal-democratic principles and procedures in order to understand why a community would be disposed to patriotically support them. It needs, in other words, to refer to the very sort of "substantive consensus on values" Habermas, in particular, seeks to avoid, at a prepolitical level on which both Habermas and Rawls are silent.[37]

5.3 Judaism and Community

It might appear strange, however, to seek a resolution to these problems in the work of Levinas. Though his ideas certainly offer an optimistic affirmation of our potential as moral agents to go beyond self-interest and the inevitable war of conflicting interests it brings in its wake, to respond with real generosity to one another, this optimism seems tempered by a deep-seated pessimism in his work toward social and political institutions that might adequately anchor this moral potential. The very idea of articulating a viable *political* sense of community seems wholly alien to Levinas. Levinas's critique of the state, for example, and its universalizing, totalizing sense of justice is well-known. The state, though necessary for justice, ultimately comes to undermine it in the way its abstract impartiality, its concern with universal principles and the rule of law, eclipses the unique individual, the face of the other, which is the ground and telos of justice, for Levinas.[38] Instead of a relationship of responsibility for the other, the perspective of the state fosters a bureaucratic administration of justice that is always, to one degree or another, "a tyranny of the universal and the impersonal."[39] Our moral potential as individuals uniquely responsible for the other as a singular being seems to be preserved only in the family, for Levinas, which he analyzes as a privileged context for such face-to-face encounters.[40] But this respite from Levinas's pessimism with regard to the state is only marginally comforting, as it only seems to make room for a genuinely ethical mode of community in our private lives, offering an ethical haven in an otherwise heartless world, but no public, institutional basis for an ethically responsible mode of community with one another.

It is considerations such as these that lead Robert Gibbs, for example, to conclude that Levinas finally lacks "a positive model for social institutions."[41] Caught up in the unsatisfactory dilemma posed by the abstract universality of the state and the concrete privacy of the family, Gibbs argues that Levinas misses the potential in the Jewish tradition itself for positive, ethically responsible modes of community. It is ironic, however, that Gibbs should emphasize the potential of the Jewish tradition in his criticism of Levinas, as it is precisely in Levinas's analysis of Jewish social life that he begins, or so I argue, to address our concerns about the sort of social institutions and modes of community that could adequately anchor without necessarily betraying our sense of justice. Though never as developed as one would like, Levinas's understanding of what we could gloss as the moral relevance of Judaism to modernity contains the seeds of an understanding of ethical modes of social life capable of mediating the distance between the private life of the family and the public life of the state, of articulating a prepolitical sense of community rich enough to nourish the political modes of community necessary to a liberal-democratic republic—a Levinasian contribution, in effect, to a theory of civil society understood as a context for the generation of social modes of life that, like Judaism, are capable of sheltering our responsibility for the other as a unique individual without forgetting the demands of justice in its universality.

5.3.1 A Jewish Understanding of Law

Levinas frames his reflections on the moral relevance of Judaism to modernity with a question. As he puts it in *Difficult Freedom*, "Can the whole of Western humanism pass for a secularization of Judaeo-Christianity? Have the rights of man and of the citizen and the new spirit that conquered in the eighteenth century not fulfilled in our minds the promises of the prophets?"[42] From a certain vantage point it would appear that they have, especially given Levinas's understanding of the uniquely moral significance of the Jewish faith. For Levinas, the word of God is revealed only in the law of God, which orders us to an unconditional sense of responsibility for the other person. Our vision of God is thoroughly ethical, accessible only in the practical observance of the law, the mundane, human tasks of caring for our neighbor. "The Bible," as he emphasizes, ". . . is a book that leads us not towards the mystery of God, but towards the human tasks of man."[43] But insofar as a modern, humanistic concern with human rights and the dignity of each individual seem to appropriate these moral concerns, it is, at least, arguable that Judaism as a particular religious faith has outlived itself, surviving only as a sentimental attachment to personally or culturally meaningful memories, not as a unique shelter for the word of God.

If modern humanism has been successful, however, in appropriating something of the core idea of the Jewish law, our unconditional sense of obligation to the other as a unique individual, it has been notoriously unsuccessful in realizing its vision of a humane society on that basis. Our memories of the flood of inhumanities witnessed this century is sufficient testimony, for Levinas, of a "crisis" of modern humanism,[44] an apparent inability to foster and sustain a sense of responsibility for the other despite the increasingly widespread acceptance of the idea of the "rights of man." There are, of course, many reasons for this "crisis". But, from Levinas's perspective, the most salient factor lies in the ways in which modern humanism may be intrinsically unprepared to serve as a bulwark against such inhumanities by having failed to adequately appropriate important dimensions of a Jewish understanding of law.

In particular, there is modernity's abstraction of law from any distinctive social mode of life in which it would be embedded. Whereas for Judaism our obligations before the law are not ultimately distinguishable from the matrix of tradition and ritual commanded of us *as* Jews, modern humanism seeks to present our duties as abstract matters of principle, incumbent on us not as a function of the particularities of our history but of our universal status as rational beings. And this is, no doubt, a gain in many ways inasmuch as it emphasizes the universality of our obligations to others, that we are responsible not merely to those close to us or like us but to any others, no matter how distant or different they may be. The potential for local modes of chauvinism, indifference to the concerns of outsiders, is always inherent in an understanding of morality closely intertwined with the cultivation of group loyalties and solidarities. Attempting to exorcize this particularly virulent form of inhumanity is surely justification enough for the modern attempt to abstract observance of the law from any particular social context.

It is considerations such as these that lead Levinas to be sympathetic with the aims and fate of modern humanism. Though it is always the face of the other as a unique individual that calls me to responsibility, the multiplicity of others, the presence of the "third party," calls me to a universal sense of responsibility before every unique individual, before humanity, in other words. "The birth of morality," as Levinas understands it, lies "in the nakedness of the face," the face of the other as "abstract man, disengaged from all culture,"[45] soliciting me to a sense of responsibility regardless of culture or history. But despite the important emphasis placed by modern humanism on the universality of our obligations, it fails to appreciate the distinctively Jewish insight into the need to anchor our rational judgments in a practical mode of life, the inability to ever adequately sever affairs of the spirit from the observance of the letter of the law, our inner life from its external trappings. "There is," Levinas observes, "a remarkable relation between the spiritual nature of ideas and the carnal nature of social habits, an element in which the final truths are preserved unaltered and from which they draw their power. . . . The bare intellect can scale great heights, but cannot endure there. . . . Truth according to Judaism finds a faithful symbolism . . . only in practical attitudes, in a Law."[46]

There are many reasons to stress this point with Levinas. It is not, for example, that far removed from the communitarian critique of liberalism we have already touched on with Sandel. Only insofar as I can see my relation to the other as an important aspect of my own identity as a member of some historical community, a community that the other helps to sustain as a fellow member, can I see the point of my obligations to the other. It is our mutual solidarity in support of shared endeavors, the common good, that establishes the importance of the other for me as one who deserves my support. But, despite the parallels, Levinas's reasons for criticizing the universalistic ambitions of modern humanism diverge from communitarian ones in, at least, one important respect. In a word, communitarian accounts of the need to anchor moral principles in social modes of life are centripetal, hinging an appreciation of the importance of others on an essentially conditional understanding of their importance to me, to projects I value but cannot pursue alone.[47] Apart from the other's involvement in such common projects it is unclear how the other can have importance to me.[48] Hence, the seemingly intractable difficulties in making sense of our commitments to a universal sense of justice and mutual responsibility from this communitarian perspective. Levinas, on the other hand, gives what amounts to a centrifugal account of our appreciation of the importance of the other. I come to appreciate the other as deserving of my consideration not insofar as I can see her/his importance to my projects and concerns but insofar as I am called to a sense of the "height" of the other, her/his unconditional authority to command my consideration. To speak with another person is to be called to understand the other as one who merits my consideration independent of her/his relevance to my concerns with my own life.

5.3.2 The Significance of Noninstrumental Communicative Interaction

This moral orientation to the other is implied in every communicative endeavor insofar as it must draw on our competence for an essentially conversational mode of deference to the other in order to secure an understanding with regard to what is said. But for this very reason we can distinguish between those communicative endeavors for which it is only an indirect implication of the act and those for which it is directly implied in the act itself, as a definitive dimension of that act in its specificity. Habermas's understanding of communicative action as a mode of coordinating social interaction is germane here. As he emphasizes, we typically speak with one another in order to get something done in the world. That we accomplish this through the medium of mutual understanding as opposed to the exercise of influence is what distinguishes communicative from strategic action. To ask someone to step out of my way is not the same as pushing her/him out of the way. But in both cases, the definitive aim of the act is getting what I want done, not securing mutual understanding as such. When I ask you to move so that I may pass, I must secure an understanding with you on what I mean to say and, consequently, be prepared to defer to you, to allow you to call what I say into question, in order to secure that understanding. But my primary concern remains getting past you.

A moral orientation to the other is an indirect implication of such instrumentally circumscribed uses of speech, as the act presupposes and draws on our capacity to defer to the other to secure understanding. But it is not directly implied in the act itself as a way of securing understanding *in order to* accomplish some strategic objective, as it is that strategic objective that is definitive of the act in its instrumentally circumscribed specificity. When I speak to you *in order to* get you to move, it is my objective of getting you moved that is definitive of the act. The deference I am bound to give you in order to secure an understanding with you is only indirectly implied in the act as its instrumentally necessary presupposition.

Only when my communicative endeavors are freed of such instrumentally determined contexts, or, at least, insofar as those instrumental contexts have been relaxed to such a point that the conversational character of speech can emerge as definitive for the act, is a moral orientation to the other directly implied in the act itself *as* a conversational sharing of speech for its own sake. Only with such noninstrumental communicative interactions do I find the conversational deference I give to the other definitive for the act itself rather than an indirect presupposition of the act, a capacity I must be prepared to draw on *in order to* accomplish my strategic purposes with speech.

Hence, it is only with my noninstrumental communicative interactions that I find the moral orientation to the other implicit in my deference to the other a potentially salient dimension of my lived experience of speech. Though indirectly implied in every communicative endeavor, it is much too indirect an implication of my instrumentally circumscribed exchanges to feature prominently in my lived appropriation of the act. When I speak to you *in order to* get something accomplished, it is what I want to get accomplished that is thematic for me. It is my strategic objective with speech that sets the context in which I will understand other aspects of the endeavor. And so, for example, in ordering a meal at a fast-food restaurant, where the instrumental exigencies of my strategic undertaking to get food define the purpose of the exchange, it also sets the context in which I can understand the person who takes my order. Focused on getting food efficiently and quickly, I cannot help but see her/him in terms that are relevant to that objective as more or less efficient, more or less helpful. My interlocutor's importance to me cannot but be an instrumental sense of importance to my strategic project in much the way a tool may have instrumental importance to me insofar as it helps me to accomplish my goals.

Only when my instrumental objectives with speech have been abandoned or relaxed for a while and my speech assumes a more directly conversational character do I find myself in a position to appreciate in a lived way my interlocutor's noninstrumental significance *as* interlocutor, not as someone who is more or less useful to my strategic aims but simply as someone who is worth attending to for her/his own sake, someone with whom I find myself sharing speech for its own sake. And so, to return to my example, it is when I set aside my strategic objectives with speech for a while that I find myself in a position to see the person behind the counter in noninstrumental terms. As we wait for my order to be delivered, with time on our hands, perhaps I comment on the weather or ask her/him about her/his job or, generally, engage in some form of casual chatter. The instrumentally circumscribed context of our interaction set aside for the moment, I find myself involved in a conversational undertaking in which I relate to her/him *as if* s/he were worthy of my consideration apart from any instrumental value s/he might have for my strategic concerns. In sharing speech with the other for its own sake, I find myself making a presumption of her/his worth that was only an indirect presupposition of my instrumentally circumscribed speech. It is here that the face of the other can become salient to me, an integral dimension of the communicative endeavor with which I am involved and I can see the person behind the counter *as* other, meriting more than my instrumentally motivated consideration.

5.3.3 Talmudic Study and Noninstrumental Modes of Communicative Interaction

In this way, we can discern the significance of social modes of life that involve me in habitual modes of interaction with others of such a noninstrumental nature, traditions and everyday acts of civility in which I find myself relating to others *as if* they were worthy of my deference—even the simple "after you," which, in its own way, recognizes the other as worthy of consideration, deserving of some, however insignificant, degree of sacrifice.[49] In this regard, we would do well to speak of the Jewish tradition of talmudic study, the study of the initially oral tradition of biblical commentary inscribed in the Talmud, whose significance Levinas has taken great efforts to appreciate in his own work. Levinas emphasizes the way in which talmudic study places me in a relation of deference to the text as inspired scripture, as the words of the other to whom I am obliged to attend. Unlike the attitudes that dominate our ideals of study today, centered in the emancipation of the student to appropriate a body of knowledge as only so much potentially useful information for her/his own projects and interests, the attitude that informs talmudic study is more in touch with the spirit of teaching that Levinas believes informs our most fundamental ethical relation with the other in which the other who teaches me is in a position of mastery in relation to me, bringing me to ideas I could not have produced on my own.[50] In contrast to the ways in which we encourage a sense of mastery in our students today, the mastery of information made available to them for their projects, talmudic study fosters an attitude of submission on the part of the student to the mastery of the text, a veneration of a text able to teach us in a way we could not possibly foresee and would only miss in viewing it exclusively from the context of our own interests. In this way, a fundamentally noninstrumental relation is established with the text. The text is not a resource I can make use of but an inspired word capable of inspiring me if only I submit to its teaching.

Implicit in this noninstrumental relation to the Talmud is a model of noninstrumental relations to others generally. The language of the Talmud is only exceptional in the way it brings out a way of reading and speaking implicit in language, per se: the ethical character of every word insofar as it is conveyed to me from the other who, by virtue of that discursive gesture, can emerge for me as one who commands my consideration. It is not surprising, therefore, to see Levinas stress the dialogical character of talmudic study. "The contribution of each person and period is confronted with the lessons from everyone else, and from the whole of the past. Hence the way that readings continually refer to origins across history going from pupil to master; hence the discussion in gatherings between colleagues questioning one another from century to century, the whole thing integrating itself as tradition into commented Scripture."[51] The Talmud, written in a style emphasizing complex deliberation of interpretive options from one generation of scholars to the next, intrinsically opens itself up to a contemporary deliberation with others in the present. It is sustained not as an object of personal study but as a social tradition of questioning and debate across the generations into the present, where my teacher is not just the text but also my fellow students, with their own unique vantage point on the text. My attitude to my companions in this tradition of study cannot be different from the attitude I maintain toward the text itself, in which I am open to the value of the others's perspective on the text, their authority to command my attention to readings that may have little relevance to the aims that guide my own.

In this way, students of the Talmud are habitually drawn into noninstrumental modes of interaction with others in which the importance of the other as interlocutor, as someone who deserves the kind of deference and consideration to which the practice of talmudic study disposes them, can become salient. And, as a practice of reading and study that draws from an ethical potential implicit in every use of speech, it can serve as a model for other communicative contexts able to develop that ethical potential in a similar way. Whenever I am institutionally disposed to relate to others with this sense of deference, I am placed in contexts where I can habitually come to appreciate the noninstrumental significance of the other as interlocutor. And, on that basis, it becomes possible to understand myself as someone responsible, in a unique way, for the others whose importance I have come to appreciate in terms of that social institution. Here we touch on Levinas's understanding of "election," the way in which I gain a sense of myself as uniquely responsible for and to the other in my communicative relationship with the other, a sense of responsibility for the other that constitutes the emergence of a morally charged sense of identity, a sense of identity that can only be fulfilled as I fulfill my obligations to the other. "To utter 'I,'" Levinas writes, "means to possess a privileged place with regard to responsibilities for which no one can replace me and from which no one can release me. To be unable to shirk (*se dérober*): this is the I."[52]

5.3.4 Election as a Bridge between a Centrifugal and Centripetal Sense of the Worth of the Other

For Levinas, this sense of election to a morally charged sense of identity is not limited to one's relations with others in social institutions. Whenever I relate to the other as a unique individual, as one who *could* address me in speech, whether it be a stranger who is suffering in the street or the televised image of a child in need I will certainly never come to know, I find myself elected to a unique and unshirkable responsibility for the other. I may be able to do nothing for them, but I sense myself as responsible anyway, as one who should help, if only I could. But taken in the context of institutional relations, such as the tradition of talmudic study we have been examining, this account of election forms a bridge, so to speak, between what I referred to as Levinas's centrifugal approach to how we come to appreciate the importance of others and a centripetal approach more characteristic of communitarian thought, a way in which we can appropriate communitarian insights in a Levinasian context. A centripetal emphasis on seeing the importance of others relative to their importance to my concerns and projects, to my sense of who I am in relation to a common tradition or form of life we share, is not so much wrong as it is one-sided. It is, perhaps, the most common way in which people with whom we share an institutional space come to matter to us. And so one student of the Talmud must matter to another to the extent that they understand who they are as wrapped up in an important way with their engagement to a tradition they each support in their own ways. They can no more be indifferent to one another than they can be indifferent to themselves inasmuch as their sense of self, by embracing their shared tradition, involves a reference to the others as members of that tradition with them. But in the context of Levinas's account of the sense of election I gain in my noninstrumental, communicative relations to the other, it is possible to recognize a centrifugal core to this otherwise centripetal account. What I gain in coming to appreciate the importance of a fellow student of the Talmud is not merely the way in which s/he matters to me in terms of her/his relevance to my particular social-institutional commitments, but the way in which s/he matters to me simply as another person, as my interlocutor, who unconditionally merits my consideration and responsibility regardless of my institutional commitments.

With Levinas, it is possible to see how the formation of a sense of who I am in a social-institutional context can involve *both* an appreciation of the other *as* other, as one who merits my consideration not merely in terms of our shared institutional commitments but simply by virtue of being my interlocutor, of soliciting my consideration in speech, *and* an appreciation of the other *as* a fellow member of a cherished institutional tradition. And, going beyond that point, it is possible to see how my fellow students of the Talmud, in becoming important to me in that relationship simply *as* other, also become important to me insofar as I am a member of that institutional tradition, concerned with its historical flourishing. Their importance to me *as* other becomes relevant to me *as* a member of an institutional tradition, in other words. My centrifugal sense of the importance of the other becomes internalized in a centripetal way in the way the other *as* other becomes important to me *as* a member of a valued institutional tradition. It underscores how my unconditional sense of election to the other can be internalized in a conditional way as a concern I have with the other as a member of a personally significant institutional tradition and, in that way, become a sense of responsibility to the other of more personal relevance to me insofar as it is relevant to my institutionally derived sense of identity. In this way, my appreciation of the importance of the other in terms of my own personally meaningful concerns and projects is given a deontological significance it lacks in what could only otherwise be a teleological account, an appraisal of the worth of the other solely in relation to her/his relevance for my own aims in life. From this Levinasian perspective it is possible, therefore, to appropriate communitarian insights regarding the need to anchor our moral responsibilities in a sense of self gained in relation to shared traditions and common projects without reducing our understanding of those moral responsibilities to those who matter to me because of their relevance to projects I value. If this otherwise conditional appreciation of the worth of the other is gained in an institutional context informed by the kind of noninstrumental, communicative relationships we see exemplified in the tradition of talmudic study, it will be an important way in which I internalize in terms of my own aims my unconditional sense of election to the other—a teleological anchoring, so to speak, of my deontological sensibilities, a way in which I can come to have a deeper personally relevant stake in my moral responsibilities.

5.4 "Ritual and Heartfelt Generosity"

It is with this anchoring of an unconditional sense of responsibility to the other in my concerns for my socially circumscribed sense of identity that we find at least a part of the practical genius of Judaism as a social mode of life—"a way of living," as Levinas puts it "that is a ritual and a heartfelt generosity."[53] Together, ritual *and* heartfelt generosity secure a public, institutional character for a mode of unconditional consideration of the other foundationally at home in more private, face-to-face encounters. And it is with such hybrid institutions, combining the public, institutional character of the state with the more private, ethical generosity of the family, that we can begin to overcome the stark dichotomy between these two modes of social life as they are presented in Levinas's work, providing an adequate institutional basis for the demands of a universal sense of justice administered by the state. It is only in relation to an appreciation of the unconditional importance of the other, cultivated in modes of social life that combine these dimensions of ritual and heartfelt generosity, that we can come to see the point of a universal sense of justice. I can only grasp the importance of being just to *any* other insofar as I can discern the worth of the other simply *as* other. Levinas's account of Judaism enables us to see how such an unconditional appreciation of the worth of the other can be anchored in modes of community that are personally meaningful to me and that, consequently, give me a personally relevant stake in being just to the other.

This concern with grounding our support of justice in a substantive appreciation of the worth of the other is also at least a part of what is at stake in Levinas's concern with "the tyranny of the universal and the impersonal" inherent in the state. His concern here is not with the way in which the state can fail to respect my uniqueness by imposing a range of impersonal restrictions on my personal liberties. The uniqueness of the individual that Levinas is concerned the state will come to eclipse is my uniqueness as a self elected to responsibility for the other as a unique individual. It is the very perspective of equality, of impartiality inherent in a universal sense of justice that would be administered by the state, that threatens to obliterate my appreciation of the other in her/his uniqueness, as my interlocutor, the one who speaks to me and in so doing commands my consideration. As all become equal as subjects under the law, all become more or less anonymous, not unique interlocutors, but merely cases to which the law must be fairly applied. But this threat that justice poses to my sense of election is not a problem that can be resolved by dismissing the perspective of an impartial administration of justice. Appearances to the contrary notwithstanding, we cannot finally separate ethics and politics in Levinas's thought. My relation to more than one other, to the "third party," demands the perspective of justice. A multiplicity of concrete others who all make moral claims on me demands an attitude of impartiality as I come to deal with their conflicting claims, a recognition of their equality as moral subjects. This is why, as Levinas puts it, "justice summons me to go beyond the straight line of justice."[54] Grounded in the demands of my personal sense of election to the other, it demands more of me than an impartial respect for fair procedures. It demands a unique sense of responsibility to the other as a basis for appreciating why any other, like the other to whom I am uniquely responsible, should deserve the same. Without this anchoring in social modes of life that foster and habituate me to these forms of personal responsibility to the other, justice cuts itself off from its own indispensable moorings. As Levinas also quite aptly puts it, getting at this connection between the universal demands of justice and the ethical demands of my personal sense of election to the other in her/his uniqueness, "justice remains justice only, in a society where there is no distinction between those close and those far off, but in which there also remains the impossibility of passing by the closest."[55] It is this "impossibility of passing by the closest" that a sense of justice abstracted from the mode of community we find in Judaism threatens to extinguish.

As we move increasingly in that direction, the law threatens to become merely a means for each of us to secure our personal liberties, our inalienable right to be indifferent to one another. The need for law is presented, as it has been in so many social contractarian views,[56] as a necessary limit on my freedom only in the service of better securing that freedom. And with this emphasis on personal liberty we are drawn increasingly into our private lives, respecting the right of the other to her/his private life insofar as that seems instrumentally conducive to the success of our own private lives, but increasingly deprived of the sort of noninstrumental relations with others that can provide the grounds for coming to appreciate the other's noninstrumental significance as unconditionally deserving of my consideration and responsibility. Levinas's observations on what he calls a "society without solidarity"[57] emergent from this tendency converge quite easily with civic republican concerns with the unqualified expansion of an increasingly individualistic attitude which, as de Tocqueville originally phrased it, "disposes each member of the community to sever himself from the mass of his fellows and to draw apart with his family and his friends, so that after he has formed a little circle of his own, he willingly leaves society at large to itself."[58] Levinas illustrates the extreme to which this individualistic withdrawal from society can lead in his image of the cafe, a place of "casual social intercourse" he presents as exemplary of modern society:

> Here you are, each at your own little table with your cup or your glass. You relax completely to the point of not being obligated to anyone or anything; and it is because it is possible to go and relax in a cafe that one tolerates (*supporte*) the horrors and injustices of a world without a soul. The world as a game from which everyone can pull out and exist only for himself, a place of forgetfulness—of the forgetfulness of the other—that is the cafe.[59]

Justice cannot survive in a world which has become a game.

But the modern world is still more than a mere game. The cafe has not overtaken all our social relations. There are still many social arenas in which noninstrumental, communicative relations with others are cultivated. And yet, we still have reasons for concern in the way our dominant arenas of "generosity" with one another have been increasingly stripped of their public, institutional character—the element of "ritual" Jewish modes of life manage to combine with generosity. Our noninstrumental social relations are increasingly organized on a thoroughly voluntaristic basis as the product of the free choices of the individuals who enter into them, giving rise to what Jean-Bethke Elshtain describes as the incoherent ideal of "nonbinding commitments"[60]—commitments that are only binding as long as they are satisfying to all concerned and so provide for equal ease of both exit and entry. Consequently, our noninstrumental social relations tend to be more casual, unstable, and, in the final analysis, circumscribed by what amounts to an instrumental understanding of the point of these noninstrumental relations—their ability to enhance our personal satisfaction with our lives. It is, of course, possible to develop an appreciation of the unconditional importance of the other in such casual, voluntaristic contexts. Our friends, for example, still matter to us in a fundamentally noninstrumental way. But because of the unstable character of these forms of interaction and the fundamentally instrumental context of concerns in which they are embedded, it is reasonable to suppose that the sense of election to the other they foster will (1) be similarly unstable, a sense of responsibility more easily given up than in a context of institutionalized ritual and tradition in which my sense of who I am is implicated in a more profound and inextricable way, and (2) be ambivalent between the noninstrumental understandings they foster between people (I gain a sense of my friends as unconditionally important to me) and the instrumental understandings one can always fall back on to decide whether to remain in a relationship or exit (I decide to remain in or leave a relationship on the basis of the personal satisfaction it affords me).

5.5 Pluralism and the Need to Make Saying Said

5.5.1 The Seeds of Chauvinism

It is the unique combination of ritual and generosity in Levinas's conception of traditionally Jewish modes of life, of centripetal, communitarian modes of identity with a centrifugal, deontological sense of election, that provides the keys to a sense of social solidarity adequate to anchor a liberal-democratic sense of justice. And yet, it could be objected that this Levinasian conception of community still contains the seeds of group chauvinism and indifference to the outsider. Whenever others come to matter to me in terms of my social-institutional relations to them, the way they belong with me in a common project that matters to us both, the seeds of intolerance to those who do not belong are sewn. Levinas's emphasis on what I have been calling a centrifugal, deontological moment in this process does not of itself obviate this threat. When I come to appreciate the unconditional importance of the other in these institutional contexts, there is nothing to impel me to extend this sense of importance to outsiders. To appreciate the unconditional importance of my fellow students of the Talmud, for example, is not necessarily to generalize that recognition to anyone I might encounter regardless of the context. It could be an occasion to merely emphasize the importance of all those who, like myself, value the study of the Talmud to the disdain of those who do not share this concern.

This is an important objection to which Levinas is particularly vulnerable. We must remember that the recognition of the worth of the other to which we are called in speaking with the other is only what Levinas describes as "an orientation" to my speech. To speak is to find oneself moved to take the other seriously, *as if* s/he mattered. But it is not to have an articulate understanding of her/his importance, an articulate idea of what Levinas describes as "the nakedness of the face," "abstract man, disengaged from all culture," which is the basis for that distinctive sense of importance. This reference of the birth of morality to "abstract man" is a significant point for him as it is what allows Levinas to argue that the presence of many others, just insofar as they are human, capable, in principle, of becoming my interlocutor, entails an impartial sense of justice. It is because the other commands my consideration only in her/his abstract humanity, "disengaged from all culture," that I realize I must extend the same consideration to all those who, like the other, also embody this abstract humanity. But without an articulate realization of this point, there is no reason why I should realize that I ought to extend that consideration. To the contrary, as my proximity to the other is always to the other in her/his specificity, my understanding of my responsibilities will tend to be equally specific, as a sense of responsibility to this or that other, not just anyone.[61]

This is particularly a problem for Levinas's account of the family. In *Totality and Infinity*, Levinas attempts to anchor a conception of human solidarity in the institution of the family. In the family, he argues, I gain a sense of election to the other as the unique son of this father[62], subject to his command. But because I am, as Levinas puts it, both "unique in the world" and a "brother among brothers," the sense of who I am that is engendered in the family "remains turned ethically to the face of the other," by which he means the face of those others who are third parties vis-à-vis my relationship with my father. Hence, Levinas concludes, a mode of human "fraternity," of universal mutual responsibility, is made possible by the family.[63] The problem with this analysis, however, should be obvious in the light of the above considerations. Levinas's analysis only works if the implicit logic of my relation to others, to the third party, is made explicit and articulate. In the absence of an articulate understanding of the fundamental equality between my "brothers" and myself or between my "brothers" and my father with respect to their right, as merely human, as interlocutors, to command my consideration, there is no reason to suppose that I should be aware of myself as belonging to the human community in the same way I am aware of myself as the unique son of this father, uniquely responsible to him. And, as far as I can see, there is nothing inherent to the institution of the family to engender such an articulate, reflective understanding of the implicit logic of my relation to the other and the others . . . which is, no doubt, why families can breed a sense of indifference to the rest of the world, a place of individualistic retreat, as easily as a sense of responsibility, generalized to humanity at large.

This is not to slight the importance of the family as a key social institution in the building of a moral sense of solidarity with others. Apart from growing up in loving and morally authoritative families, combining the authority to command me as the child of these parents with a form of unconditional consideration for my uniqueness as a developing person, it is difficult to imagine how children could develop a unique sense of themselves that would be open to a sense of responsibility toward others. It is through my sense of election as a beloved child of this father and/or mother that I gain an initial sense of myself that is personally meaningful and fulfilling to me insofar as it has been shaped through the attention of parents who genuinely care for me as a unique individual and is also receptive to the idea that my unique sense of self cannot be maintained apart from a recognition of the moral authority of the other (lived, at first, only as the authority of my parents). Insofar as I have gained a sense of who I am in my family in which I can see the assumption of responsibility to the other as a fulfillment of my sense of who I am, I can internalize my developing sense of the unconditional worth of the other person, can come to have a personal stake in my responsibilities to the other, as a matter of my personal integrity. In this way, the formation of my sense of identity in a family affects what I characterized in relation to Levinas's conception of Judaism as the centripetal internalization of my centrifugal sense of the importance of the other, a way in which I come to have a personally relevant stake in my sense of responsibility to the other, a way in which that sense of responsibility is anchored in my understanding of who I am. As no one has, as yet, suggested a plausible substitute for families that could provide the same combination of loving nurture and moral authority, the importance of the family as a social institution is beyond question.[64]

But the problem still remains, for families as well as for other social institutions, no matter how well they institute noninstrumental, communicative relationships capable of anchoring a deontological sense of the importance of the other in a teleological sense of my own self-importance, my personal integrity: without an articulate recognition of the unconditional importance of the other *as* other, there is no guarantee that my consideration of the other will "gesture beyond itself" toward all my fellow citizens and, ultimately, humanity. At most, we have the necessary condition for the possibility of such a gesture in the way I find myself called to a sense of the unconditional worth of those who share a valued social institution with me. Without being turned in an articulate way to the face of the other *as* other, however, I lack a basis for seeing the face of any other as worthy of my consideration. Only an articulate recognition of the moral worth of the other *as* other is sufficient to this "gesture beyond itself."

5.5.2 Jewish Universalism

This is where the case of Judaism, as Levinas understands it, has another instructive role to play in our consideration of the issue of community. An articulate understanding of the worth of the abstract humanity of the other is a constitutive dimension of Jewish modes of life—a Jewish universalism that is not inconsistent with the particularism of its traditions and rituals.

> That is our universalism. In the cave that represents the resting place of the patriarchs and our mothers, the Talmud also lays Adam and Eve to rest: it is for the whole of humanity that Judaism came into the world. We have the reputation of considering ourselves to be a chosen people, and this reputation greatly wrongs this universalism. The idea of a chosen people must not be taken as a sign of pride. It does not involve being aware of exceptional rights, but of exceptional duties.[65]

In particular, this involves duties to "the stranger" that may decisively trump my loyalty to those close to me. Levinas emphasizes this point in a most dramatic way in his talmudic commentary on the story of David's execution of seven of Saul's descendants. After three years of famine, God told David that Saul's persecution of the Gibeonites many years before was the major reason for the famine. After the Gibeonites demand that seven of Saul's descendants be nailed to the rock of the Mountain of Saul for retribution, David hands them over to a most brutal execution. Levinas comments: "Let passersby know this: in Israel, princes die a horrible death because strangers were injured by the sovereign. The respect for the stranger and the sanctification of the name of the Eternal are strangely equivalent. And all the rest is a dead letter."[66]

Though necessary, it is not sufficient to overcome the threat of chauvinism inherent in centripetal, communitarian modes of appreciating the importance of the other to merely emphasize a centrifugal, deontological moment in that process. As long as my appreciation of the unconditional importance of the other in her/his abstract humanity remains inarticulate, a logic that is only implicit in my noninstrumental, communicative relationships, my more articulate solidarity with those close to me will be likely to trump that inarticulate sense of gravity in my relations with strangers for which I am unprepared to make sense. Only a reflective articulation of that implicit deontological logic in discourses and practices constitutive of our forms of life provides a sufficient basis, *not* to exorcise this threat of group chauvinism, but, at least, to resist it—to enable us to understand why we should resist it. This reflective articulation of the implicit logic of our responsibility to the other is, as Levinas might put it, a matter of making the significance of saying said, of sheltering our sense of the moral significance of the other to which we are called in the act of saying what is said to the other in what is said. Making the significance of saying said in a tradition that not only enacts a mode of generosity with the other but also reflectively articulates this generosity in an articulate manner is a way of sheltering the implicit universalism of our responsibility to the other in particular modes of life that are important to us, a way of transforming the particularity of those modes of life from breeding grounds for chauvinism and indifference to the stranger into self-conscious training grounds for a more unlimited sense of responsibility to all humanity.

5.5.3 Jewish Pluralism

In appreciating this point, however, we must not overlook the significance of Levinas's thesis concerning the irreducibility of the saying to the said.[67] In particular, our inability to ever adequately articulate the sense of the moral importance of the other to which we find ourselves called in speaking with the other impels us to adopt a distinctively critical and pluralistic model of community. It enables us to recognize how Levinas's account of Judaism avoids the sort of dogmatic, monolithic traditionalism that would, in the final analysis, have no place in a pluralistic, democratic culture. And, in this way, we may be able to see how Levinas's account of Judaism not only is normatively relevant to modernity as a model of community we ought to cultivate in order to secure a social base of support for a liberal-democratic sense of justice, but is also relevant in a realistic and feasible way to modernity as well, a model of a community that remains viable in our increasingly pluralistic world.

To begin, there is a critical sense of pluralism that is constitutive of the life of Judaism as Levinas understands it that gives to its traditions a distinctively nondogmatic and open character. As the word of God is, for Levinas, essentially revealed in the law of God, which orders us to an unconditional responsibility for the other, and as the grounds of this responsibility in an unconditional sense of the worth of the other transcend any thematic account we might give of it, Levinas is logically drawn to stress the potentially unlimited ways in which the significance of God's word can be appropriated. The Holy Scriptures speak to a "pluralism of persons and generations" in the way their meaning is disseminated in terms of a multiplicity of different readers with different perspectives and concerns, none able to exhaust the depth of meaning posed in the Scriptures.[68] This pluralism quite reasonably gives rise to the way in which the tradition of talmudic readings is maintained in an open spirit of debate and questioning in which the point of the debates seems not so much to reach any firm conclusions about a univocal meaning of the text, which, as Levinas insists, does not exist anyway, but to open up a field of multiple interpretations that can, in an unpredictable way, correct and nourish one another. This is a way of maintaining tradition by putting it up for question, a practical way in which Judaism appropriates Levinas's philosophical strategy of "unsaying" the said in order to emphasize the way in which the moral significance of the other always transcends what can be said. The debates themselves unsay each attempt to say univocally what the Scriptures mean in the way they draw one from one position to another without a conclusive resolution. In this way, a critical pluralism is maintained internal to the tradition antagonistic to both the dogmatism of some presumptively absolute vantage point on the truth and the subjectivism of the denial of truth and consequent rejection of argument and debate as pointless. This Jewish mode of pluralism goes a long way to overcoming our otherwise quite justifiable concerns with the potentially oppressive character of tradition by establishing a form of tradition that is genuinely critical and inclusive.

Beyond this mode of pluralism internal to Judaism as a tradition, there is also another sense of pluralism implicit in Levinas's work that centers on the relation of Judaism to other modes of social life and expression. In relating the Holy Scriptures of Judaism to a potential of language itself to signify a sense of responsibility to the other beyond anything that can be explicitly said, Levinas lays the ground for a recognition of the manifold discourses that may, in diverse ways, shelter this sense of responsibility. In this regard, Levinas speaks of "a religious essence of language, a place where prophecy will conjure up the Holy Scriptures, but which all literature awaits or commemorates, whether celebrating it or profaning it."[69] As with the pluralism internal to Judaism, this external pluralism does not culminate in an uncritical celebration of every mode of cultural expression. Levinas defends the distinctive insights of Judaism, for example, in relation to Christian and humanistic discourses. It is not that every culture has articulated our sense of responsibility to the other equally well or with the same insights. Though every attempt to make the significance of saying said must ultimately betray it, there are, as always, degrees of betrayal. As with the internal mode of pluralism, therefore, there are grounds for continuing debate and critical reflection on the value of various culturally specific contributions. And, in keeping with the principle of the inadequacy of every said to our sense of moral importance of the other, there is no more reason to expect any univocal conclusions from this debate than from the one internal to Judaism. In this way, the ground is laid for a critically informed pluralism that is open to the irreducibly distinctive insights of various cultures, forever anticipating the site of a universal culture that would appropriate the specific contributions of all, but aware that this universal site is always "to come," that the only way to shelter a properly universal sense of responsibility is in the particularity of distinctive modes of life.

> This is what is represented by the Jewish concept of Israel, and the sense that it is a chosen people (*et de son élection*). It is not "still anterior" to the universalism of a homogenous society in which the differences between Jew, Greek and barbarian are abolished. It already includes this abolition, but remains, for a Jew, a condition that is at any moment still indispensable to such an abolition, which in turn at any moment is still about to commence (*recommencer*). . . . a particularism. Like that of Abraham. The salvation of human universality perhaps once more requires paths that do not lead to a great metropolis."[70]

5.5.4 The Hope for a Human Community in an Overlapping Consensus

In stressing the many paths that lead to "the salvation of human universality," Levinas sketches a model of human community that need not entail the transcendence of cultural pluralism. Though a Levinasian model of community does entail the kind of "substantive consensus on values" Habermas takes pains to avoid in his own work, an articulate consensus on the moral worth of the other person, it does not entail that we must come to or make sense of this value in the same way. The many paths that lead to the salvation of human universality are, at best, overlapping in Levinas's account, in much the way Rawls speaks of an overlapping consensus in his work: an agreement on the same values for different reasons. It is unrealistic to expect people of diverse backgrounds and traditions to come to agree on the moral worth of the other person for the same reasons. But it may not be unrealistic to hope that all of our various attempts to articulate an understanding of what is morally significant in life may overlap on a shared recognition of the moral worth of the other person for different reasons. Some may speak of it in religious terms, articulating the worth of the other as a child of God, while others speak of it in secular terms, articulating the worth of the other as an autonomous being or in other diverse idioms we may not be able to anticipate. And while each will undoubtedly have good reason to criticize the shortcomings of each other's different frameworks of interpretation, this disagreement is consistent with the kind of overlapping consensus envisioned here.

This is the hope for human community at the heart of Levinas's account of Judaism. It is a hope that is grounded in his account of our ethical proximity to the other as an unavoidable dimension of our communicative relations with others that may be articulated in diverse, always more or less inadequate ways. As we find ourselves called to a sense of the moral worth of our interlocutors as a condition for making sense of our unavoidable communicative commitments, we have reason to suppose that every culture must construct, in its own distinctive way, some articulate sense of the worth of the other as the point of its communicative commitments. And though we have no reason to suppose that these culturally diverse accounts should be similar to or consistent with one another, the responsiveness of such accounts to our shared condition as communicative agents, bound to one another with a sense of obligation that defies strategic intelligibility, gives us reason to hope that we might, for very different reasons, be able to see the point of supporting one another despite our differences in a shared commitment to the substantive moral worth of the other person. Though Habermas's doubts about the feasibility of such a substantive consensus under modern circumstances cannot be dismissed out of hand, it is arguable that he has overstated the case against its feasibility, missing the way in which an overlapping consensus need not entail the abandonment of one's own distinctive "comprehensive doctrine," but only a recognition of the way it is, perhaps, not as entirely alien to others as one might, at first, suppose. Indeed, if Habermas is right in asserting the feasibility of a moral consensus on deliberative procedures, grounded in our unavoidable commitment to such procedures as communicative agents, then the substantive point of those procedures must be articulated in some way in order to make sense of it as a properly *moral* consensus. An intelligible sense of moral obligation does not come to us as a purely procedural affair that would enable us to imagine, as Habermas does, a consensus on the moral point of view sustained entirely at the level of formal procedures of discourse. If there is to be any sort of moral consensus at all, therefore, it must be articulated in terms of the substantive point of those procedures.[71]

We should not expect, however, and there is nothing in Levinas's work that leads us to expect, a consensus on *how* to articulate the substantive point of our obligations to one another. And, for this reason, we have no reason to expect a consensus on the precise determination of those obligations insofar as a determination would depend, in part, on how one articulates what it is about the other person that makes her/him worthy of our moral consideration. In particular, as Taylor argues in his essay considering the question of a possible world consensus on human rights, we may not even be able to expect a consensus on even the seemingly indispensable idea of the individual as a bearer of subjective rights, as this particular way of articulating our obligations to others, as duties to respect those rights, turns on a particular "philosophy of human nature," a social-contractarian perspective on the relation between the individual and society, that is not universally embraced.[72] As I argue in chapter 4, it is important to keep in mind the indeterminate character of the "height" of the other person, which, though it provides the moral point to a liberal-democratic system of private and public rights, could plausibly be articulated in different terms as well. And though we might disagree as to whether we could be faithful to the moral importance of the other without recognizing a system of rights that would place the private and public autonomy of the individual at the center of our understanding of our obligations to the other,[73] such disagreements are beside the point. In an *overlapping* consensus on the moral worth of the other person, we should expect such disagreements because of the different reasons that lead us to such a consensus, as well as because of our ongoing concern to improve our understanding of our responsibilities to the other in the light of our different understandings. A human community that would be based in such a consensus need not exclude such disagreements. To the contrary, it must feed on them, with the adherents of every "comprehensive doctrine" denying themselves the complacency of believing their particular point of view to be the final word on the question of our responsibilities to one another. As the final word always belongs to the other, I must defer to the judgment of the other before coming to a final conclusion on the adequacy of any point of view. And as I am other to the other, the other must, in turn, defer to my judgment, establishing us both in an ongoing process of deliberation that can never end insofar as we are each other to one another, always there to demand more of each other. In this way, any overlapping consensus on the worth of the other person must remain fluid and open-ended, its content and character always subject to redetermination as we come to terms again and again with the potential value of this or that particular mode of articulation.

For this reason as well, we should not expect our understanding of the moral worth of the other person that would be the subject of an overlapping consensus to be "freestanding," as Rawls understands it, justified in a public way without any reference to the comprehensive doctrines which flourish in a community. The idea of the moral worth of the other is nourished in institutional practices of noninstrumental, communicative deference to the other and the attempts of those engaged in such practices to reflectively articulate the point of those practices. We cannot, therefore, turn a blind eye to these reflective traditions of consideration for the other in our public lives if we are to come to an overlapping consensus on the worth of the other adequate to our public sense of responsibility to the other. With his idea of the freestanding character of a shared conception of justice, however, Rawls appears to blind himself to these reflective traditions in the way he recommends restraint in our public use of reason. We should refrain, he advises, from an appeal to reasons that would refer beyond our shared political values to aspects of our comprehensive doctrines that might be controversial in the wider political community. In fairness to Rawls, it must be said that the point of this sense of restraint is a clear and justifiable one. He conceives of a public use of reason as the discourse of those in or seeking offices of state concerned with "public political discussions of constitutional essentials and basic matters of justice."[74] A public use of reason, for Rawls, is one in which we speak for or to the political community as a whole. It is, therefore, important that we offer reasons for our positions "that others as free and equal also might reasonably be expected to reasonably endorse."[75] Otherwise we effectively put those we could not reasonably expect to reasonably endorse our reasons beyond the range of our deliberations, excluding them from our consideration and so failing to provide the kind of consideration for their point of view that a recognition of the moral worth of the other commands of us. If I simply insist to the secular proponent of abortion rights, for example, that God forbids abortion, I have essentially denied the relevance of her/his secular point of view on the subject, dismissed it out of hand.

But as we recognize a justifiable point to such restraint, it is important that we are also clear about its limitations. Indeed, Rawls has come some way toward this end with his recent insistence on conceiving a public use of reason in an appropriately "wide" manner. We cannot, he argues, construe the commitment to restraint in our public use of reason too narrowly, to exclude any and every reference to comprehensive doctrines that might appear controversial, as there are occasions, he notes, in which such references can be redeemed in a purely political way. He cites the theological references of the abolitionist and civil rights movements as two important references to comprehensive doctrines in our political history that could be and have been so redeemed.[76] In proposing a "wide" conception of public reason, Rawls appears to make important and valid concessions to his ideal of a freestanding conception of justice, admitting the need for a robust shared conception of justice to draw on, at least in a provisional way, aspects of comprehensive doctrines that have not yet been translated into shared political currency. We cannot and should not seek to immunize the overlapping consensus of a political community from the insights of its various comprehensive doctrines as, at least on occasion, those insights are necessary to its ongoing and progressive transformation. It was, in part, the religious references of abolitionists and civil rights leaders reminding the public that African Americans were, as much as any white person, children of God that brought Americans to a more adequate consensus on racial equality. Similarly, an overlapping consensus on the substantive moral worth of the other person as the point of our obligations to the other will undoubtedly need to be worked and reworked in terms of the various interpretations of that moral worth that are embodied in our various comprehensive conceptions of the good of human life. We should, therefore, conceive of a public use of reason that would contribute to the development of an overlapping consensus on the moral worth of the other as widely as possible, avoiding the misleading characterization of its subject as freestanding.[77] Though we always need to consider the point of view of our fellow citizens in the sorts of reasons we offer for our public commitments, engaging with them in a way that shows respect for their point of view, we also need to be generous in our appraisal of the sort of reasons we are willing to entertain in a public discourse with the other. Speaking of the other as a child of God, for example, may turn out to be, in some form, not merely a provisionally valuable way of reminding ourselves of our fundamental equality as citizens but, perhaps, an indispensable way of articulating the moral dignity of the other person that underlies that ideal of equality. At the very least, we cannot know that on the front end. Regardless of our beliefs concerning the existence of God, we should, therefore, be open to the way such references may capture a crucial dimension of the significance of our moral intuitions in a way that may be impossible without them.[78] More generally, we need to be open to the potential value of the contributions of any comprehensive doctrine to our shared public life, whether or not we share a commitment to those doctrines. Such openness need not and should not be uncritical. But it is an indispensable element in any public discourse that would be genuinely responsive to the other.

5.5.5 Liberal Neutrality and the Need to Rebuild Civil Society

A Levinasian account of community does not, therefore, entail the abandonment of our commitment to pluralism. But it does entail the abandonment of certain understandings of the liberal ideal of political neutrality that insist that we distance ourselves from any evaluative judgments concerning the normative value of various cultures and modes of life, neither supporting nor inhibiting the efforts of individuals to maintain their traditions. The Jewish sense of pluralism we have been considering lives and thrives in such evaluative judgments. Critically attentive to the ways in which different cultures, in different and not altogether equal ways, may shelter our universal sense of responsibility to the other, it is a conception of pluralism based in a recognition of our need to offer public support for those modes of life that, like Judaism, nourish and shelter our universal sense of responsibility to the other in distinctive ways. Though striving "to secure equal opportunity to advance any permissible conception (of the good)," what Rawls calls "neutrality of aim,"[79] remains a laudable ideal insofar as we have no grounds to restrain any pursuit of the good that is consistent with justice and, indeed, shows respect for the moral worth of the other person in our respect for her/his life projects, we cannot refrain from distinguishing those traditions and modes of life that are merely consistent with justice from those that are significant in maintaining a sense of the importance of justice in a community. The latter deserve not only our respect but also our active support, even at the risk of establishing unequal opportunities for different modes of life.

In a time of increasingly individualistic sentiments in which a market mentality emphasizing self-gain above all else has come to dominate so many aspects of our life, culminating in what Cornel West has loosely but aptly termed the "gangsterization" of culture,[80] the ties that bind us together in a sense of community with one another are becoming increasingly precarious. But these are the ties that establish our moral importance to one another, our sense of why it is important to be just to one another. If we are to safeguard the communitarian conditions of a liberal-democratic society, we must, therefore, be prepared to provide a degree of support for those practices and institutions that build moral solidarity between us that we would not give to those that are only consistent with liberal-democratic principles. Associations that foster noninstrumental, communicative relationships between people are essential to a liberal-democratic society. As Robert Putnam has argued, it is not good for the citizens of a democratic republic to bowl alone.[81] And as Habermas among others has argued, the renewal of our opportunities for modes of association with one another that are dominated neither by the economic imperatives of the market nor the imperatives of power in the state is crucial for the renewal of our sense of social solidarity. Indeed, the tripartite model of state, market economy, and life-world advanced by Habermas has stimulated some of the most valuable contemporary reflections on the importance of our civic life and the threat posed to it by the "gangster" mentality of the market and the "tyranny of the universal and impersonal" inherent in the use of state power. Both eclipse the face of the other in the way they eclipse a noninstrumental, communicative relationship with the other, substituting, as Habermas analyzes it, the systemic steering mechanisms of money and power for the communicative coordination of our social endeavors.[82]

We need to go beyond a Habermasian conception of civil society, however, in also recognizing the importance of associations that articulate the substantive moral worth of the other person. They provide, in diverse ways, the moral resources for an articulate recognition of the need to extend our social solidarity to the stranger, the moral vocabularies to draw on in coming to a reflective appreciation of the universal logic of our ethical proximity to the other that is only implicit in our noninstrumental, communicative relationships. Habermas and those following his lead have resisted a recognition of this moral dimension of the crisis of modern civil society as a part of their resistance to anything that would smack of a "substantive consensus on values," proposing instead what Seyla Benhabib has described as a "participatory" approach to community which emphasizes the renewal of "political agency and efficacy" as an alternative to a communitarian emphasis on "value revival."[83] But in appreciating the need to make the significance of saying said, as Levinas would put it, we can also appreciate the futility of attempting to abstract civic-political concerns with increasing agency and participation in civil society from concerns with a substantive moral renewal in civil society. It is probably no accident that the civil rights movement emerged from African American churches in which an unqualified idea of the equality of every individual as a child of God was prominent or that the trade union movement emerged in America from a civic-republican tradition that stressed a conception of the dignity of the individual as a citizen that was deemed inconsistent with wage labor.[84] Abstracted from such contexts as these, which can, in different ways, form the basis of a robust overlapping consensus on the substantive moral worth of the other person, participation in civil society of itself lacks the resources to develop the potential implicit within it of a genuinely moral solidarity with the other sufficient to our support of liberal-democratic politics and principles.

What is entailed in supporting the practices and institutions that can rebuild moral solidarity between us will vary, of course. Often the most appropriate measures of support can only be offered in the guise of private citizens acting with one another to strengthen our associative life for ourselves. State legislation cannot rebuild our bowling leagues and P.T.A.s for us. But we should not refrain from state support when it is necessary and appropriate. Michael Walzer, for example, gives several examples of state action that have and could strengthen our associative life in civil society, such as the Wagner Act of the 1930s, which "actively fostered union organization," tax exemptions and matching grants for religious and civic organizations to undertake many of our social-welfare services from day-care centers to nursing homes, and plant closing laws designed to defend local communities from the moral and civic indifference of the unfettered forces of the market.[85] To these proposals, I would add a state-mandated reduction of working hours to free more time for involvement in the associative life of civil society.[86] The use of state power can be and often has been detrimental to institutions within civil society. But it is important to recognize the ways in which it can and must be used to establish the legal and economic conditions for the flourishing of our associative life. And though all of these examples of state initiatives could be justified on grounds that are more congenial to liberal concerns with neutrality, it is needlessly awkward, not to mention duplicitous, to limit our reasons for them in this way when a case can be made for their importance in communitarian terms that are not so congenial. Indeed, it is probably self-defeating to do so, as one of the values of these sorts of initiatives lies precisely in raising public awareness of the need to renew our moral solidarity with one another by rebuilding the institutions in civil society necessary to cultivate it. Defending a reduction in working hours entirely in terms of the need to reduce unemployment, for example, makes it only that much more likely that the time gained for working people will not go into rebuilding civil society, and an opportunity will be missed for focusing attention on it as a public concern.

The basic ideal that animates liberal concerns with neutrality in all their forms is a valid one. We should respect the equal right of all to pursue their own conceptions of the good in their own ways as long as it is consistent with what justice demands of us. Our respect for the private autonomy of the individual is a part of what we are called to in our recognition of the "always positive value" of the face of the other. But our concerns with equal consideration here should not blind us to the unequal moral and civic importance of the different modes of communal life we may choose to build as private citizens and the consequent need to offer different levels of support for different sorts of practices and institutions depending on our assessment of their importance. Engaging in a public assessment of the moral and civic importance of various modes of social life can be, of course, a politically dangerous affair, inviting all manner of unjustifiable social privilege, if not outright oppression. But the insight behind the need for such a public assessment is in no way invalidated by the political dangers posed by it. Indeed, if those of us with liberal-democratic commitments refrain from contributing to that public assessment out of a misguided concern with neutrality, that assessment will reflect only the contributions of those without such commitments—and so much the worse for liberal democracy.

◆

Despite my criticisms of the limitations of his work, I believe Habermas has aptly grasped the major moral and political imperative of our time more than most in his concerns with the renewal of conditions in civil society capable of strengthening our ties of solidarity with one another. As he notes, this solidarity was a presupposition of the socialist and social-democratic movements of the nineteenth and early twentieth centuries—a mode of working-class solidarity that would be formed in "the subcultural forms of life of industrial workers," intensified in the "cooperative relationships within the factory" and drawn on as a basis for the generation of a radically democratic, self-organized mode of social life. "But," as he continues, "since then these subcultures have largely disintegrated. And it is somewhat doubtful whether their power to create solidarity can be regenerated in the workplace. Be that as it may, what was previously a presupposition or a condition of the utopian idea of a laboring society has now become a theme for discussion."[87] The moral relevance of Judaism, as Levinas understands it, to modernity lies principally in the contribution it can make to that discussion, in helping us to clarify the conditions and character of a mode of community capable of rebuilding the forms of social solidarity that we must presuppose in any pursuit of justice but that we, unlike our socialist and social-democratic predecessors, can no longer take for granted.

Notes

1. Michael Sandel, *Democracy's Discontents* (Cambridge, Mass.: Harvard University Press, 1996), 343. *Democracy's Discontents* is the most fleshed out account of Sandel's civic-republican vision of community.

2. Jürgen Habermas, "Citizenship and National Identity," in *Between Facts and Norms*, trans. William Rehg (Cambridge, Mass.: The MIT Press, 1996), 500.

3. Levinas, *Difficult Freedom*, trans. Seàn Hand (Baltimore: The Johns Hopkins University Press, 1990), 212, and *Difficile Liberté: Essais sur le judaïsme* (Paris: Editions Albin Michel, 1976), 276.

4. Sandel, "The Procedural Republic and the Unencumbered Self," *Political Theory* 12 (1984): 90. Also see his *Liberalism and the Limits of Justice* (New York: Cambridge University Press, 1982), from which most of the points of "The Procedural Republic" were taken.

5. Sandel, "The Procedural Republic," 82. For Rawls's early conception of the priority of the right to the good, which was the immediate reference of Sandel's critique, see *A Theory of Justice*, (Cambridge, Mass.: Harvard University Press, 1971), ch. 1, no. 6.

6. See Rawls, *A Theory of Justice*, ch. 2, no. 11.

7. See Rawls, *A Theory of Justice*, 73-74.

8. See Rawls, *A Theory of Justice*, 150-151.

9. See Sandel, "The Procedural Republic," 89. Also see *Liberalism and the Limits of Justice*, 96-103.

10. Sandel, "The Procedural Republic," 90.

11. For Sandel's account of a "constitutive" community and its relation to this argument, see "The Procedural Republic," 87 & 89-90. Also see *Liberalism and the Limits of Justice*, 149-152.

12. See Robert Nozick, *Anarchy, State, and Utopia* (USA: Basic Books, 1974), ch. 7, especially 167-174.

13. Charles Taylor, "Cross-Purposes: The Liberal-Communitarian Debate," in *Liberalism and the Moral Life*, ed. Nancy Rosenblum (Cambridge, Mass.: Harvard University Press, 1989). For Montesquieu quote see page 165.

14. Habermas, "Citizenship and National Identity," in *Between Facts and Norms*, 499-450, *Faktizität und Geltung*, (Frankfurt am Main: Suhrkamp, 1992), 641-642, and "Struggles for Recognition in the Democratic Constitutional State," in *Multiculturalism: Examining the Politics of Recognition*, ed. Amy Gutman (Princeton, N.J.: Princeton University Press, 1994), 135. On the "nonrestrictive" sense of "neutrality" that Habermas believes is possible with a liberal political culture, see "Citizenship and National Identity," 308-314, and "Struggles for Recognition in the Democratic Constitutional State," 122-128.

15. John Rawls, *Political Liberalism*, (New York: Columbia University Press, 1993), 202. Rawls denies that these revisions of his earlier efforts were undertaken as a response to communitarian critiques of his work. Rather, he explains, they were adopted as a response to problems in his earlier account of the stability of a just society. Basing the social support of a just regime in what he would come to characterize as a comprehensive doctrine that would be shared by all, Rawls came to see this approach as inadequate to a pluralistic society, such as we have today, in which we cannot rely on any widespread agreement on comprehensive doctrines, in which an array of competing comprehensive doctrines about human life and its value is "the normal result of the exercise of human reason within the framework of the free institutions of a constitutional democratic regime." But, as he himself admits, others have seen this aspect of his work as a reply to communitarian critics, and it is, undoubtedly, the most promising place to look for an account in Rawls's political theory that could answer them. See *Political Liberalism*, xvii-xix.

16. See Rawls, *Political Liberalism*, 176 & 13.

17. See Rawls, *Political Liberalism*, 12 & 40.

18. Rawls, *Political Liberalism*, xviii & 50.

19. Habermas, "Struggles for Recognition in the Democratic Constitutional State," 132-133.

20. See Habermas, *Between Facts and Norms,* 461, 302 & 488.

21. Rawls, *Political Liberalism*, 16 & 50.

22. See Rawls, *Political Liberalism*, 17.

23. Habermas, *Between Facts and Norms*, 340-341.

24. See Habermas, *Between Facts and Norms,* 461.

25. He observes that the idea of autonomy is the "dogmatic core" of his work. See *Between Facts and Norms,* 445-446.

26. Habermas, *Between Facts and Norms*, 455.

27. Habermas, *Between Facts and Norms*, 104.

28. Habermas, *Between Facts and Norms*, 445.

29. Habermas uses the terms "moral" and "ethical" in such a way that they correlate respectively with deontological or unconditional authority for anyone and a telelogical or conditional authority for anyone who shares a particular set of life aspirations; the "right" and the "good," in other words.

30. Habermas, "Citizenship and National Identity," 498.

31. See Habermas, *Between Facts and Norms*, 298 & 505, and "Struggles for Recognition in the Democratic Constitutional State," 134-135.

32. Habermas, *Between Facts and Norms*, 107.

33. See Habermas, "Struggles for Recognition in the Democratic Constitutional State," 142. Habermas qualifies this judgment as made from "the moral point of view," but I doubt he would or could sharply distinguish this from a legal-political point of view. Even though he is at pains in *Between Facts and Norms* to insist on the separation of a political point of view on the legitimacy of laws from a moral point of view concerning universalizable norms of action, whether or not they can or should be institutionalized as enforceable laws (laws can be legitimate, for example, for a particular community that shares particular desires and aspirations and regulates its members lives in terms of those shared values without being universally authoritative for anyone and everyone—the hallmark of moral judgments), both of these points of view are derived from the more fundamental discourse principle, which demands a more general sense of impartiality tailored to the specific conditions of each context of judgment (moral or political). Thus, even though a moral point of view is not always relevant to each and every political question it would be incoherent for someone committed to the principle of democracy on the basis of the discourse principle to decline taking a moral point of view on political questions when it is relevant, as in the case of immigration.

34. Habermas, *Between Facts and Norms*, 118. In addition to adding emphasis on the word "legitimately" I have also eliminated Habermas's original emphasis on the phrase "equal weight" as I mean to draw the reader's attention to a different aspect of his claim than he does.

35. Habermas, *Between Facts and Norms*, 263.

36. See Rawls, *Political Liberalism*, 194, for his characterization of reasonableness as a liberal political virtue.

37. Commenting on a version of this argument I presented in a paper at the December 1998 meeting of the Eastern Division of the American Philosophical Association, Kenneth Baynes raised a question concerning my apparent neglect of Habermas'ss understanding of the importance of civil society for a democratic polity. Though I will address the concept of civil society and what I believe are the limitations of Habermas's understanding of it later in the chapter, it is probably a good idea to quickly note my reasons for neglecting it here before proceeding. In recognizing the importance of civil society, it is true that Habermas recognizes that the social conditions of a liberal democracy go deeper than its political culture, but not in a way that would constructively address the questions raised here. For

one, it also remains true that the only *shared* sense of community a democratic polity requires for Habermas is a political form of community where citizens share a commitment to liberal-democratic principles and procedures. In keeping with Habermas's aversion to any substantive consensus on values, he understands civil society as an arena in which diverse groups articulate and pursue competing values. In this way, I believe it is fair to say that he restricts his understanding of the shared sense of community a democratic polity requires to the political sphere as I argue here. And, second, if my basic conclusion is sound, that a democratic community's support of liberal-democratic principles and procedures needs to be anchored in a shared sense of the substantive value or importance of those principles and procedures, then an appeal to civil society will *only* be helpful if it is understood as the site for the articulation and clarification of a shared sense of the substantive value of its constitutional principles, the arena in which the citizens of a democratic political community work out their substantive understandings of what is at stake in their constitutional principles. But Habermas has always resisted such a conception of civil society, preferring instead a conception that mirrors his procedural understanding of democracy and morality—a conception of civil society as the arena for the informal and unstructured flows of communication required for democratic deliberation. The implication of my argument is that a democratic civil society needs to be more (but not less) than this: not merely the site of informal and unstructured flows of communication, but the site of the convergence of these flows of communication in a shared sense of the substantive value of democratic principles and procedures. It is this more substantive conception of civil society that I will explore later in this chapter.

38. See *Totality and Infinity*, trans. Alphonso Lingis (Pittsburgh: Duquesne University Press, 1969), 241-243, for a concise discussion of Levinas's critical appraisal of the state, the dimension of the political, and the judgment of history.

39. Levinas, *Totality and Infinity*, 242.

40. For Levinas's analysis of the family, see *Totality and Infinity*, 267-269 & 274-285.

41. Robert Gibbs, "A Jewish Context for the Social Ethics of Marx and Levinas," in *Autonomy and Judaism*, ed. Daniel H. Frank (Albany: State University of New York Press, 1992), 174. Though I believe Gibbs is mistaken in this assessment of Levinas's work I am very much indebted to his analysis of Levinas's understanding of social institutions and the possibilities for ethical modes of sociality.

42. Levinas, *Difficult Freedom*, 278.

43. Levinas, *Difficult Freedom*, 275. For more on Levinas's understanding of the moral character of religion that is not, as he puts it, "the forever primitive form of religion," see *Totality and Infinity*, 77-79.

44. See Levinas, *Difficult Freedom*, 281.

45. Emmanuel Levinas, "Meaning and Sense," in *Collected Philosophical Papers*, trans. Alphonso Lingis (Dordrecht: Martinus Nijhoff, 1987), 101.

46. Levinas, *Difficult Freedom*, 274.

47. This is not to say that communitarian accounts of the importance of the other reduce the importance of the other to an instrumental significance. I do not understand my fellow citizens as important and deserving of my respect and consideration merely because I need their cooperation to attain things I enjoy on my own independent of them, as I might value the cooperation of others in support of such things as our local police force that enable all of us to enjoy greater security in our private lives. The other is not a mere means to the end of my private satisfaction with life. Rather, as Taylor so clearly brings out with his distinction between common and convergent goods in "Cross-Purposes: The Liberal-

Communitarian Debate," a common sense of the good is something that can only be enjoyed with others as, for example, I can only take pride in the achievements of my country *as* a citizen, with my fellow citizens. But this point still preserves what I am calling the centripetal character of the significance of the other to me.

48. Except, of course, in the indirect way we have already discussed, as a function of the fact that our common attachment to *universal* liberal-democratic principles makes it important to "us" that those who are not a part of our community be treated as having the same or a similar sense of worth. But this response is inadequate for the reasons we have examined. For another example of this approach to the problem of our relations with others who do not belong to our community, see Richard Rorty, "Postmodernist Bourgeois Liberalism," *The Journal of Philosophy* (1983), and my "Putting Ourselves Up for Question: A Postmodern Critique of Richard Rorty's Postmodernist Bourgeois Liberalism," *The Journal of Value Inquiry* 29 (1995): 241-253, for a critical discussion of the shortcomings of Rorty's particular approach.

49. See Levinas, *Otherwise than Being*, trans. Alphonso Lingis (The Hague: Martinus Nijhoff, 1981), 117. Also see Stephen L. Carter, *Civility: Manners, Morals, and the Etiquette of Democracy* (New York: Basic Books, 1998), who argues that acts of civility should be construed as elementary ways of acknowledging the moral worth of the other person.

50. See Levinas, *Totality and Infinity*, 69.

51. Levinas, *Beyond the Verse: Talmudic Readings and Lectures*, trans. Gary D. Mole (Indianapolis: Indiana University Press, 1994), xiii.

52. Levinas, *Totality and Infinity*, 245, and *Totalité et Infini*, (La Haye: Martinus Nijhoff, 1961), 223.

53. Levinas, *Difficult Freedom*, 212.

54. Levinas, *Totality and Infinity*, 245.

55. Levinas, *Otherwise than Being*, 159.

56. "In particular, modern political theories since Hobbes deduce the social order from the legitimacy, the incontestable right, of freedom." Emmanuel Levinas, "Philosophy and the Idea of Infinity," in *Collected Philosophical Papers*, 57.

57. See Levinas, *Nine Talmudic Readings*, trans. Annette Aronowitz (Indianapolis: Indiana University Press, 1990), 111.

58. Alexis de Tocqueville, *Democracy in America,* vol. 2 (New York: Vintage Books, 1960), 104.

59. Levinas, *Nine Talmudic Readings*, 112, and Emmanuel Levinas, *Du Sacré au Saint: Cinq Nouvelles Lectures Talmudiques* (Paris: Les Éditions de Minuit, 1977), 42.

60. Jean-Bethke Elshtain, "Feminism, Family, and Community," *Dissent* 29 (fall 1982): 445.

61. Also see chapter 3 for my discussion of the abstract humanity of the other and the way our sense of obligation to the other is always, at first, a partiality for the other in her/his specificity.

62. Or, I would add, daughter of this mother. Levinas's preoccupation with paternity is unintelligible to me, though the debate surrounding Levinas's sexism is not one I am either prepared or inclined to take on here. For my purposes, I believe a reference to a child of this father and/or mother could be substituted without distortion for Levinas's reference to sons and fathers.

63. See Levinas, *Totality and Infinity*, 279

64. I trust it is clear from the level at which I have pitched my brief analysis in this paragraph that I do not intend to take a position on the question of the ideal structure of the family. Though, undoubtedly, a decent empirical and intuitive case has been made in the current literature on the family for the superiority of two-parent families for the raising of children (a point with which any parent who has struggled on without the support of a partner, even for a weekend, could probably agree—it *is* a lot easier to do a good job with raising kids with someone else rather than alone), my analysis only insists on the importance of children discovering themselves as elected to someone who genuinely loves them. My point is just that the sort of combination of loving consideration and moral authority currently provided by the best sorts of families, be they single parent, two-parent, heterosexual or homosexual parents, is probably not available, at least to the same degree, for children in other social institutions such as state orphanages or communal child-raising groups. For a review of the literature arguing for the two-parent family as an ideal, see Barbara Dafoe Whitehead's "Dan Quayle Was Right," *The Atlantic Monthly* (April 1993): 47-84. For a nicely balanced argument for the importance of the family as a social institution and a consideration of the political dimensions of the "family values" debate, see Sylvia Ann Hewlett and Cornel West's *The War against Parents* (Boston: Houghton Mifflin, 1998).

65. Levinas, *Difficult Freedom*, 176.

66. Levinas, *Nine Talmudic Readings*, 27.

67. See chapter 3 as well as chapter 6, where I return to this issue.

68. See Levinas, *Beyond the Verse*, xiii. Though Levinas does not relate this pluralism directly to his thesis regarding the saying and the said, it is reasonable to suppose a connection in the way I have elaborated it. Levinas's emphasis on the way the revelation of the Scriptures implicates each person in her/his uniqueness, as a distinctive reading posed from her/his perspective, is convergent with his claims regarding the moral significance of the word of God and his account of how the moral significance of my speech with the other cannot be appropriated except in a mode of election, the assumption of a unique sense of responsibility.

69. Levinas, *Beyond the Verse*, xi.

70. Levinas, *Difficult Freedom*, 177 & 288, and *Difficile Liberté* (Paris: Editions Albin Michel, 1976), 231.

71. My argument here is similar to the argument Joshua Cohen advances in his "Pluralism and Proceduralism," *Chicago-Kent Law Review* 69 (1994): 589-618. "If . . . pluralism does not defeat a procedural consensus, then neither does it exclude a deeper and broader (substantive) overlapping consensus" (600). But the level at which I am concerned with a "substantive consensus on values" is less demanding than the level at which Cohen operates. His concern is with a consensus on Rawls's substantive political principles such as the difference principle, which deals with social and economic inequalities. My concern is only with a consensus on the basic dignity of the other person, which gives us the moral point of being fair to the other in the way demanded by the difference principle. It could, therefore, be agreed to while still disagreeing over what substantive principles should govern our economic and social inequalities.

72. See Charles Taylor, "A World Consensus on Human Rights?" *Dissent* (summer 1996), in particular, pages 16-17.

73. Actually, some varieties of communitarian thought come pretty close to making a case for an alternative to a rights-based understanding of our duties as citizens. Taylor cites examples of Asian thought, Confuscian and Buddhist, as alternatives. The language of rights has, after all, been exploited as a justification for denying any meaningful sense of

obligation to our fellow citizens (not to mention outsiders) as much as for supporting them. So there may be a case to make for the superiority of alternative articulations. We cannot know without examining them in detail.

74. For Rawls's "wide" conception of public reason, see *Political Liberalism*, l - lvii, "Introduction to the Paperback Edition," l, for the quote. For a good critique of Rawls's initial conception of public reason (before he widened it) that makes a case, as I have, for the need to keep our conception of an overlapping consensus that would form the basis for a public use of reason fluid and subject to redetermination through ongoing deliberation, see Thomas McCarthy, "Kantian Constructivism and Reconstructivism: Rawls and Habermas in Dialogue," *Ethics* 105 (October 1994), 44-63.

75. Rawls, *Political Liberalism*, li & l.

76. See Rawls, *Political Liberalism*, li-lii.

77. There is, however, a sense in which a conception of the moral worth of the other person that would be the subject of an overlapping consensus might still be characterized as freestanding. Insofar as aspects of various comprehensive doctrines that are deemed essential, in some form, to such a conception come to be acknowledged as public dimensions of an overlapping consensus and cast in an appropriately civic form that can be endorsed without having to convert, wholesale, to any particular comprehensive doctrine, then it could be said that though the conception of moral worth in question was constructed in terms of the various comprehensive views, it can now be said to stand alone apart from them as a purely civic conception. This is true, I think, and is an important element in a political community gaining a common discursive ground upon which to conduct their public deliberations in a spirit of what Rawls characterizes as "reciprocity" and "civic friendship." (See Rawls, *Political Liberalism*, li.) But this point should not distract us from the need, at any given point in the ongoing determination and redetermination of that overlapping consensus, to justify our contributions to that process in ways that will not allow us to always reasonably refrain from making reference to our own comprehensive doctrines. And this is the only point I am trying to make in this context.

78. I am not claiming that religious language is indispensable in our public life but merely suggesting it as a possibility to illustrate the general need to be open to contributions to public life derived from comprehensive doctrines we might not share. There are, of course, some who would take the argument a step farther and claim that religious language really is indispensable to our public life, as Stephen Carter appears to, for example, in his work, *Civility* (see page 31, for example). Levinas, on the other hand, does not appear to endorse the idea, at least in any unequivocal way. Though he insists on the religious character of our sense of moral obligation to the other, the point seems to be that the sense of transcendence that we evoke in religious references to God are grounded in a sense of transcendence which opens up in our proximity to the other, by which he means, I believe, the way the moral authority of the other, the "height" or alterity of the other, defies presentation and is "otherwise than being" in this sense. (More on this issue in the next chapter.) In this way, Levinas thinks the significance of religion from within our human relationship to the other rather than the other way around. As he puts it, our proximity to the other is not "a 'proof of God's existence' but 'the fall of God into meaning'" ("Diachrony and Representation," in *Time and the Other*, trans. Richard A. Cohen [Pittsburgh: Duquesne University Press, 1987], 115). "The Other is not the incarnation of God, but precisely by his face, in which he is disincarnate, is the manifestation of the height in which God is revealed" (*Totality and Infinity*, 79). And, as with the significance of saying, this religious reference to God is not said, is not explicit in my proximity to the other. Though Levinas insists that

my responsibilities are always undertaken "'in the name of God.' . . . The word God is still absent from the phrase in which God is for the first time involved in words. It does not state at all 'I believe in God'" (*Otherwise than Being*, 149). But for this very reason, there is a value to religious language for Levinas in articulating this transcendent dimension of our moral proximity to the other. Speaking of the other as a child of God, speaking of ourselves as commanded to the other by God makes salient the absolute and unconditional nature of the moral authority of the other and our obligation to the other in a way that is, *perhaps*, unequaled by any secular discourse. And so the moral value of religious language is recognized by Levinas. But its *indispensable* value remains undecided in his work, as far as I can make it out at least.

79. Rawls, *Political Liberalism*, 193.

80. See Cornel West, "The Crisis in Contemporary America," part 2 of *The Culture of Community: A Series of Public Conversations* (New Jersey Committee for the Humanities, 1993), 20.

81. See Robert Putnam, "Bowling Alone," *Journal of Democracy* 6 (January 1995): 65-78.

82. For Habermas's "classic" statement on these issues, see "The New Obscurity: The Crisis of the Welfare State and the Exhaustion of Utopian Energies," in *The New Conservativism* (Cambridge, Mass.: The MIT Press, 1989). For the most sustained and systematic development of these ideas into what remains the most sophisticated theory of civil society available today, see Jean L. Cohen and Andrew Arato, *Civil Society and Political Theory* (Cambridge, Mass.: The MIT Press, 1992).

83. See Seyla Benhabib, *Situating the Self*, (New York: Routledge, 1992), 77.

84. For a nice overview of the civic-republican roots of the trade union movement in the United States, see Sandel, *Democracy's Discontent*, chs. 5-6.

85. See Michael Walzer, "The Communitarian Critique of Liberalism," *Political Theory* 18, no. 1 (February 1990): 16-18, and "Socializing the Welfare State," in *Democracy and the Welfare State*, ed. Amy Gutman (Princeton, N.J.: Princeton University Press, 1988).

86. See Pierre Rosanvallon, "The Decline of Social Visibility," in *Civil Society and the State: New European Perspectives*, ed. John Keane (London: Verso Press, 1988), 209, who connects this initiative with the need to rebuild institutions of civil society.

87. Jürgen Habermas, "The New Obscurity: The Crisis of the Welfare State and the Exhaustion of Utopian Energies," 67-68.

Chapter 6

The Epistemic Viability of the Appeal to the Face of the Other

In the preceding four chapters I have advanced an argument for the utility of expanding Habermas's procedural understanding of communicative action to embrace Levinas's substantive appeal to the face of the other to whom speech is addressed. With respect to our understanding of the place of care in our moral lives, our ability to make sense of the properly moral or unconditional authority of the moral point of view, the common root of our respect for the liberties of the ancients and moderns, and the need for a sense of community sufficient to our support of liberal-democratic principles, Habermas's postmetaphysical approach to moral and political theory comes up short in ways that can be constructively addressed with Levinas's appeal to the face of the other. As I put the point most simply at the beginning of chapter 4, Habermas's postmetaphysical perspective is just more trouble than it is worth.

To be fair, however, there are serious questions that have been raised concerning Levinas's appeal to the face of the other that ought to be addressed as well if we are to adequately appraise the philosophical value of his insights. In particular, I address three questions in this chapter that all deal with the epistemic viability of Levinas's work: first, its openness to argumentative justification, as raised by Max Pensky's criticism that Levinas's work "runs out of gas" when pressed for a theoretical elaboration of its insights and Habermas's related criticism that "arguments will not suffice" for any substantive appeal to the good; next, the question of the internal coherence of Levinas's account of the other as raised by Jacques Derrida in his ground-breaking essay on what Levinas understands as the *metaphysical* character of his work, "Violence and Metaphysics"; and finally, the question of the epistemic role experience plays in the validation of Levinas's account as raised by Todd May's charge that Levinas's account of the other succumbs to what Wilfred Sellars called "the myth of the given." Carefully attending to each of these related though distinct concerns with the epistemic viability of Levinas's work, we should be able to better appraise the philosophical status of his appeal to the face of the other, defending not only, as I have up till now, its relevance for moral and political theory, but also its credibility and coherence as a position we can acknowledge and work with theoretically without sacrificing our epistemic integrity.

6.1 Moral Theory and the Recourse to "Subtler Languages"

6.1.1 Taylor and Levinas's "Subtler Languages"

To begin, Max Pensky raises questions concerning the way Levinas's account appears to go beyond the bounds of what can be theoretically enunciated. Levinas's appeal to the face of the other, Pensky argues, "runs out of gas precisely at the point where we push it to get a theoretical elaboration of the moment of recognition of vulnerability of an other itself . . . (and) does not so much lie 'outside' moral theory but actively resists incorporation into any system of philosophical concepts." Citing approvingly from Habermas's response to Taylor's charge that discourse ethics is unable to answer the question, "Why be moral?" he assimilates Levinas's work to "the rhetorically moving, exemplary representation of the novelist or the quietly insistent intuitions of common sense," which, unlike philosophical argument, are capable of moving us to an appreciation of "the ultimate meaning and value of human life." He concludes that Levinas's work is best thought of as a form of "radical moral pedagogy, whose end is not to convince but to sensitize toward where we draw the limits of our moral theory," in a substantive relation to the vulnerability of the other that defies theoretical elaboration.[1]

Pensky's conclusions draw from and echo Habermas's own conclusions regarding the philosophical status of Taylor's invocation of the substantive sources of our moral intuitions. As Levinas's appeal to the face of the other is to a particular good that exemplifies Taylor's idea of constitutive goods generally, we may usefully think of Pensky's conclusions with Levinas as an application of the point Habermas makes with Taylor that any appeal to a substantive notion of the good must transcend the limits of what can be accomplished through philosophical argument. Noting that Taylor's interests lie not merely with describing the goods that are constitutive for our modern sense of identity but in justifying them as "ineluctable and authoritative for us," Habermas argues, "An ethics of the good that discloses the order of constitutive goods as a publicly accessible reality can realize this ambitious argumentative goal. But under the premises of postmetaphysical thinking, this route is closed to us." Modernity has lost its public access to substantive goods with the multiplication of our cultural and ethical points of view on the world. The publicly accessible goods of a less pluralistic age, belief in the authority of God, for example, can now only be understood as private, ethical commitments—hence, Taylor's appeal to the "subtler languages" of modern art and literature to disclose in a more personally resonant way the sources of our moral intuitions that have become publicly inaccessible to us. Though Habermas does not question the importance of the arts in moving or sensitizing us to the importance of our moral ideals, he stresses the way such a move to aesthetic modes of experience abandons philosophical argument that is insufficient to that end. "Arguments," Habermas concludes, "will not suffice to open the eyes of the 'value-blind' children of modernity to the efficacy of the highest goods; that requires the world-disclosing power of an evaluative language that first lifts the scales from our eyes."[2] In appealing to the substantive point of our moral intuitions, it would appear, therefore, that Taylor and Levinas both abandon the terrain of argument in favor of aesthetic invocations designed more to move or sensitize us to that which lies, or ought to lie, beyond the pale of any properly argumentative, philosophical theory.

Taylor appears, moreover, to support Habermas's contention by stressing the limits of our ability to justify the validity of our claims regarding any substantive good. "There is nothing we can do," he admits, to "convince someone who saw none of the point of our moral beliefs . . . to 'prove' we are right to such a person. . . . I can only convince you by my description of the good if I speak for you, either by articulating what underlies your existing moral intuitions or perhaps by my description moving you to the point of making it your own."[3] It is here that the "subtler languages" of modern art and literature become important in enabling us to articulate goods for which we have lost a publicly available language. What Taylor means to refer to here is the way in which modern art and literature have lost many dimensions of a public order of shared understandings that could once be drawn on to express ideas and sentiments. Shakespeare, for example, could take for granted the medieval doctrine of correspondences between the human and natural order in evoking the horror of regicide: "the night in which Duncan is murdered is an unruly one, with 'lamentings heard i' the air; strange screams of death,' and it remains dark even though the day should have started."[4] The doctrine of correspondences constitutes for him a publicly available set of meanings that enable him to express in a publicly intelligible way the importance of Duncan's murder in terms of sympathetic events in nature. Lacking widespread beliefs in the correspondences, modern writers can only get at similar ideas in a personally resonant way. Baudelaire, for instance, is still able to write a poem dealing with the correspondences, but he cannot take them for granted in the way Shakespeare did. At most, he can attempt to get at "some personal vision he is trying to triangulate through this historical reference, the 'forest of symbols's that he sees in the world around him. But to grasp this forest, we need to understand not so much the erstwhile public doctrine (about which no one remembers any details anyway) but, as we might put it, the way it resonates in the poet's sensibility."[5] In this way, Baudelaire may produce a vision we can acknowledge for ourselves insofar as he articulates something we may share in an inarticulate way with him or his poem succeeds in moving us to make it our own. But our access to Baudelaire's vision is limited to the way in which his personally resonant language resonates with us as well, the extent to which the particular triangulation of symbols that constitutes his poem can open up for us in a personally relevant way the unique vision he is trying to share.

What holds true of Taylor's "subtler languages" also appears to hold true of Levinas's articulation of the face of the other. Levinas attempts to articulate an intuition regarding the unconditional importance of the other person that has been, most notably, the province of theological languages that are no longer publicly available—the idea of the other person as a child of God, for example. Without denying the religious, particularly Jewish, inspiration behind his work, he has, nonetheless, always sought for nonreligious, philosophical modes of expression for that inspiration, turning, in particular, to the phenomenological tradition as a way of access to our lived experience of the other.[6] But the idioms Levinas has adopted to articulate this lived experience, the references to the "face" of the other, the "height" and "vulnerability" of the other, come together to form a highly personal vision of the moral worth of the other, a unique expression of an intuition that is no longer publicly available. His work can, to this extent, give one the impression of poetry as much as philosophy. Bringing his own "subtler language" to bear on the articulation of a phenomenon that has lost its public modes of articulation, Levinas's project can only be convincing in the way Taylor elaborates it, by "speak(ing) for you . . . by articulating what underlies your existing moral intuitions or perhaps by . . . moving you to the point of making it your own."

6.1.2 The Need to Distinguish Issues of Articulation and Justification

We should be careful, however, in our appraisal of the epistemic status of such personally resonant articulations of the good. It is not, after all, as if we are dealing with purely subjective expressions of taste immune to rational, critical evaluation. Taylor, for instance, properly stresses the distinction between the subjective manner of our expression of substantive goods and the matter or content of what is expressed that is intended, at least, as nonsubjective, "something beyond the self."[7] Though only accessible through the personally resonant languages of their expression, the substantive goods articulated there are presented as matters of objective importance that we should be able to see for ourselves through the optics of the artist's "subtler language." Levinas's understanding of his own work as phenomenological is, undoubtedly, an expression of the same general concern to adopt an unavoidably subjective mode of access to nonsubjective matters. It constitutes an "intentional analysis" of the horizons within which our experience of the other is given its sense, an articulation of the significance of our lived experience, of the gravity or seriousness with which I am called to respond to the other in speech.[8] As with all phenomenology, Levinas's work is an attempt to be rigorous with our subjective experience, to offer an account of our lived experience that will make sense of it and, in that way, speak for us.

Lacking a publicly available language for its articulation, we should not, of course, expect Levinas's particular language of personal resonance to speak for everyone. The terms of its articulation are too unique and bound to specific cultural, religious, and philosophical traditions to be compelling for most of us.[9] But though the terms of Levinas's articulation of the face of the other are limiting, it does not follow that the subject matter that is expressed in that articulation is limited as well. To the contrary, we have good reason to believe that the insight Levinas is trying to articulate in his own personally resonant way is far from limited in its capacity to resonate with and illuminate our lived experience of the other. Though it may be articulated in quite different ways, a point Levinas himself anticipates with his analysis of the saying and the said, the face of the other remains, in some form or another, an indispensable dimension of our moral experience. This has been the key theme running throughout the arguments of chapters 2-5. Whether we are trying to understand the relation between care and justice, make sense of the unconditional authority of the moral point of view, construct a balanced account of the liberties of the ancients and moderns, or grapple with the need to anchor our sense of justice in a sense of community, we cannot adequately come to terms with the moral intuitions that guide these considerations without a recognition of the substantive worth of the other person as the ground of our sense of justice, the point of the moral point of view, the common root of our respect for the public and private liberties of the other, and the subject of the sort of overlapping consensus that would adequately anchor a sense of justice in a community. As we have seen, trying to negotiate these issues without a substantive sense of the moral worth of the other as an essential dimension of our moral experience puts us at an irreparable disadvantage, leaving us without the resources we need to adequately understand them.

This indispensable role of the face of the other in our moral experience is, moreover, perfectly comprehensible. As we saw in chapter 3, a substantive sense of the moral worth of the other person is an essential condition for making sense of the unconditional authority of the moral point of view. It is, in effect, an essential condition for having an intelligible moral experience. No one who feels the gravity of a moral point of view onto life can, therefore, be blind to the face of the other. And, as it is in the very act of speech that we are encumbered with the unconditional sense of deference to the other that is at the heart of the moral point of view, it is clear that we will find no one who does not at least find her/himself *called* to a sense of the unconditional worth of the other person as a condition of making sense of her/his commitments as a communicative agent. Though every historical community must find its own way of articulating the point, the substantive value of its communicative commitments depending on the distinctive discursive resources available to it, the value we find ourselves called to articulate in this way is, in some form or other, a good toward which no one can be absolutely indifferent. Levinas's distinctive articulation of that good will not speak for everyone. But we have reason to believe that the good he articulates is a sense of the good to which every communicative agent finds her/himself ineluctably called.

"Arguments will not suffice," as Habermas correctly reminds us, "to open the eyes of the 'value-blind' children of modernity to the efficacy of the highest goods." For that we need Taylor's subtler languages capable of articulating such goods in what must remain a personally resonant way. But arguments *will* suffice to show our need for an articulation of a sense of the unconditional worth of the other in the conditions for the intelligible appropriation of our commitments as communicative agents. And arguments *will* suffice to show the inadequacy of any account of our moral experience that eclipses this substantive good. Though the *articulation* of the face of the other must go beyond what could be established on the basis of theoretical arguments, the *justification* of that good as indispensable to our moral experience and called for in any intelligible appropriation of communicative action need not. Habermas's and Pensky's criticisms miss this distinction, reasoning as if the nontheoretical character of the articulation of a substantive good made it inconceivable that any properly theoretical work could be done with the insights articulated there. But this supposition is unfounded. It will, of course, primarily be the business of artists and poets to create personally resonant and compelling articulations of matters of substantive importance in life. Philosophers typically do not have what it takes for that. But this does not mean that *what* is articulated there is irrelevant to philosophical concerns or that philosophers do not have a relevant role to play in helping us to understand what is at stake there. It is the justification of the insights developed in those articulations, the clarification of their relevance to our moral experience along with an analysis of the limits and extent of their validity, that is the properly theoretical task.

When we begin to have reason to suppose that a good is indispensable to moral experience and grounded in a universally relevant condition of human life, such as we have with the "always positive value" of the face of the other, we also begin to have reason to acknowledge its clarification and analysis as an essential task of moral philosophy, understanding that task, as Habermas does, as one that is committed to the clarification and justification of the moral point of view.[10] If that means we must have recourse to subtler languages of personal resonance to articulate such goods, as Taylor and Levinas do, then we must also accept a certain blurring of the boundaries between theory and art, acknowledging at least a need to make theoretical use of artistic idioms when more publicly available languages of expression fail us. But this does not mean, as Habermas seems to think, that we have abandoned theoretical reflection and argument for something else. Subtler languages of personal resonance only provide the necessary starting points for our theoretical reflections, which must, as Habermas insists, go beyond them, seeking arguments to justify the insights we find articulated there. Often, of course, we will not find such arguments and will be forced to conclude that the insights in question, however compelling they may be *for us*, are only valid for particular forms of life, valid ethical but not moral insights. My point here is just that with regard to Levinas's insights regarding the face of the other, we do not find ourselves in such a situation. When pushed to theoretically clarify and justify the moral importance of the face of the other, we do not "run out of gas." Far from it. But it is important to be clear about what we can and cannot accomplish theoretically and the need to draw on nontheoretical idioms when, as in this case, we have theoretically compelling reasons to do so.

6.2 The Metaphysical Limits of Intelligibility

We have, then, good reason to regard Levinas's appeal to the face of the other as an important and necessary contribution to moral theory, amenable to argumentative clarification and justification, rather than as a transgression of its proper limits. But in making a case for the theoretical importance of this appeal we also need to consider the coherence of the appeal itself. In what is, for many, one of the more frustrating aspects of his work, Levinas lays great emphasis on the way the face of the other is "absolutely other (*autre*)," "infinite" in the way it defies conceptual comprehension, alien to the "province of representation," and, as he expresses it in the title of his last major work, "otherwise than being."[11] This is what Levinas characterizes as the metaphysical dimension of his work, the way our proximity to the other involves us in a relationship "toward an alien outside-of-oneself, toward a yonder."[12] The face of the other effects a rupture with what can be known, indeed, is such a rupture, an unsurpassable mystery[13] that resists assimilation to any conceptual framework that might otherwise render it intelligible. As such, Levinas confronts himself with what can only appear, at least at first, to be the impossible task of speaking about what cannot be said, conceiving what defies conceptual comprehension, making intelligible a mystery defined most essentially by the way it effects a rupture with intelligibility.

It is for this reason that Derrida concludes that, with his distinctively metaphysical conception of our proximity to the other, Levinas deprives himself of the conditions for the possibility of a coherent discourse about the other, limiting himself to "a language of pure invocation, pure adoration, proffering only proper names in order to call to the other from afar." Drawing on Heidegger's thesis that there must be a practically or discursively articulated "clearing" for anything to appear *as* the thing that it is, Derrida argues that "thought—or at least the precomprehension of Being—*conditions* . . . the *recognition* of the essence of the existent (for example someone, existent *as* other, *as* other self, etc.). It conditions the *respect* for the other *as what it is*: other." Or, to put the same point somewhat differently, without some interpretive framework which allows us to grasp the other *as* other, that enables us to make the presence of the other intelligible in terms of the practical or conceptual resources available within that framework, no recognition, let alone respect, for the other is possible. It is in this aspiration to transcend the interpretive frameworks that constitute the conditions of intelligibility for our world that Derrida finds evidence of an underlying empiricism in Levinas's metaphysical account of the other. "The true name of this renunciation of the concept," Derrida suggests, " is *empiricism*. . . . It is the *dream* of a purely *heterological* thought at its source. A *pure* thought of *pure* difference. . . . We say the *dream* because it must vanish *at daybreak*, as soon as language awakens."[14] As soon as we attempt to speak of the face of the other, in Levinas's sense, it slips through our fingers, becoming, at best, the vague memory of a dream that forever escapes us.

In a recent appropriation of his critique, John Caputo has extended Derrida's point to argue that although Levinas's discourse on the other should not be dismissed, it cannot be taken "literally" either. It can, rather, only be taken hyperbolically, as making an "excessive statement" meant to draw our attention to something we should not overlook; not the truth but, as Caputo puts it, a "fabulous tale" whose aim is an inspirational or prophetic one to make "irresponsibility look as bad as possible and . . . responsibility look as good" as possible.[15] Reading Levinas's work in this way, as an inspirational discourse whose object is not, indeed, cannot be the truth of what it speaks, Caputo illustrates how Derrida's critique of Levinas leads to the same conclusion as Pensky's and Habermas's. It is possible to admire Levinas's work for its morally uplifting tone, its prophetic rhetoric. But it cannot be taken seriously or "literally" in the way it is intended, as a philosophical attempt to make a case for a set of claims about the moral worth of the other that is, as all claims are, subject to rational assessment.

6.2.1 The Rupture with Intelligibility Effected by Our Proximity to the Other

Before asking after the coherence of Levinas's metaphysical account of the other, it is important to clarify *why* he is drawn to such an apparently incoherent project. What is it about the face of the other that resists straightforward articulation? What is it about our conversational deference to the other that "cannot," as Levinas puts it, "be interpreted on the basis of disclosure (*dévoilement*)"?[16] To see his reasons, it is important to recall that Levinas basically agrees with the Heideggerian perspective Derrida invokes in his critique of him. Nothing is able to be present *as* what it is apart from a context of interpretation that is constituted in terms of our practical involvement with the world, the "projection" of our possibilities for "Being," as Heidegger puts it, which establishes a "clearing" in which things can present themselves *as* what they are. And so, to take one of Heidegger's famous examples, a hammer can only present itself *as* a hammer in the way it is "ready-to-hand" for projects in which it can be *used* as a hammer. My, or Dasein's, practical involvement with the world establishes a practical understanding of the world that *is* an "existential" interpretation of it presupposed by every thematic interpretation.[17]

The intelligibility of the world is constituted, most primordially, in terms of our practical interests and concerns with the world, what Heidegger refers to as our "circumspective" concern, which enables things to disclose themselves as significant in terms of their relevance to our concerns. But, as Heidegger argued, my concerns with the world ultimately rest on my care for myself, for the projection of my own possibilities for existing. The hammer only discloses itself *as* a hammer insofar as it is relevant to "making something fast" that is relevant to "providing shelter" for myself. A coin only shows itself *as* a coin insofar as it is relevant to commercial exchanges in which I can obtain what I need or desire, and so on.[18] Though this point need not be construed to entail the priority of self-interest ordinarily construed in terms of selfishness,[19] it does imply what Levinas gets at with his slogan of "the reduction of the other to the same," that the intelligibility of the world is established only through the assimilation of what is other than me to the context of my own concerns and interests.[20]

In my proximity to the face of the other, however, my concerns and interests are called into question in a way that is impossible for anything made intelligible in terms of them. This is not to say that the things I comprehend in terms of my projects cannot resist those projects. A hammer can be too small for my needs. I may not have enough coins to purchase what I want. But this is, at best, a conditional form of resistance that only makes sense against the background or on the assumption of my concerns and interests, a way of calling into question only the instrumental feasibility of realizing my interests. What becomes intelligible to me in terms of my practical involvement with the world may be disclosed as insufficient to my needs. But in my proximity to the other I find my interests and concerns called into question in a uniquely unconditional way.[21] There I find myself called to assess not merely the instrumental feasibility of my projects but whether they *ought* to be pursued at all. Levinas shares with Kant and the deontological tradition that follows him the idea that our properly moral obligations to the other are not hypothetically imperative, a prudential explication of what is necessary to our interests, but categorically imperative, an unconditional explication of what simply ought to be done.[22] As such, the unconditional moral authority of the face of the other appears to transcend what is intelligible in terms of the context of my concerns and interests with the world and myself. Rather than being intelligible in terms of such a context, it makes sense to say that it effects a rupture with it, calling into question the propriety of the projects in terms of which it is constituted.

Hence, there is the necessity of a discourse that is hyperbolic not in Caputo's sense of a "fabulous tale" whose aim is inspirational, but in the sense of attempting to say more than can be made intelligibly present in order to draw attention to the way we are claimed by an unconditional sense of obligation whose complete intelligibility transcends our practically constituted horizons of intelligibility. This is, more or less, the sense in which Levinas speaks of his work as hyperbolic: "Here the human is brought out (*s'saccuse*)," he writes, "by transcendence, or the hyperbole . . . a hyperbole in which it breaks up and *falls upward* (*tombe vers le haut*), into the human."[23] Levinas's hyperbolic discourse exploits the resources of language to say more than what can be made present, proceeding through paradox, or, as Levinas puts it, in unsaying itself, denying the limitations of the themes in terms of which the unconditional authority of the other is presented to us.[24] When, for example, Levinas speaks of the "ethical resistance" of the other person to my projects as "the resistance of what has no resistance,"[25] we find his discourse unsaying itself in the way it denies the limitations of the theme in terms of which that resistance is presented, emphasizing the way the *ethical* resistance being invoked exceeds any sense of objective resistance to which the theme of resistance would ordinarily be adequate. Here we find another sense in which the moral significance of saying transcends what is said, and what is said always, to one extent or another, betrays our orientation to the other in saying.[26] It is this hyperbolic, metaphysical dimension of the significance of our moral orientation to the other that cannot be adequately said, cannot be made present as a theme that would be intelligible in terms of any practically constituted horizon of interpretation.

"Language," he notes, "is the possibility of an enigmatic equivocation for better or worse, which men abuse."[27] And Levinas's own "enigmatic equivocation(s)" *would* be an abuse, would say *less* than what can be made intelligible, if it were not for what he characterizes as "the empirical event of obligation to another."[28] Abstractions that would otherwise break up under the force of their own self-defeating logic into vacuity, into a loss of significance, break up instead toward a signification that exceeds any theme, the being-for-the-other of our sense of moral obligation. As such, Caputo is right that Levinas's discourse cannot be taken literally. It is not an incoherent attempt to give an accurate description of something that cannot become present. But it is not, for that reason, merely a "fabulous tale." It is, rather, an attempt to make sense of our moral response to the other in a way that must exploit the resources of language to say more than what can be made present and, in so doing, draw our attention to the concrete way we are held by a sense of authority that exceeds our presence, that "cannot be interpreted on the basis of disclosure."

It is at this level that Levinas's work remains phenomenological, constituting an "intentional analysis" of the horizons within which our lived experience of a distinctively unconditional sense of obligation can emerge for us. Though it is true that Levinas makes a case for the way those horizons exceed the bounds of what can be intelligibly presented in experience and known as such, his work remains, nevertheless, a phenomenological exposition of lived experience, in this case, of how experience appears to gesture beyond itself toward an unconditional sense of authority that cannot be intelligibly contained within experience. His work forms, if you will, a phenomenological analysis of how we live the rupture with what can be made intelligible within experience that is effected by our ethical proximity to the other. It constitutes an interpretation of "the empirical event of obligation to another" as significant in a way that cannot be adequately made present, a proposal for an interpretive context in which to make sense of our lived experience of the gravity with which the other comes to us as interlocutor that cannot itself be adequately explicated in terms of what discloses itself to us as practically intelligible[29] within our lived experience.

6.2.2 The Hermeneutics of the Face of the Other

It must be admitted, however, that Levinas's interpretation of our lived experience of obligation could only aspire to be adequate if that lived experience were originally given *as* an experience *of obligation*, with a, more or less, determinate significance his interpretation can aim to articulate. As Heidegger reminds us, all discursive interpretation presupposes an "existential" interpretation that has already prethematically articulated the phenomenon in question in terms of our practical involvement with it. I can only speak adequately of the hammer *as* a hammer insofar as I have what he calls a "fore-conception" of the hammer in terms of my practical involvement with it, an interpretation that "is carried out primordially not in a theoretical statement but in an action of circumspective concern."[30] In this way, we come back to Derrida's point that it would be impossible to even recognize, let alone respect, the other *as* other apart from an interpretive context that allowed the other to become intelligible to us in a determinate way. And, moreover, it is clear upon reflection that our lived experience of obligation *is* available to us in a way that lends itself to discursive articulation precisely insofar as it is emerges for us in a practical context that lends itself to a particular interpretation. As I have stressed since chapter 1, the face of the other is always, for Levinas, the face of my interlocutor, the one who speaks to me. My obligation to the other is, first and foremost, a conversational obligation to defer to the other, to take what the other says to me with a degree of importance equal, at the very least, to my concerns with myself. My sense of the gravity or importance of my response to the other is a sense of the importance of a response that is intelligible to me in terms of the role it plays in the context of a social practice of conversation that is a practical possibility of mine. It is this practical context of a communicative, ultimately conversational, relationship with the other that establishes a determinate significance for my lived experience of obligation to the other *as* an obligation to defer to the other, to hear and genuinely respond to the concerns of the other. This is a point Levinas himself supports in his own way. He repeatedly emphasizes my proximity to the other as a mode of signification.[31] It is an orientation to the other, the establishment of a relationship between myself and the other in which the other is originally, though not thematically, signified as interlocutor. It is this practical involvement with the other that provides a context in which the other can appear *as* interlocutor, and a sense of the importance of my deference to the other *as* interlocutor can emerge for me. It is only as an experience that has already been practically interpreted in this way that our lived experience of obligation to the other can lend itself to a particular thematic interpretation of it.

It is in this sense that we should interpret Levinas's claim that "ethics is an 'optics.'"[32] Only a moral discourse can enable us to adequately articulate the unconditional character of the sense of obligation that emerges in our communicative proximity to the other. Only an account of the "always positive value" of the face of the other is adequate to the unconditional sense of the gravity of my response to the other. Levinas's account of the face of the other makes sense of this gravity in the way Taylor speaks of an account of moral sources making sense of our moral intuitions by "articulating what makes these responses appropriate."[33] Levinas's appeal to his distinctively substantive moral language makes sense of our lived experience of obligation to the other insofar as it enables us to see, to make intelligible to ourselves, the unconditional character of our response to the other *as appropriate*. It enables us to see, in a way in which Habermas's procedural analysis does not, how taking up the communicatively based imperative to respond to the other *as* a constitutive dimension of a moral point of view onto life is appropriate, how taking that imperative with that unconditional degree of importance is appropriate.

To recognize how ethics may be an optics in this sense is also, however, to recognize another dimension in which, just as Derrida points out, Levinas's account must be committed to an interpretive framework that enables our lived experience of obligation to become intelligible to us in a determinate way. Indeed, even to speak of a lived experience of "obligation" is already to begin to situate it in terms of a deontological vocabulary developed largely since the eighteenth century.[34] It is already to be caught up in a distinctive theoretical interpretation of our relationship to the other, to see that relationship in terms of a problematic unique to that interpretative tradition. To claim that ethics is an optics is, in effect, to claim that no other historically available linguistic resource is adequate to the lived significance of our experience of obligation, that among competing vocabularies, only a morally weighted one that allows us to speak of what we ought to do regardless of our own interests, even in opposition to our interests, is capable of making sense of the gravity with which our communicative proximity to the other seizes us, of enabling us to see how our lived experience of that gravity is not inappropriate.

But this is not a point that Levinas needs to contest. He can agree with us that our proximity to the other is always situated in terms of a practical context of interpretation that enables it to have a distinctive significance *and* that its significance can only be discursively articulated in terms of the conceptual resources of a unique interpretive tradition. Recognizing the other *as* other is always going to be a hermeneutic endeavor, and there is no point in quibbling about it. *If* Levinas is right, however, that it is only a distinctively ethical, deontological discourse that is able to make sense of our proximity to the other, then he still has grounds to claim that its ultimate intelligibility transcends any context of interpretation constituted in terms of our own concerns and interests and is metaphysical in this specific sense of the term. All he needs to say is that there is a dimension of the significance of our practically interpreted experience of obligation to the other that cannot be made intelligible in terms of any practically constituted interpretive context. Insofar as its articulation demands a uniquely moral interpretive framework, we can see that it involves a sense of obligation that resists my concerns and interests in a way no practically intelligible thing can. This is not to endorse the incoherent idea that we can make what is fundamentally unintelligible intelligible but only that our otherwise communicatively intelligible experience of obligation to the other involves or gestures toward a metaphysical significance that transcends the limits of what is practically intelligible.

This metaphysical limit of intelligibility can, moreover, itself be made intelligible through the interpretive resources of a moral discourse that exploits the hyperbolic possibilities of language to gesture at more than can be made present. It is the interpretive necessity of this hyperbolic framework that makes the limits of the practical intelligibility of our lived experience of obligation intelligible to us, that circumscribes this rupture with intelligibility in an intelligible way by situating it within a determinate context of interpretation. Ethics is an optics in precisely the way it enables us to make intelligible to ourselves a distinctive limit to our practical intelligibility of the world. This is the unique value of a deontological moral vocabulary for Levinas: enabling us to intelligibly demarcate the limits of the intelligibility of our lived experience of obligation to the other. We do not need, therefore, to understand what Levinas is doing as a matter of saying what cannot be said or presenting what cannot be intelligibly presented but only of saying the limits of what can be intelligibly presented, of constructing an interpretive framework capable of articulating this limit *as* a distinctively moral limitation to our comprehension of the world in terms of our own concerns and interests, a limit where our care for ourselves is not merely called into question in a conditional way, but an unconditional way that is without precedent in the world insofar as it is practically intelligible to us.

6.3 The Face of the Other and the Myth of the Given

In considering the previous objection, we had occasion to see the importance of Levinas's phenomenological reference to lived experience, to what he characterizes as "the empirical event of obligation to another." But in appealing to lived experience to give us a reason to be moral, a justification for taking a moral point of view onto life with an unconditional degree of importance, are we not succumbing to what Wilfred Sellars characterized as the "myth of the given," the mistake of every mode of empiricism in thinking that the fact of an experience can, on its own, provide us with good reason to adopt an epistemic position?[35] This is the heart of the question raised by Todd May's assessment of Levinas's work. "Ethical justification," he argues, "attaches to something other than experiences *as experiences*."[36] The fact of having a particular experience taken on its own lacks the epistemic authority to justify any claim. At most, our lived experience of the face of the other may have what May refers to as a "constitutive" role to play in our adoption of a moral point of view. Much as Habermas argued with respect to Taylor's reference to substantive goods, May concludes that our lived experience of the other may have a causal or motivational importance in moving us to be moral. But it cannot provide us with a *reason* to be moral.[37]

May illustrates his point with a consideration of the way he believes Levinas's position commits the "naturalistic fallacy" of illicitly attempting to derive what *ought* to be the case from what *is* the case, the respect and consideration we *ought* to give the other from the *fact* that we experience the other as worthy of such consideration. But our experience of the other as worthy, he argues, no more justifies treating the other with respect than an experience of the other as "vile or unworthy" would justify indifference to the other. Though our experience surely may be relevant to *explaining* why we treat the other one way or another it is not relevant to *justifying* that treatment. "It is not the fact of something's being an experience, of whatever kind, that offers ethical justification for a relation to otherness. Ethical justification attaches to something other than experiences *as experiences*."[38] Indeed, as Sellars argued, no justificatory value can be attributed to experience *as experience*. Experience can play a justificatory role in relation to our beliefs only insofar as it is embedded in "the logical space of reasons, of justifying and being able to justify what one says." And so, to cite one of Sellars examples, knowing that what I am aware of is green presupposes a knowledge that what I am aware of "is a reliable symptom" of a thing's being green. I must be able to say something as to why what I am aware of ought to be taken as I take it, in this case, as green. There are many circumstances in which the experience of something as green would not be taken as a reliable symptom and, hence, as knowledge, of a thing's being green—say, for instance, perceiving a thing as green under unusual lighting or the perception of someone who is known to be red/green color blind. To appeal to one's experience as a reason for one's belief is to place it in this "logical space of reasons" where the epistemic authority it possesses is entirely a function of what can be said for that authority.[39]

It is for considerations such as these that May concludes, "ethical justification comes inescapably from within ethical discourse, within what might be called, with Wittgenstein, a language game. To say that a responsibility is justified is to say that it is in accordance with other responsibilities that are themselves justified." In appealing to an experience that would transcend the level of what can be said and not be caught up, therefore, in the exigencies of our various language games, Levinas excludes himself from the arena in which his appeal could have justificatory value. "Normative appeal outside of the said to a founding saying is either useless or illicit. . . . saying . . . is a cog in the machine that performs no function."[40] Or, at least, no epistemic function.

With this point there can be no argument. Considered completely apart from anything said about it, our lived experience of speaking with the other, of saying, *is* "a cog in the machine that performs no function." Only as said, as articulated in a plausible interpretation of the sense of worth to which we are called in our lived experience of speaking with the other, can saying play any epistemic role at all in moral discourse. To the extent that Levinas's distinction between the saying and the said suggests that there is no need for saying to be said, it is, as we discussed in chapter 3, untenable. That is why I have understood Levinas's references to the moral significance of saying as a reference to our lived experience of finding ourselves called to a sense of the unconditional worth of the other that *needs to be said*. It is only as said that it can serve as a reason why we should adopt a moral point of view onto life, why we should take up our communicatively based sense of obligation to the other with such an unconditional sense of importance. Only as an articulate proposition about the worth of the other can it play a role in justifying our commitment to care for the concerns of the other, to consider them equal in importance to our own. Apart from that all we have is what Levinas gets at as an inarticulate sense of gravity in our relationship with the other, what I have tried to gesture at as a lived presumption of the worth of the other in the way we find ourselves bound to defer to the other *as if* s/he were unconditionally worthy of our consideration, but certainly not the kind of articulate proposal that could serve as a justification for anything. Only insofar as that inarticulate presumption of the worth of the other is interpreted as a uniquely moral sense of worth can it play an epistemic role in our moral discourse.

As so interpreted, however, it plays an indispensable epistemic role. As said, the experience of saying is anything but "a cog in the machine that performs no function." To the contrary, it is an unavoidable opening onto a recognition of the moral worth of the other that gives us the point of our moral beliefs, the reason why we consider the adoption of a morally framed discourse about certain issues, a moral point of view onto them, of such importance. Without a lived experience of the other person in which I find myself called to what can plausibly be interpreted as a sense of the unconditional worth of the other, our language games about morality would be only *games* whose sense of unconditional importance would be lost. To this extent, it would make a great deal of difference to our moral beliefs should we lack such an experience or, as May suggests hypothetically, it were to be replaced by an equally fundamental experience of the other as "vile or unworthy," as we would be deprived of our reason for taking our moral beliefs as seriously as we ought. At best, we might construe them as principles of enlightened self-interest for a world in which we, unlike those with Gyges ring[41], cannot pursue our own desires indifferent to the concerns of others and hope to always get away with it. But, as Plato demonstrated long ago,[42] we could have no reason for continuing to appreciate their importance on those occasions when we could plausibly get away with injustice. We could not construe the moral point of view as unconditionally authoritative for us, but only as a prudentially expedient perspective to take onto life, applicable to many, perhaps even most, but certainly not all occasions. When our questions only concern the assumption of this or that responsibility, they may be adequately answered, as May stresses, in terms of "other responsibilities that are themselves justified." But when they begin to concern the assumption of a sense of responsibility to the other that is at the basis of our sense that we ought to be concerned with our duties to the other at all, we begin to have a real epistemic need for more than that. It is here that the sense of worth to which I find myself called in my lived experience of speaking with another person comes to possess epistemic relevance, providing us with a reason why we should consider the assumption of our putative responsibilities to the other worth the trouble.

To be clear, however, May is right that it is not *as* an experience that our lived experience of saying comes to have epistemic relevance, but only *as* said, as interpreted as a call to a uniquely moral sense of the worth of the other. The epistemic relevance of saying is only established in the said as we make a case for our interpretation of its significance. Levinas's own moral interpretation of that experience *is*, at a practical level, a matter of placing it in "the logical space of reasons, of justifying and being able to justify what one says." It is an attempt to provide reasons for the epistemic relevance of that experience to our moral beliefs in much the way our beliefs that certain observational states of affairs are reliable symptoms of certain facts provide reasons for the epistemic relevance of those observational states of affairs. By offering a plausible interpretation of our lived experience of speech *as* a matter of finding oneself ineluctably called to a sense of the *moral* worth of the other, Levinas attempts to establish the epistemic relevance of saying to our moral discourse *in the said*.

In making this point we must remember, of course, that the epistemic cogency of that interpretation of our lived experience of speech can itself only be established in the said as well. Levinas may be right to insist that "ethics is an optics," that only a uniquely moral interpretation of our lived experience of speaking with another person is capable of making good sense of that experience. But we cannot appeal to that experience as a "self-authenticating, non-verbal episode" that would transparently authorize the interpretation we make of it, as this would return us to the very heart of the myth of the given, the idea that experience can play a direct and discursively unmediated role in our epistemic life.[43] By contrast, the validity of Levinas's interpretation of our lived experience of the other can only be established in a discursively holistic way, through its capacity to respond to the open-ended array of questions and issues that could motivate our interest with it. The examination I have undertaken here of the contribution it can be seen to make to our understanding of different facets of our moral experience and the connection between morality and language can be understood as part of such a holistic assessment, an attempt to say why we have good reason to accept its epistemic cogency in relation to some of the questions it can help us to constructively address. Just as the epistemic relevance of our lived experience of speech can only be established in terms of an interpretation that makes a case for its relevance, so the epistemic authority of that interpretation can only be established in terms of a holistic assessment of its ability to make a constructive contribution to our understanding of the issues it would purport to illuminate. As May's comments serve to remind us, we can never leave "the logical space of reasons, of justifying and being able to justify what one says." But this does not entail that we should abandon Levinas's account of the face of the other, only that we should understand it in such a way that it can be accommodated within that "logical space of reasons"—not as a discursively unmediated appeal to an experience of saying wholly beyond the said, but as an attempt to establish the epistemic relevance of our experience of saying within the said, in terms of what can plausibly be said about it.

6.4 Are We Duped by Morality?

In closing, however, it is important to be clear about the precise justificatory role Levinas's account of the face of the other can play in our moral discourse. It can, as I have stressed, establish the point of the moral point of view, the reason why we should take the moral point of view with an unconditional degree of importance. Anyone who shares in a sense of the unconditional worth of the other person has a good reason to defer to the other in the way the moral point of view demands. Searching for an analogy, it is not that different from justifying the distinctive degree of deference and respect we give someone who holds public office by reference to our recognition of the civic importance of the office s/he holds. Anyone who shares with us a sense of the civic importance of that public office will have a good reason to give the officeholder a degree of deference and respect that might be inappropriate to others.

But, as we saw in chapter 3, our sense of the moral worth of the other also requires articulation in terms of an account as to *why* the other is unconditionally deserving of my consideration in this way. As Taylor makes this point, it is applicable to any sense of importance. I cannot just feel something to be important without being able to say anything about why it is important. I may enjoy wiggling my toes in warm mud, to return to Taylor's curious example, but I cannot regard it as important without an account that articulates why it is important. The justificatory force of an appeal to our sense of the moral importance of the other person as the point of the moral point of view will, therefore, be undermined without something that can be said for why the other should assume such importance for us. Just as we could not articulate our sense of the civic importance of public office as a reason for our deference to the officeholder without alluding, if only implicitly, to our sense of why public office assumes such importance for us, so we cannot articulate our sense of the moral importance of the other as a reason for our unconditional deference without saying something as to why the other assumes such importance for us.

We run into a significant hitch here, however. Whereas it is not hard to articulate our sense of the civic importance of public office—presumably, in terms of the role it plays in the institutionalization of our ideals of democratic self-government—the articulation of our sense of the unconditional importance of the other person leads us beyond what can be thematically presented and made intelligible. Attending to why the other assumes such an unconditional degree of importance for us must lead us to a sense of authority the other comes to have in relationship to us that can only be metaphysical in the sense that Levinas stresses in his work, a sense of "height" that cannot be made present, that is absolutely or infinitely other insofar as it calls my interests into question in an unconditional way that is unintelligible in terms of any practically constituted context of interpretation. We do not run out of things to say here, but what we can say must exploit what Levinas characterized as the hyperbolic capacity of language to say more than what can be made present, to gesture at what can only remain insistently other. But in speaking of the "height" of the other in this way, Levinas also resolutely seeks to avoid the temptation of so much traditional metaphysical and theological discourse to objectify this sense of alterity, to present it as an elevated world behind the scenes, a realm of Platonic ideas or a Kingdom of Heaven. Though sensitive to the metaphysical dimensions of the face of the other, Levinas shares with Nietzsche a disdain for this "otherworldly" sense of metaphysics.[44] In looking to a world behind the scenes to explain the sense of the infinite we encounter in the face of the other, we sacrifice its insistent alterity to our search for intelligibility. We fail to respect the limit of intelligibility we encounter in the "height" of the other.

In his own work, Levinas seeks to address this limit not by eclipsing it in terms of a world behind the scenes that would give it a false sense of intelligibility, but by making it salient as a uniquely moral limit to intelligibility. By attending phenomenologically to the rupture it effects with our search for intelligibility and the way that rupture is lived by us as a moral sense of authority, Levinas does not seek to explain the sense of alterity we encounter in the face of the other, but rather to draw our attention to it and let it show itself as insistently other. Despite its metaphysical dimensions, then, Levinas's articulation of the face of the other remains thoroughly phenomenological, seeking to address the question of why the other assumes such an unconditional degree of importance for us only by attending to a sense of authority that opens up for us in our communicative proximity to the other as a rupture with intelligibility, a sense of alterity that is lived as an unfathomable right of the other to command my unconditional consideration. To this extent, the only justificatory role Levinas's appeal to the face of the other can play in our moral discourse is phenomenological as well. It does not attempt to speculatively elucidate the ultimate grounds of the moral worth of the other *in her/himself* in relation to a transcendent world behind the scenes that would bestow such importance on the other, but only to clarify how the other becomes unconditionally important *for us* within the limits of our communicatively circumscribed experience of the other.

In his preface to *Totality and Infinity*, Levinas begins by asserting that "everyone will readily agree that it is of the highest importance to know whether we are not duped by morality."[45] In some ways, I believe, this simple question frames all of Levinas's meditations on the moral significance of our proximity to the other. By the time one has finished reading Levinas, however, it may still be unclear in what way he may have plausibly answered it. If we are asking this question in a traditionally metaphysical sense, asking after what it is about the other person *in her/himself* that deserves our moral consideration, then Levinas's account of the other leaves the question deliberately unanswered as a way of respecting the limit to intelligibility we reach in the face of the other. Perhaps our moral sensibilities are a not yet entirely explained effect of natural selection and there is nothing about the other in her/himself that really merits our moral consideration. Perhaps, as John Caputo playfully entertains, our sense of the moral worth of the other is just an effect of indigestion or some other natural cause we have yet to uncover.[46] Given the phenomenological character of Levinas's appeal to the face of the other, there is nothing in it, as far as I can see, that rules out such possibilities.[47]

Acknowledging such possibilities does not, however, undermine the epistemic value of Levinas's account. It may be that what *causes* us to come to a sense of the moral worth of the other person is ultimately its uniquely adaptive value in a process of natural selection in which other forms of living our relationship to the other person cannot compete. In fact, given the adaptive value of developing stable forms of communicative interaction with others, we have reason to suppose that something like this may very well be true. The development of stable forms of communicative interaction bring with them a form of unconditional deference to the other that can only be lived intelligibly by communicative agents in relation to a sense of the unconditional worthiness of the other to that deference. Our openness to the "always positive value" of the other person may, therefore, be explicable in a thoroughly naturalistic way as a plausible product of the operation of natural selection. But, if Levinas is right, that does not change the fact that the other person has come through that process of natural selection to be unconditionally important *to us* in a way that transcends the naturalistic frame of reference of the "struggle for life" that gave it birth.[48] And it is the other person's unconditional importance *to us* that gives us a *reason* to be moral, a reason to suppose we are not duped by morality when we give the other a form of consideration not strictly entailed by the intelligent pursuit of our self-interest. Insofar as we are communicatively bound to one another as interlocutors, we find ourselves called to an unconditional sense of our importance to each other, a sense of moral solidarity with each other that is knit into the very fabric of human intercourse with one another. This is the most basic lesson of Levinas's uniquely phenomenolgical form of metaphysics.

In speaking with another person, we find ourselves called to a sense of the unconditional importance of our interlocutor, a sense of the moral worth of the other that emerges precisely in the communicative relationship that is established between us. It is in the relationship between myself and the other that the moral worth of the other emerges for me. It is a fact about the other person only insofar as s/he emerges *as* other to me in this communicative relationship, as my interlocutor. At one point in his essay, "God and Philosophy," Levinas makes a point about God that is analogous to the point I am suggesting here concerning the moral worth of the other. There he suggests that we think of the ethical relationship to the other as "the improbable field where the Infinite is in relationship with the finite without contradicting itself by this relationship, where on the contrary it alone *comes to pass* (*se passe*) as Infinity."[49] This is a theologically unorthodox idea inasmuch as it seems to suggest that God, the infinite, does not exist apart from our human relationship to the other person, that God only "comes to pass" as God in that relationship. But this is an idea that is congenial to Levinas's understanding of the ultimately ethical significance of religion. For Levinas, our attempts to speak of God are ultimately a matter of trying to speak of a sense of transcendence that opens up for us in our ethical relationship to the other, the insistent alterity of the unconditional authority of the other that marks a limit to our comprehension of the world. To say, as Levinas does, that "I am here" for the other always "in the name of God" is to say that I am here for the other in the name of an authority that is mysterious to me, wholly other.[50] To bestow the name of God upon this mystery is only our way of inadequately striving for a way of doing justice to our relationship with it, a mode of hyperbole that, even still, fails to make it intelligible.

By conceiving God in this way, however, as an event of transcendence that "comes to pass" as God only in the finitude of our relationship to our fellow human beings, Levinas does not mean to make God any less real. Far from it. It is, for him, only a way of acknowledging that we cannot make sense of the reality of God apart from the way in which we find ourselves called to care for one another. It is the Jewish idea that the revelation of God only "comes to pass" in the law of God that orders us to the other person and that the reality of God is, perhaps, not best thought of independent of this revelation. I believe the logic of Levinas's insights into the face of the other suggest an analogous point. The "height" or moral authority of the other person only "comes to pass" in my relationship to the other, as I attempt to articulate the sense of unconditional importance of the other to which I find myself called in my communicative proximity to the other. Apart from that relationship, the other person is only one, very insignificant aspect of nature, hardly worth the trouble of even a petty sacrifice of my interests and enjoyment with life. But in the context of a communicative relationship, the other is infinitely more than that. S/he is no mere part of nature but my interlocutor, the one who commands my consideration with a mysterious, yet inescapable, mode of authority and importance. And that authority and importance are not addressed to nature. They are only addressed *to me* as a categorical mode of authority over me, an unconditional form of importance to me, a sense of election for me. But, as with Levinas's reflections on God, this is not to suggest that the moral worth of the other person is any less real than we might have otherwise been inclined to suppose. It is only to suggest that it is best not thought of independent of the sense of gravity that "comes to pass" in our relationship to the other, that it does not really matter what the other person is as a part of nature or as an unseen metaphysical participant in a world behind the scenes. All that matters is that in our human, communicative relationships with one another, we find ourselves inescapably called to an unconditional sense of importance to one another. And it is here that we find the point of the otherwise needless sacrifices morality demands of us, the resources sufficient to make sense of why it is important to be responsible for one another, and, in that way, to know we are not duped by morality.

Notes

1. Pensky, "The Limit of Solidarity," paper presented at the annual meeting of the Society for Phenomenology and Existential Philosophy, October 1994, 28, 30 & 31. The second quotation is from a passage in which Habermas is responding to Taylor cited by Pensky. See Habermas, *Justification and Application*, trans. Ciaran Cronin (Cambridge, Mass.: The MIT Press, 1993), 75.

2. Habermas, *Justification and Application*, 74. Taylor takes the phrase "subtler language" from Shelly. See Taylor, *The Ethics of Authenticity* (Cambridge, Mass.: Harvard University Press, 1991), ch. 7 and *Sources of the Self* (Cambridge, Mass.: Harvard University Press, 1989), part 5.

3. Taylor, *Sources of the Self*, 87.

4. Taylor, *The Ethics of Authenticity*, 83.

5. Taylor, *The Ethics of Authenticity*, 83-84.

6. See, for example, his interview in *Face to Face with Levinas*, ed. Richard A. Cohen (Albany: State University of New York Press, 1986), 17-19.

7. See Taylor, *The Ethics of Authenticity*, 87-88.

8. Though Levinas breaks with many of the conventions of phenomenological analysis as classically articulated by Edmund Husserl (but, then again, what genuinely influential phenomenological work has not?), he has, nevertheless, always been clear about the

essentially phenomenological nature of his work. See Levinas, *Totality and Infinity*, trans. Alphonso Lingis (Pittsburgh: Duquesne University Press, 1969), 28-29 and Levinas, *De Dieu qui vient a l'idée*, 2d ed. (Paris: Librarie Philosophique J. Vrin, 1986), 139-143. Note that even where Levinas describes, as an alternative to the transcendental search for foundations, what he characterizes as the way of "emphasis" or "hyperbole," he still insists on the phenomenological character of his work. "There are hyperboles in which notions are transformed. To describe this mutation is also to do phenomenology" (142). This is not to downplay, however, the serious questions that Levinas's phenomenology raises for the very idea of phenomenology. See, in particular, Steven G. Smith, "Reason as One for Another: Moral and Theoretical Argument," in *Face to Face with Levinas*, 53-71. These are points we shall come to broach as we deepen our understanding of the epistemic status of Levinas's work with our consideration of the objections of Derrida and May.

9. I would venture to say that it is the way Levinas's articulation of the face of the other is embedded in specific philosophical traditions, most notably that of European phenomenology, that is most limiting for his account. Not many of us are familiar enough with Heidegger's conception of human existence as a mode of being-in-the-world, for instance, to enable those aspects of Levinas's articulation that are embedded in a polemic with Heidegger (such as the metaphysical aspects of his account of the other to which we will attend shortly in considering Derrida's objections to the epistemic coherence of Levinas's project) to resonate with us. Other aspects of his articulation stressing the vulnerability and height of the other are, I believe, able to speak for more of us.

10. See Habermas, *Justification and Application*, 77 & 76. "Moral theory is competent to clarify the moral point of view and justify its universality, but it can contribute nothing to answering the question, 'Why be moral?'" The gist of my argument here could be boiled down to the simple point that moral theory cannot fulfill its tasks of clarifying and justifying the moral point of view *without* addressing the question, "Why be moral?" with an appeal to the face of the other.

11. See *Totality and Infinity*, 33 (*Totalité et Infini*, [La Haye: Martinus Nijhoff, 1961], 3), 48-52 & 194, "Diachrony and Representation," in *Time and the Other*, trans. Richard A. Cohen (Pittsburgh: Duquesne University Press, 1987), 114-118, and *Otherwise than Being*, trans. Alphonso Lingis (The Hague: Martinus Nijhoff, 1981).

12. Levinas, *Totality and Infinity*, 33.

13. See *Time and the Other*, 69-70, where Levinas speaks of the alterity of death in these terms. But, as the argument of that work indicates, they are equally applicable to the alterity of the other person.

14. Jacques Derrida, "Violence and Metaphysics: An Essay on the Thought of Emmanuel Levinas," in *Writing and Difference*, trans. Alan Bass (Chicago: The University of Chicago Press, 1978), 147, 137-138, & 151.

15. See John D. Caputo, *Against Ethics* (Indianapolis: Indiana University Press, 1993), 18, 82 & 68.

16. Levinas, *Otherwise than Being*, 179, and *Autrement qu'être ou au-delà de l'essence* (La Haye: Martinus Nijhoff, 1974), 226.

17. See Martin Heidegger, *Being and Time*, trans. John Macquarrie & Edward Robinson (New York: Harper and Row, 1962), div. 1, ch. 3, sect. 18, and ch. 5, sect. 31-33. For Levinas's qualified agreement with Heidegger's analysis, see his *Time and the Other*, in particular, 62-64, where the dissent he lodges is, on the whole, a minor one concerning the priority of what Levinas characterizes as our involvement with the world as an "ensemble of nourishments" over the Heideggerian understanding of our involvement with the world

as a "system of tools." In either case, however, Levinas and Heidegger agree that the world becomes present for us only in terms of our practical involvement with it, our possibilities for being that are opened up for us in terms of it.

18. See Heidegger, *Being and Time*, 116-117.

19. John Rawls's distinction between an interest *in* the self and an interest *of* the self is helpful here. Heidegger's thesis only implies the priority of interests *of* the self (or Dasein, as he would put it), the interests that are mine and that I care for as a part of my care for myself. But these interests that are mine need not always be interests *in* the self, interests in doing things for myself as opposed to others. See Rawls, *A Theory of Justice*, (Cambridge, Mass.: Harvard University Press, 1971), 127.

20. This theme runs throughout Levinas's work. For an example in which he relates it explicitly to Heidegger, see *Time and the Other*, 99.

21. See Levinas, "Philosophy and the Idea of Infinity," in *Collected Philosophical Papers*, trans. Alphonso Lingis (Dordrecht: Martinus Nijhoff, 1987), 50-51.

22. See Emmanuel Levinas, *Outside the Subject*, trans. Michael B. Smith (Stanford, Calif.: Stanford University Press, 1994), 158, where he describes the "imperative of assuming responsibility" for the misery of the Other as "categorical."

23. Levinas, *Otherwise than Being*, 184, and *Autrement qu'être*, 231.

24. See Levinas, *Otherwise than Being*, 181.

25. See Levinas, *Totality and Infinity*, 199.

26. See chapter 3 for my initial analysis of this issue, where I posed it in terms of the way the other as interlocutor always reserves the right to call into question whatever is said. In the final analysis, I would not want to sharply distinguish these two modes in which the saying transcends the said from one another, however. It is in reserving to her/himself the unconditional right to question what is said that the other is constituted as interlocutor, and it is in the unconditionality of this right that the metaphysical dimension of my orientation to the other is constituted.

27. Levinas, "Phenomenon and Enigma," in *Collected Philosophical Papers*, 66.

28. Emmanuel Levinas, "God and Philosophy," in *The Levinas Reader*, ed. Seán Hand (Cambridge, Mass.: Basil Blackwell Inc., 1989), 180.

29. In speaking of what is "practically intelligible" I mean to speak of what is intelligible in terms of a context of interpretation provided by one's practical involvement with the world in the Heideggerian sense discussed above.

30. See Heidegger, *Being and Time*, 200. Also see 191 for his thesis on the dependence of interpretation on a "fore-conception."

31. See, for example, *Totality and Infinity*, 204-209, "Discourse Founds Signification."

32. See Levinas, *Totality and Infinity*, 29.

33. See Taylor, *Sources of the Self*, 8.

34. Though, of course, its roots extend as far back as the Mosaic law.

35. See Wilfred Sellars, "Empiricism and the Philosophy of Mind," in *Science, Perception and Reality* (New York: The Humanities Press, 1963), 169.

36. Todd May, *Reconsidering Difference* (University Park: The Pennsylvania State University Press, 1997), 140.

37. In fact, May believes the experience of the other as Levinas understands it, involving a metaphysical reference to what is infinitely other, could not play even a constitutive role in our moral experience. He argues instead that "the ethical experience lies at least as much in what we can recognize of ourselves in the other as in what we cannot" (146). It is only because I can understand the suffering of the other that I can meaningfully respond to it. But

this is not a point Levinas would reject. May sees a difference between Levinas and himself on this point only because he identifies Levinas's understanding of the infinite alterity of the other with incomprehensible difference. In this way, May is able to assimilate Levinas's sense in which the other is infinitely other to the way in which a bat's auditory experience is infinitely different from our own and, to that extent, incomprehensible to us. (See pages 142-143.) Following this logic, Levinas betrays his own ideas in even speaking of the "face" of the other, for a face is, after all, something we can relate to and understand on the model of our own. The only truly other would be a bat or, even better, an utterly alien form of intelligence we could scarcely recognize as sentient. But Levinas's position need not lead to such absurdities. It is not the other person that is infinite in Levinas's account but the "height," the moral authority of the other. In our responsibility to the other we find ourselves responsible to someone like ourselves, whose needs and fears are comprehensible to us, making it possible for us to meaningfully respond to them. What transcends our comprehension is the unconditional authority with which the other person calls us to be responsible, how another person, just insofar as they are other to me, could claim that kind of authority. May's concerns about the infinite character of Levinas's account of the other are, therefore, unfounded.

38. May, *Reconsidering Difference*, 140.

39. Sellars, "Empiricism and the Philosophy of Mind," 168-169. Though May does not go into Sellars's ideas in any detail, they are an essential part of the philosophical context in which his arguments are framed. See, in particular, page 149, where May refers to Sellars's "myth of the given" in a footnote (note 36) to elucidate the general significance of his argument against Levinas.

40. May, *Reconsidering Difference*, 146 & 149.

41. I make reference here to Plato's famous ring that confers invisibility on all who wear it and, consequently, the capacity to commit any injustice without fear of repercussion. See book 2 of *The Republic*.

42. See, once again, book 2 of *The Republic*, in which Glaucon and Adaimantus make their case for the value of a life of injustice when justice is construed only as a matter of enlightened self-interest among those too weak to practice "perfect" injustice.

43. See Sellars, "Empiricism and the Philosophy of Mind," 169.

44. For Levinas's rejection of the idea of a "world behind the scenes" as it arises as a theme in philosophical discourse, see *Otherwise than Being*, 8 & 185. Also see *Difficult Freedom*, trans. Seán Hand (Baltimore: The Johns Hopkins University Press, 1990), 280, where he deals with this tendency in theological discourse in a very pointed way: "This was the century in which God died—that is to say, in a very precise sense, in which a certain discourse on God became increasingly impossible. . . . One still hears it in certain assemblies where one does not hesitate when faced with phrases such as 'God wished, God chose, God ordered'; we are told about God as we might be told about someone's doctor or mother-in-law. This is a language that must be forbidden when we do not know how to designate the appropriate place, even when addressing very young people, at the risk of making them lose everything on the day on which the literal meaning of this language will appear hollow and impossible to them. This is a day that has probably already come."

45. Levinas, *Totality and Infinity*, 21.

46. Caputo's playful reference to indigestion is his way of underscoring our absolute ignorance regarding the ultimate basis of what calls us to the aid of the other in our moral sensibilities. See *Against Ethics*, 31 & 85.

47. . . . which entails, by the way, that there is nothing in Levinas's account of the other that is, in principle, inconsistent with a naturalistic account of morality as an evolutionary product of natural selection, as long as the implications of this perspective are carefully assessed, as having bearing on the genesis and explanation of our moral sensibilities, not the justification (or, as they are often taken to imply, the *lack* of justification) for adopting a moral point of view with the unconditional degree of seriousness it demands. Thanks to Todd May, who initially suggested the possibility of a rapprochement between an evolutionary account of morality and Levinas's insights in correspondence with me.

48. I am taking the phrase, "struggle for life," from the title of Darwin's magnum opus, *On the Origin of Species by Means of Natural Selection or the Preservation of Favored Races in the Struggle for Life*. That a "struggle for life" might give rise to a perspective onto life that transcends it is only paradoxical insofar as we misconceive this struggle for life as a struggle among organisms all selfishly acting so as to preserve their own lives at the expense of the others. But it must be remembered that, insofar as it has relevance to the operation of natural selection, the "struggle for life" does not require (though it *may* encourage) selfish organisms only acting to ensure their own survival. The "struggle for life" takes place at the level at which the most adaptive organisms (regardless of the selfish or altruistic character of their behavior) are selected by nature to survive and reproduce at the expense of those less well adapted. There will always be winners and losers in this "struggle" depending on the rates at which organisms can perpetuate their own genetic makeup into succeeding generations. But the winners need not be only those that are selfishly acting to benefit themselves. Sometimes, organisms that are prepared to benefit others, even to their own detriment, are better adapted to win in the sense of perpetuating their genetic makeup. On this point see, for example, Richard Dawkins's discussions of the evolution of "kin selection" and "reciprocal altruism" in his classic text, *The Selfish Gene* (New York: Oxford University Press, 1989), especially chs. 6, 7, 10 & 12. Putting this point in terms of Dawkins's framework: the organisms produced by "selfish" genes need not themselves be selfish in order to enable their genes to replicate and flourish down through the generations. For a more recent and comprehensive examination of the evolution of altruism both in a biological sense of behavior which benefits others to the detriment of the organism in question and a psychological sense of a conscious concern for the well-being of others, see Elliott Sober and David Sloan Wilson, *Unto Others: The Evolution and Psychology of Unselfish Behavior* (Cambridge, Mass.: Harvard University Press, 1998).

Finally, of course, evolutionary accounts of altruism in terms of being well disposed toward my genetic kin and those who reciprocate in my other-regarding behavior fall far short of accounting for a genuinely moral point of view that regards every other person as deserving of my consideration. The evolutionary plausibility of the moral point of view as a function of the evolution of language, as I have suggested here, remains, therefore, just that—nothing more than a suggestion, and a rather speculative one at that. My only point is that it is a suggestion that is, in principle, consistent with the operation of natural selection, of the "struggle for life."

49. Levinas, "God and Philosophy," in *The Levinas Reader*, 184, and Levinas, "Dieu et la Philosophie," in *De Dieu Qui Vient A L'Idée*, 123.

50. See Levinas, *Otherwise than Being*, 149.

Bibliography

Arendt, Hannah. *Between Past and Future: Eight Exercises in Political Thought.* New York: Penguin Books, 1954.

Aristotle. *The Basic Works of Aristotle.* Ed. Richard McKeon. New York: Random House, 1941.

Austin, J. L. *How to Do Things with Words.* Cambridge: Harvard University Press, 1962.

Benhabib, Seyla. *Situating the Self: Gender, Community and Postmodernism in Contemporary Ethics.* New York: Routledge, 1992.

Blum, Lawrence. "Gilligan and Kohlberg: Implications for Moral Theory." *Ethics* (April 1988): 474-477.

Brandom, Robert. *Making It Explicit: Reasoning, Representing, and Discursive Commitment.* Cambridge, Mass.: Harvard University Press, 1994.

Caputo, John. *Against Ethics: Contributions to a Poetics of Obligation with Constant Reference to Deconstruction.* Indianapolis: Indiana University Press, 1993.

Carter, Stephen L. *Civility: Manners, Morals, and the Etiquette of Democracy.* New York: Basic Books, 1998.

Castoriadis, Cornelius. *Philosophy, Politics, Autonomy: Essays in Political Philosophy.* Ed. David Ames Curtis. New York: Oxford Press, 1991.

Cohen, Jean L., and Andrew Arato. *Civil Society and Political Theory.* Cambridge, Mass.: The MIT Press, 1992.

Cohen, Joshua. "Pluralism and Proceduralism." *Chicago-Kent Law Review* 69 (1994): 589-618.

Cooke, Maeve. *Language and Reason: A Study of Habermas's Pragmatics.* Cambridge, Mass.: The MIT Press, 1994.

Dawkins, Richard. *The Selfish Gene*. New York: Oxford University Press, 1989.

de Tocqueville, Alexis. *Democracy in America*, vol. 2. New York: Vintage Books, 1960.

Derrida, Jacques. "Signature, Event, Context." In *Limited Inc., ed.* Gerald Graff. Evanston, Ill.: Northwestern University Press, 1988.

———. "Violence and Metaphysics: An Essay on the Thought of Emmanuel Levinas." In *Writing and Difference*, trans. Alan Bass. Chicago: The University of Chicago Press, 1978.

Dummett, Michael. "What Is a Theory of Meaning? (II)." In *Truth and Meaning: Essays in Semantics*, ed. Gareth Evans and John McDowell. Oxford: Clarendon Press, 1976.

Elshtain, Jean-Bethke. "Feminism, Family, and Community." *Dissent* 29 (fall 1982): 442-449.

Gibbs, Robert. "A Jewish Context for the Social Ethics of Marx and Levinas." In *Autonomy and Judaism*, ed. Daniel H. Frank. Albany: State University of New York Press, 1992.

Gilligan, Carol. *In a Different Voice*. Cambridge, Mass.: Harvard University Press, 1982.

Gilligan, Carol, and Joel Michael Murphy. "Moral Development in Late Adolescence and Adulthood: A Critique and Reconstruction of Kohlberg's Theory." *Human Development* 23 (1980): 77-104.

Gottlieb, Roger. "Levinas, Feminism, Holocaust, Ecocide." In *Artifacts, Representations and Social Practice*, ed. Carol Gould and Robert Cohen. Dordrecht: Kluwer Academic Publishers, 1994.

Gutman, Amy, and Dennis Thompson. *Democracy and Disagreement*. Cambridge, Mass.: The Belknap Press of Harvard University Press, 1996.

Habermas, Jürgen. "A Reply." In *Communicative Action: Essays on Jürgen Habermas's The Theory of Communicative Action*, ed. Axel Honneth and Hans Joas. Cambridge, Mass.: The MIT Press, 1991.

———. *Between Facts and Norms: Contributions to a Discourse Theory of Law and Democracy*. Trans. William Rehg. Cambridge, Massachusetts: The MIT Press, 1996. *Faktizität und Geltung: Beiträge zur Diskurstheorie des Rechts und des demokratischen Rechtsstaats*. Frankfurt am Main: Suhrkamp, 1992.

———. *Communication and the Evolution of Society*. Trans. Thomas McCarthy. Boston: Beacon Press, 1979.

———. "Justice and Solidarity: On the Discussion Concerning 'Stage 6.'" *The Philosophical Forum* 31 (fall-winter 1989-90): 32-52.

———. *Justification and Application: Remarks on Discourse Ethics*. Trans. Ciaran Cronin. Cambridge, Mass.: The MIT Press, 1993. *Erläuterungen zur Diskursethik*. Frankfurt am Main: Suhrkamp Verlag, 1991.

———. *Moral Consciousness and Communicative Action*. Trans. Christian Lenhardt and Shierry Weber Nicholsen. Cambridge, Mass.: The MIT Press, 1990.

————. *Postmetaphysical Thinking: Philosophical Essays.* Trans. William Mark Hohengarten. Cambridge, Mass.: The MIT Press, 1992.

————. "Reconciliation through the Public Use of Reason: Remarks on John Rawls's Political Liberalism." *The Journal of Philosophy* 92, no. 3 (March 1995): 109-131.

————. "Reply to Skjei." *Inquiry* 28 (1985): 111-130.

————. "Struggles for Recognition in the Democratic Constitutional State." In *Multiculturalism: Examining the Politics of Recognition,* ed. Amy Gutman. Princeton, N.J.: Princeton University Press, 1994.

————. "The New Obscurity: The Crisis of the Welfare State and the Exhaustion of Utopian Energies." In *The New Conservativism.* Cambridge, Mass.: The MIT Press, 1989.

————. *The Theory of Communicative Action.* vol. 1: *Reason and the Rationalization of Society.* Trans. Thomas McCarthy. Boston: Beacon Press, 1984. *Theorie des kommunikativen Handelns.* Band 1, *Handlungsrationalität und gesellschaftliche Rationalisierung.* Frankfurt am Main: Suhukamp Verlag, 1981.

Heidegger, Martin. *Being and Time.* Trans. John Macquarrie and Edward Robinson. New York: Harper and Row, 1962.

Hendley, Steven. "From Communicative Action to the Face of the Other: Habermas and Levinas on the Foundations of Moral Theory." *Philosophy Today* (winter 1996): 504-530.

————. "Liberalism, Communitarianism, and the Conflictual Grounds of Democratic Pluralism." *Philosophy and Social Criticism* 19 (1993): 293-316.

————. "Putting Ourselves up for Question: A Postmodern Critique of Richard Rorty's Postmodernist Bourgeois Liberalism." *The Journal of Value Inquiry* 29 (1995): 241-253.

————. "Reconsidering the Limits of Democracy with Castoriadis and Lefort." In *Reinterpreting the Political: Continental Philosophy and Political Theory,* ed. Lenore Langsdorf and Stephen H. Watson with Karen A. Smith. Albany: State University of New York Press, 1998.

Hewlett, Sylvia Ann, and Cornel West. *The War against Parents.* Boston: Houghton Mifflin Company, 1998.

Kant, Immanuel. *Fundamental Principles of the Metaphysics of Morals.* Trans. T. K. Abbott. Amherst, N.Y.: Prometheus Books, 1988.

Kohlberg, Lawrence, Dwight R. Boyd, and Charles Levine. "The Return of Stage 6: Its Principle and Moral Point of View." In *The Moral Point of View.* Cambridge, Mass.: The MIT Press, 1990.

Kymlicka, Will. *Liberalism, Community, and Culture.* Oxford: Clarendon Press, 1991.

Lefort, Claude. *The Political Forms of Modern Society.* Ed. John Thompson. Cambridge, Mass.: Polity Press, 1986.

————. *Democracy and Political Theory.* Trans. David Macey. Minneapolis:

University of Minnesota Press, 1988.

Levinas, Emmanuel. *Beyond the Verse: Talmudic Readings and Lectures*. Trans. Gary D. Mole. Indianapolis: Indiana University Press, 1994.

———. *Collected Philosophical Papers*. Trans. Alphonso Lingis. Dordrecht: Martinus Nijhoff, 1987.

———. *De Dieu qui vient a l'idée*. 2d ed. Paris: Librarie Philosophique J. Vrin, 1986.

———. *Difficult Freedom: Essays on Judaism*. Trans. Seán Hand. Baltimore: The Johns Hopkins University Press, 1990. *Difficile Liberté: Essais sur le judaïsme*. Paris: Editions Albin Michel, 1976.

———. *In the Time of the Nations*. Trans. Michael B. Smith. Indianapolis: Indiana University Press, 1994.

———. *Nine Talmudic Readings*. Trans. Annette Aronowicz. Indianapolis: Indiana University Press, 1990. *Du Sacré au Saint: Cinq Nouvelles Lectures Talmudiques*. Paris: Les Éditions de Minuit, 1977.

———. *Otherwise than Being or Beyond Essence*. Trans. Alphonso Lingis. The Hague: Martinus Nijhoff, 1981. *Autrement qu'être ou au-delà de l'essence*. La Haye: Martinus Nijhoff, 1974.

———. *Outside the Subject*. Trans. Michael B. Smith. Stanford, Calif.: Stanford University Press, 1994.

———. *The Levinas Reader*. Ed. Seán Hand. Cambridge, Mass.: Basil Blackwell Inc., 1989.

———. *Time and the Other*. Trans. Richard A. Cohen. Pittsburgh: Duquesne University Press, 1987.

———. *Totality and Infinity*. Trans. Alphonso Lingis. Pittsburgh: Duquesne University Press, 1969. *Totalité et Infini*. La Haye: Martinus Nijhoff, 1961.

Levinas, Emmanuel, and Richard Kearny. "Dialogue with Emmanuel Levinas." In *Face to Face with Levinas*, ed. Richard A. Cohen. Albany: State University of New York Press, 1998.

Lyotard, Jean-François. *Just Gaming*. Trans. Wlad Godzich. Minneapolis: University of Minnesota Press, 1998.

———. *The Differend*. Trans. Georges Van Den Abbeele. Minneapolis: University of Minnesota Press, 1988.

Marsh, James. *Critique, Action and Liberation*. Albany: State University of New York Press, 1995.

May, Todd. *Reconsidering Difference*. University Park: The Pennsylvania State University Press, 1997.

McCarthy, Thomas. "Kantian Constructivism and Reconstructivism: Rawls and Habermas in Dialogue." *Ethics* 105 (October 1994): 44-63.

———. "Reflections on Rationalization in *The Theory of Communicative Action*." In *Habermas and Modernity,* ed. Richard Bernstein. Polity Press, 1985.

Nozick, Robert. *Anarchy, State, and Utopia*. USA: Basic Books, 1974.

Pensky, Max. "The Limits of Solidarity: Discourse Ethics, Levinas, and the Moral

Point of View." Paper presented at the annual meeting of the Society for Phenomenology and Existential Philosophy, October 1994, and forthcoming in *Philosophy Today*.

Peperzak, Adriaan. "Presentation." In *Re-Reading Levinas*, ed. Robert Bernasconi and Simon Critchley. Bloomington: Indiana University Press, 1991.

Plato. *The Collected Dialogues of Plato*. Ed. Edith Hamilton and Huntington Cairns. Princeton, N.J.: Princeton University Press, 1961.

Putnam, Robert. "Bowling Alone." *Journal of Democracy* 6 (January 1995): 65-78.

Rawls, John. *A Theory of Justice*. Cambridge, Mass.: Harvard University Press, 1971.

———. *Political Liberalism*. New York: Columbia University Press, 1993.

———. "Reply to Habermas." *The Journal of Philosophy* 92, no. 3 (March 1995): 132-180.

Rehg, William. *Insight and Solidarity: A Study in the Discourse Ethics of Jürgen Habermas*. Berkeley: University of California Press, 1994.

Rorty, Richard. "Postmodernist Bourgeois Liberalism." *The Journal of Philosophy* 80 (1983): 583-589.

Rosanvallon, Pierre. "The Decline of Social Visibility." In *Civil Society and the State: New European Perspectives*, ed. John Keane. London: Verso Press, 1988.

Sandel, Michael. *Democracy's Discontents*. Cambridge, Mass.: Harvard University Press, 1996.

———. *Liberalism and the Limits of Justice*. New York: Cambridge University Press, 1982.

———. "The Procedural Republic and the Unencumbered Self." *Political Theory* 12 (1984): 81-96.

Sellars, Wilfred. "Empiricism and the Philosophy of Mind." In *Science, Perception and Reality*. New York: The Humanities Press, 1963.

Sober, Elliott, and David Sloan Wilson. *Unto Others: The Evolution and Psychology of Unselfish Behavior*. Cambridge, Mass.: Harvard University Press, 1998.

Smith, Steven G. "Reason as One for Another: Moral and Theoretical Argument." In *Face to Face with Levinas*, ed. Richard A. Cohen. Albany: State University of New York Press, 1986.

Taylor, Charles. "A World Consensus on Human Rights?"*Dissent* (summer 1996): 16-21.

———. "Cross-Purposes: The Liberal-Communitarian Debate." In *Liberalism and the Moral Life*, ed. Nancy Rosenblum. Cambridge, Mass.: Harvard University Press, 1989.

———. "Language and Society." In *Communicative Action: Essays on Jürgen Habermas's Theory of Communication*, ed. Axel Honneth and Hans Joas. Cambridge, Mass.: The MIT Press, 1991.

———. *Sources of the Self*. Cambridge, Mass.: Harvard University Press, 1989

————. *The Ethics of Authenticity.* Cambridge, Mass.: Harvard University Press, 1991.

————. "The Politics of Recognition." In *Multiculturalism: Examining the Politics of Recognition*, ed. Amy Gutman. Princeton, N.J.: Princeton University Press, 1994.

Trey, George. "Communicative Ethics in the Face of Alterity: Habermas, Levinas and the Problem of Post-Conventional Universalism." *Praxis International* 11 (January 1992): 412-427.

Vetlesen, Arne Johan. "Worlds Apart? Habermas and Levinas." *Philosophy and Social Criticism* 23, no. 1 (1997): 1-20.

Walzer, Michael. "Socializing the Welfare State." In *Democracy and the Welfare State*, ed. Amy Gutman. Princeton, N.J.: Princeton University Press, 1988.

————. *Spheres of Justice: A Defense of Pluralism and Equality.* New York: Basic Books Inc., 1983.

————. "The Communitarian Critique of Liberalism." *Political Theory* 18, no. 1 (February 1990): 6-23.

West, Cornel. "The Crisis in Contemporary America." Part 2, *The Culture of Community: A Series of Public Conversations.* New Jersey Committee for the Humanities, 1993.

Whitehead, Barbara Dafoe. "Dan Quayle Was Right." *The Atlantic Monthly* (April 1993): 47-84.

Wong, David. "On Care and Justice within the Family." *Contemporary Philosophy* 15, no. 4: 21-24.

Index

179

About the Author

Steven Hendley is associate professor of philosophy at Birmingham-Southern College. He is the author of *Reason and Relativism: A Sartrean Investigation* and several articles on issues in contemporary moral-political philosophy and social theory.